Romantic Nationalism in India

National Cultivation of Culture

Edited by

Joep Leerssen (*University of Amsterdam*)

Editorial Board

VOLUME 31

The titles published in this series are listed at *brill.com/ncc*

Romantic Nationalism in India

*Cultivation of Culture and the Global
Circulation of Ideas*

By

Bob van der Linden

BRILL

LEIDEN | BOSTON

Cover illustration: 'Vande Mataram' by P. S. Ramachandra Rao. Chromolithograph published by Rao Brothers, Coimbatore (1937). Courtesy of Erwin Neumayer, Vienna.

Library of Congress Cataloging-in-Publication Data

Names: Linden, Bob van der, author.
Title: Title: Romantic nationalism in India : cultivation of culture and the global
    circulation of ideas / by Bob van der Linden.
Other titles: Cultivation of culture and the global circulation of ideas
Description: Leiden ; Boston : Brill, [2024] | Series: National cultivation of culture,
    1876-5645 ; volume 31 | Includes bibliographical references and index.
Identifiers: LCCN 2024006178 (print) | LCCN 2024006179 (ebook) |
    ISBN 9789004694798 (hardback) | ISBN 9789004694804 (ebook)
Subjects: LCSH: India–Civilization–European influences. |
    Nationalism–India–History. | Romanticism–India. |
    India–History–British occupation, 1765-1947.
Classification: LCC DS423 .R66 2024 (print) | LCC DS423 (ebook) |
    DDC 320.540954–dc23/eng/20240312
LC record available at https://lccn.loc.gov/2024006178
LC ebook record available at https://lccn.loc.gov/2024006179

Typeface for the Latin, Greek, and Cyrillic scripts: "Brill". See and download: brill.com/brill-typeface.

ISSN 1876-5645
ISBN 978-90-04-69479-8 (hardback)
ISBN 978-90-04-69480-4 (e-book)
DOI 10.1163/9789004694804

Printed by Printforce, United Kingdom

To the memory of Ma

∵

You say our religion is no religion, our poetry no poetry, our philosophy no philosophy. We try to understand and appreciate whatever Europe has produced, but do not imagine that we despise what India has produced. If you studied our music as we do yours, you would find that there is melody, rhythm, and harmony in it, quite as much as in yours. And if you would study our poetry, our religion, and our philosophy, you would find that we are not what you call heathens or miscreants, but know as much of the Unknowable as you do, and have seen perhaps deeper into it than you have!

DWARKANATH TAGORE to Friedrich Max Müller, Paris (1846)

• • •

'You don't need to pull down in order to move forward. This is the fatal mistake of the present day'.

'There has to be a rubble clearing before we breathe, and think, free'.

'You can not annihilate an entire tradition. Our culture, our *sanskriti* ...'

'Culture is akin to cultivation Baba. Of the land and the mind. But when you talk of your culture, your *sanskriti*, all this, you don't think of agriculture do you?'

'Do you?'

'Our, our ... tradition ... has made the custodians of culture and cultivation strangers to each other. Let us begin now, once again, to talk of culture not as *sanskriti* but as *krishti*, as cultivation that removes the weeds, prepares the land and furrows it'.

SASWATI SENGUPTA, *The Song Seekers* (2011)

∴

Contents

Preface

'Romantic nationalism' has recently emerged as an important category for the study of European cultural nationalist movements that primarily aimed to establish nations as moral communities and preceded or accompanied state-oriented political nationalisms.[1] But is this phenomenon distinctive to Europe alone, as is commonly claimed?[2] By discussing Romantic nationalism in (British) India, this book argues to the contrary that the category may be used globally (and especially in Asia), albeit to different degrees and in various ways of course due to the existence of local (civilizational) traditions, which were often redefined in the imperial encounter at the same time. No doubt, India is the right starting point for such a dialogue because it was central to both the Enlightenment search for the origins of language, music and man ('Everything, yes, everything without exception has its origin in India', wrote Friedrich von Schlegel in 1803) and European Romanticism ('Stick to the East', Madame de Staël told Lord Byron, for 'it was the only poetical policy'). It is generally known that the European discoveries of the Indo-European language family and, closely related, the concept of Aryanism were essential to the emergence of European Romantic nationalist thought. But how did European Enlightenment and Romantic ideas (about India) relate to Indian Romantic nationalism?[3]

This book is to a great extent about the global circulation of ideas. The formation of Indian nationalism was more complicated and intellectually global than understood by historians of earlier generations, who were largely preoccupied with political nationalism – and within India often so from a nationalist perspective, either elitist or subaltern. Particularly since the early nineteenth century, ideas from around and about the world, including European Orientalist ones about India, were adopted and modified in view of Indian

---

1   The main and pioneering work in the field is: Joep Leerssen, ed., *Encyclopedia of Romantic Nationalism in Europe*, two volumes, Amsterdam: Amsterdam University Press, 2018. Cf. J. C. Eade, ed., *Romantic Nationalism in Europe*, Canberra: Australian National University, 1983 and Miroslav Hroch, "National Romanticism" in Balázs Trencsényi and Michal Kopeček, eds., *Discourses of Collective Identity in Central and Southeast Europe 1770–1945, volume II: National Romanticism: The Formation of National Movements*, Budapest: Central European University Press, 2007: 4–18.
2   See especially: Joep Leerssen, "Introduction" in Leerssen, ed., *Encyclopedia*, volume one: 41–43.
3   I spell 'Romantic' with a capital R to emphasize its meaning, beyond that of powerful emotion, as a global cultural and intellectual movement.

cultural and intellectual traditions. Thus, over time, nationalist ideas were empowered with qualities, meanings and nuances that could not be found in Europe. Simultaneously, however, the self-esteem of the Indian intelligentsia was generally demoralized because of the confrontation with European civilization, the fact that the state was authoritatively in colonial hands and processes of modernization at large. As a result of this historical context, then, this volume maintains that 'cultivation of culture' was morally and spiritually more important to the making of (the) nation(s) and Romantic nationalist thought in India than in Europe.[4]

Without any doubt, the topic of Indian Romantic nationalism is complex and wide-ranging. To begin with, the questioning of Indian civilizational identity by colonialism diverged from what (had) happened in Europe, where all emerging nations shared one civilization: the same Judeo-Christian culture, with Greek and Roman antiquity as a common imagined frame of reference. Likewise, the great number of Indian languages and scripts, as well as sacred traditions (Hindu, Muslim, Sikh, Buddhist, Jain and Parsi), make Indian Romantic nationalism more complicated than the European case. As a synthesis of literature from different fields of research that aims to address a readership beyond the South Asian specialist, therefore, *Romantic Nationalism in India* merely presents a preliminary overview. Yet, I trust that it is useful for further comparative (Asian) studies. Although it mainly concerns the nineteenth and early twentieth centuries, I will repeatedly point out afterlives of Indian Romantic nationalist thought, sometimes up to the present, to underline an important continuity in modern Indian history. The text is dominantly focused on northern India because I am most familiar with this region. I will be pleased if this volume stimulates further research that makes the topic into a deeper subcontinental one.

The urge to write this book came unexpectedly. What sparked it off was an invitation to give a keynote at the conference 'Rethinking the Dynamics of Music and Nationalism', organized by the Study Platform on Interlocking Nationalisms (SPIN) led by Joep Leerssen, at the University of Amsterdam in September 2017. The topic of my lecture was at the forefront of my mind: 'Music, Culture and Nationalism: India and Empire in Global History'. For over time, indeed, I found that the study of music provides an excellent lens for the understanding of what intellectually happened in India and

---

4 Besides Leerssen, ed., *Encyclopedia*, see on the concept of 'cultivation of culture' in Europe: Joep Leerssen, *National Thought in Europe: A Cultural History*, Amsterdam: Amsterdam University Press, 2018 (third revised and expanded edition; first published in 2006) and "Nationalism and the Cultivation of Culture", *Nations and Nationalism*, 12, 4, 2006: 559–578.

globally during the imperial encounter.[5] Through this event, I came to know about Leerssen's fascinating work on 'cultivation of culture' and 'Romantic nationalism' in Europe. Hence, in the following year, I decided to participate in another SPIN-conference: 'Cultural Mobilization: Cultural Consciousness-Raising and National Movements in Europe and the World', which was again held in September at the University of Amsterdam. While in my 2017-lecture, I had emphasized that the concept of Romantic nationalism worked equally in British India, at least in relation to modern national music making, I now focused on the idea of cultivation of culture among the Sikhs: 'The Making of the Sikh "Nation": Cultivation of Culture and Identity Politics'.[6] Afterwards, Joep Leerssen welcomed me as a guest researcher at SPIN. In February 2020, then, I gave an informal presentation under the same title as this volume at a staff seminar of the University of Amsterdam's European Studies department and I basically followed up from there in writing during the corona pandemic.

With this project, I feel that an important dimension of my research has come full circle. In my *Moral Languages from Colonial Punjab: The Singh Sabha, Arya Samaj and Ahmadiyahs* (2008), I investigated the period of Indian socio-religious reform, which is generally seen as congruent with the early stage of cultural nationalism. My contribution was the term 'moral languages' in replacement of 'religion' to clarify cultural and intellectual change among Indians under colonial rule. *Romantic Nationalism in India* revisits this period and indisputably the Indian Romantic nationalist preoccupation with the cultivation and revival of the nation as a moral community greatly corresponds with the moral languages of Indian reformers. Thus, I believe I have gained a clearer understanding of what happened in (British) India due to the imperial encounter, especially from a global perspective.

In the footnotes I have mentioned the names of several colleagues to whom I am grateful for their feedback. Special thanks to Yousuf Saeed for arranging the images from *Tasveer Ghar* ('House of Pictures'), a most welcome digital archive of South Asian popular visual culture.[7] I consider the inclusion of these art works important because such representations played a significant role in the dissemination of Romantic nationalist ideas among a largely illiterate

---

5 Among my publications in this field, see particularly: *Music and Empire in Britain and India: Identity, Internationalism, and Cross-Cultural Communication*, New York: Palgrave Macmillan, 2013 and "Non-Western National Music and Empire in Global History: Interactions, Uniformities, and Comparisons", *Journal of Global History*, 10, 3, 2015: 431–456.
6 This experience partially inspired me also to compile *Cultivating Sikh Culture and Identity: Art, Music and Philology*, London: Routledge, forthcoming.
7 http://www.tasveerghar.net.

population. Additionally, they provide a long-term historical perspective to the subject. Although Joep Leerssen's work motivated me to write this volume, the appearance of a manuscript one day on his desk must have surprised him as much as it did myself. Thanks a lot, Joep, for the inspiration, support and your enthusiast response to my invitation to write an Afterword. I hope that this book will contribute to the incorporation of the category of Romantic nationalism in the writing of global history. Last but not least, a loving thank-you to Emily de Klerk for preparing the map and copyediting the text, and above all, of course, for the wonderful way of life that we have created together.

While this book contains a great number of names of individuals, communities and movements that will be mostly unknown to those uninitiated in South Asian history, I have included an extended chronology catered to the text. A map shows the geographical location of the most important cities, regions and languages. I have used the 'corrupt' terminology of Indian city names and regions that was in use during colonial times, for instance Bombay, Calcutta, Madras and Ceylon in preference to the contemporary Mumbai, Kolkata, Chennai and Sri Lanka. Likewise, I have opted for the anglicized names of individuals, such as Bankim Chandra Chatterjee instead of Bankimchandra Chattopadhyay. Although the term 'untouchable' is now considered condescending and offensive, it was used during most of the period discussed in this book and, hence, rather than the current 'Dalit' or official 'Scheduled Caste', I decided to retain it throughout for any member of a wide range of lower caste Hindu groups and any person outside of the caste system. Finally, I have included birth and death dates only in those cases in which it was needed to clarify historical time.

Figures

Chronology

Ancient India

Indian (Hindu) nationalists have continually harked back to the past to define modern India. The Vedic period (roughly 1500 to 600 BCE) became a critical reference point for them, symbolizing the Golden Age of the Aryans, who with their Brahminical tradition (Sanskrit, Vedas and caste system) supposedly civilized the original inhabitants of the subcontinent. The Indus Civilization, which was discovered in 1924, preceded the Vedic period. Its discovery reinvigorated the discussion about the Indian past and identity.

3000–1500 BCE	Period when the Indus Civilization arose and flourished.
2000–1000 BCE	The so-called Aryan migrations into the subcontinent occur, that is, of steppe pastoralists, speaking an Indo-European language.
1500–1200 BCE	The *Rig Veda*, the first book of the Vedas, is composed.
500 BCE–500 CE	*Manu Smriti* ('The Laws of Manu'), the Ramayana and the Mahabharata are compiled.
200 BCE–480 CE	Ajanta Buddhist cave paintings are made.
100 BCE–250 CE	Period of the Tamil Sangam literature.

Medieval India

From the sixth century onwards, *bhakti* (devotional) saints throughout the subcontinent have questioned the Brahminical tradition, while celebrating the direct communion between devotee and God instead. As the *bhakti* movement transcends the different religious communities, many Indian nationalists believed that it represented the true soul of India. The 'Greater India' of the Chola Empire inspired not only Tamil nationalists, but also Rabindranath Tagore and other Indian nationalists. In the twentieth century, Chaulukya architecture is adopted as the main revivalist architectural style by Jains and nationalist Hindus.

400–500	Playwright and dramatist Kalidasa writes numerous works in Sanskrit that are primarily based upon the Vedas, the Ramayana and the Mahabharata. The play *Shankuntala* and the poem *Meghaduta* are his most famous works.

999–1026   Mahmud of Ghazni raids palaces and temples in north-western India
            and sets a trend for subsequent Muslim invaders.
940–1244   Chaulukya dynasty rules parts of what are now Gujarat and Rajasthan
            in north-western India.
985–1016   Emperor Rajarajachola creates the thalassocratic Chola Empire, linking
            south India with Southeast Asia.
1346–1565   Vijayanagara kingdom rules in south India.
1469   Birth of Guru Nanak, the founder of Sikhism.
1498   Vasco da Gama reaches India.

The Mughals and the British East India Company

Under the third Emperor Akbar (r. 1556–1605), the Mughal Empire covered a
large part of the subcontinent. In 1632, the fifth Emperor Shah Jahan commissioned the building of the Taj Mahal, the tomb for his favourite wife
Mumtaz Mahal. East Indian Company rule was firmly established after the
British defeated the Marathas (in 1818) and the Sikhs (in 1849). Since the late
nineteenth century, a canon was created of national heroes, including Maharana Pratap Singh, Shivaji and Sikh Guru Gobindh Singh, who all three fought
against the Mughals. Following the Indian Revolt of 1857, which greatly challenged British rule, the last Mughal Emperor Bahadur Shah Zafar was exiled to
Burma.

1526   The Mughal dynasty is founded by Babur, a descendant of Tamerlane.
1576   Rajput leader Maharana Pratap Singh almost defeats the Mughals at the
            Battle of Haldighati.
1674   Coronation of Shivaji as leader of the Marathas, who afterwards create
            an empire that dominated a large portion of the subcontinent and are
            credited to a large extent for ending Mughal rule.
1788   William Jones pioneers the idea of the Indo-European language family.
1799   Maharaja Ranjit Singh establishes a Sikh Empire, which in 1849 was the
            last major region of the subcontinent to be annexed by the British.
1816   Discovery of the Dravidian language family by Francis Whyte Ellis.
1849   Annexation of Punjab; end of Sikh Empire.
1857   Indian Revolt.

British India

Indian reforms and Romantic nationalist thought greatly overlap in the context of processes of colonial state formation and modernization at large. In course, competing nations (Bengali, Tamil, Rajput, Maratha, Sikh and so on) are defined. The partition of Bengal in 1905 triggers the *swadeshi* (self-rule) movement and boosts Indian nationalism. Following the ideology of Hindutva ('Hindu-ness'), Hindu chauvinists champion the idea of the creation of a Hindu nation. In 1947, the antagonism between Hindus and Muslims leads to the partition of British India into India and Pakistan.

1858	The British Crown abolishes the East India Company and assumes direct rule.
1875	Dayanand Saraswati founds the Hindu reform movement Arya Samaj ('Noble Society') and calls for a return to the Golden Age of the Vedas; Sayyid Ahmad Khan sets up Muhammadan Anglo-Oriental College in Aligarh to foster the education of Indian Muslims.
1881	Theosophical Society establishes its headquarters in Adyar near Madras; first Indian census taken.
1885	The Indian National Congress (INC) is founded in Bombay.
1893	Swami Vivekananda receives great acclaim at the World's Parliament of Religions at Chicago's Columbian Exposition.
1905	Partition of Bengal; INC launches *swadeshi* movement; Japan defeats Russia in war.
1906	The Muslim League is founded to protect the political rights of Indian Muslims.
1909	Morley-Minto reforms introduce a separate electorate for Indian Muslims; Gandhi publishes *Hind Swaraj*.
1913	Rabindranath Tagore is awarded the Nobel prize in literature; Dadasaheb Phalke releases India's first silent film *Harishchandra*; foundation of the Ghadar party in San Francisco.
1915	Provisional government of India is established in Kabul, Afghanistan.
1919	Gandhi's anti-Rowlatt-Act *satyagraha* campaign.
1919–1924	Khilafat movement seeks to unite Indian Muslims in pan-Islamic agitation and overlaps with Gandhi's Non-Cooperation Movement (1920–1922).
1925	Establishment of the Hindu right wing Rashtriya Swayamsevak Sangh.
1930	Muhammad Iqbal gives the presidential Address to the Muslim League annual conference in Allahabad, supporting a separate nation-state in the Muslim majority areas of the subcontinent.

Independent India

Under independent India's first prime minister Jawaharlal Nehru (1947–1964), the development of an over-centralized Sovjet-style national government leads to the call for, and the creation of, separate states based on language. From the 1990s onwards, aggressive Hindu majority politics increasingly turn the over two hundred million Indian Muslims into pariahs of the nation.

1947	Partition of British India into India and Pakistan.
1948	Gandhi is assassinated by the Hindu extremist Nathuram Godse.
1956	The politician and anti-caste reformer Bhimrao Ramji Ambedkar converts to Buddhism.
1990	The Indian Parliament accepts the recommendation of the Mandal Commission that 27 per cent of all posts in the central government be reserved for the 'Other Backward Classes', to add to the 22,5 per cent already set apart for Scheduled Castes and Tribes.
1992	Hindu nationalists demolish the fourteenth century Babri Masjid ('Mosque of Mughal Emperor Babur'), which is supposedly built on the birthplace of God Rama in Ayodhya, to clear the way for the construction of a Hindu temple.
2014	Narendra Modi of the Hindu right wing Bharatiya Janata Parishad is elected prime minister of India.

Map

FIGURE 1   Map

Introduction

Indians we all are, and therefore our only possible perfection consists in the development of the Indian nature we have inherited from our fore-fathers. Centuries of real development, of civilisation, of noble fidelity to all the highest ideals men can worship, have fixed for ever the national character of India; and if we be not true to that character, if we be not genuine Indians, we can never be perfect men, full and strong men, able to do a true man's part for God and motherland. Our forefathers are our best models and patterns; they alone can show us what our common Indian nature can and ought to be. We must copy their greatness and their goodness; truly worthy are they of affectionate and reverent imi-tation, for were they not men of renown in their day, men of highest saintliness, of Indian genius and learning and love of learning, of might and valour or the dread field of battle – saints, scholars, heroes? ... Look to your forefathers, read them, speak of them; not in unworthy men-dicant eloquence, nor yet in vulgar boasting about our ancient glories while we squat down in disgraceful content with our present degeneracy, nor least of all in miserable petty controversy with the hireling liars who calumniate our dear India. No! but to learn from them what you ought to be, what God destined Indians to be.

ANANDA K. COOMARASWAMY, *Essays in National Idealism* (1909)[1]

∴

In the above paragraph, the Ceylonese-English art historian and Indian nation-alist Ananda Kentish Coomaraswamy replaced the words Irish(men)/Ireland with Indian(s)/India in a text from a pamphlet issued by the Gaelic League, which was founded in 1893 to encourage the preservation of Irish culture, music, dance and language. The references to national character, the mother-land and a glorious past with heroic forefathers are typical to the language of Romantic nationalism and, no doubt, Coomaraswamy remains important for

---

1 Ananda K. Coomaraswamy, *Essays in National Idealism*, New Delhi: Munshiram Manoharlal, 1981 (first published in 1909): vii–viii.

© BOB VAN DER LINDEN, 2024 | DOI:10.1163/9789004694804_002

the discussion of its Indian incarnation. Like most leading European Romantic nationalists (Byron, Foscolo, Hugo, Lamartine, Mickiewicz, Pushkin, Solomos, de Staël, Wordsworth and so on), he became involved in socio-political reforms. In 1905, he founded the Ceylon Social Reform Society and became its first president, as well as the co-editor of its journal, *The Ceylon National Review*, which ran from 1906 to 1911. According to a manifesto printed in the journal's inaugural issue, which was surely written by Coomaraswamy, the society was dedicated to restraining 'the thoughtless imitation of unsuitable European habits and customs' and to resisting Eastern nations' loss of 'individuality' resulting from 'the adoption of a veneer of Western habits and customs'.[2] Disproportionate devotion to and investment in Western aesthetic ideals, it continued, had resulted in the 'neglect of the elements of superiority in the culture and civilization of the East'.[3] The Ceylon Social Reform Society, therefore, was especially eager 'to encourage the revival of native arts and sciences' and 'to re-create a local demand for wares locally made, as being in every respect more fitted to local needs than any mechanical Western-manufactured goods are likely to become'.[4]

In 1906, Coomaraswamy visited India for the first time and, ever since, he devoted himself to its cultural revitalization. In particular, he made it his mission to educate the West about Indian art.[5] In this, he was much inspired by the ideas of William Morris, the spiritual leader of the British Arts and Crafts Movement. In 1907, in fact, he took over the Essex House Press – which basically was a continuation of Morris's Kelmscott Press – and, accordingly, his *Mediaeval Sinhalese Art* (1908) was printed by hand upon the press that Morris had used for the printing of the Kelmscott Chaucer. Alike Morris, Coomaraswamy hated commercialism and asserted a vision of a future society that would retrieve certain medieval values. Thus, for instance, his description of Ceylon's kingdom of Kandy as 'a society organized on the basis of personal relations and duties' recalls Morris's Romantic account of medieval Europe.[6] Comparable to many late Romantic nationalists in Europe, Coomaraswamy detested capitalist practices – and the doctrine of utilitarianism, which seemed to underlie it – and urbanization. He nostalgically

---

2   Anonymous, "Ceylon Social Reform Society: Manifesto", *Ceylon National Review*, no. 1, January 1906: ii.

3   Ibid.

4   Ibid.: iii.

5   Among his main works on Indian art are *Rajput Painting* (1916), *The Dance of Śiva* (1918) and *History of Indian and Indonesian Art* (1927).

6   Ananda K. Coomaraswamy, *The Indian Craftsman*, London: Probsthain & Co, 1909: 4.

believed that the 'true' India was to be found in its 'village communities' and that the most devastating blow inflicted by colonial rule was not economic ruin, but the vulgarization and destruction of India's artistic traditions. For him, aesthetics and craftsmanship had to precede profit. While assuming that 'nations are made by artists and by poets, not by traders and politicians',[7] Coomaraswamy saw the cultivation of Indian arts and crafts as a national, even international,[8] project to be guided by an ideal of community as an organic whole, a work of art. Subsequently, he became preoccupied with the antiquity and spirituality of India's Hindu art and, through his many writings and as curator in the Museum of Fine Arts in Boston between 1917 and 1947, he overall propagated a rather Romantic image of Indian art to the world.

As a follow-up to Joep Leerssen's grand project on Romantic nationalism in Europe,[9] this book explores to what extent and in which ways Romantic nationalist ideas, like those mentioned above, mingled and were transformed in India from the early nineteenth century and into the twentieth. In doing so, it not only takes a comparative approach with Europe, but it also aims to lay a foundation for the further study of Romantic nationalism in Asia. For, in general, Asian elites and newly emerging middle classes from Istanbul to Tokyo during this period gropingly worked out what it meant to be modern, and they often did so in a Romantic, albeit increasingly anti-imperial/Western, nationalist idiom, as well as in interaction between each other.[10] No matter how small the segment that these groups constituted among the different Asian populations, their cultural initiatives were decisive to the emergence of nations and nationalism.

---

7   Coomaraswamy, *Essays in National Idealism*: ii.
8   On Coomaraswamy's internationalism: Bob van der Linden, *Music and Empire in Britain and India: Identity, Internationalism, and Cross-Cultural Communication*, New York: Palgrave Macmillan, 2013: 20–28.
9   Joep Leerssen, ed., *Encyclopedia of Romantic Nationalism in Europe*, two volumes, Amsterdam: Amsterdam University Press, 2018.
10   On the wider Asian historical context, see for instance; Nicole Cuunjieng Aboitiz, *Asian Place, Filipino Nation: A Global Intellectual History of the Philippine Revolution, 1887–1912*, New York: Columbia University Press, 2020; Cemil Aydin, *The Politics of Anti-Westernism in Asia: Visions of World Order in Pan-Islamic and Pan-Asian Thought*, New York: Columbia University Press, 2007; C. A. Bayly, *The Birth of the Modern World, 1780–1914: Global Connections and Comparisons*, Oxford: Blackwell, 2004; Rebecca E. Karl, *Staging the World: Chinese Nationalism at the Turn of the Twentieth Century*, Durham, NC: Duke University Press, 2002; Bob van der Linden, "Non-Western National Music and Empire in Global History: Interactions, Uniformities, and Comparisons", *Journal of Global History*, 10, 3, 2015: 431–456; Pankaj Mishra, *From the Ruins of Empire: The Revolt Against the West and the Remaking of Asia*, London: Allen Lane, 2012.

4

The departure point is Joep Leerssen's definition of Romantic nationalism as: 'the celebration of the nation (defined in its language, history and cultural character) as an inspiring ideal for artistic expression; and the instrumentalization of that expression in political consciousness-raising'.[11] Thus, while critical of the argument that nationalist appeals to culture merely serve political legitimation, I am specifically concerned with cultural nationalism – that is, the texts and reflexive practices that have the nation as the chief source of inspiration for intellectuals and artists – as an end in itself. Rather than upon political organization and autonomy, Romantic nationalists were largely focused on the cultivation of the nation as a moral community. Also, they increasingly adhered to historicism as a surrogate religion, whereby they habitually argued for the revival of a Golden Age of the nation. In the process, significantly, nationalist revivals repeatedly overlapped with the 'moral languages' of socio-religious reform movements that overall preached modernization from within, while seeking to reconcile tradition with the idea of progress.[12] On the whole, Romantic (cultural) nationalism emerged in the early phase of a national movement, before an explicitly political nationalism (that is, state-seeking) had appeared. At the same time, of course, it remains difficult to separate the two, and Romantic nationalism often converged with political nationalism over time.

On the other hand, Romantic nationalism is an ideal-typical concept and, despite the obvious parallels with what happened in Europe, it no doubt worked out differently in the Indian context. This, among other things, because the British colonial rulers were fundamental to processes of cultivation of culture in India. Following the foundation of the Asiatic Society of Bengal (1784) by the hyperactive polymath William Jones,[13] numerous similar institutions encouraged the study of Indian culture. While the first scholarly efforts were generally the 'hobbies' of European civil servants and missionaries, after the British Crown replaced the East India Company (EIC) in 1858, knowledge production was increasingly formalized during colonial state formation, as exemplified by the *Imperial Gazetteer of India* (1881) and the decennial census of India, of which the first complete one was taken in 1881. The

11   Joep Leerssen, "Introduction" in Leerssen, ed., *Encyclopedia*, volume one: 36.

12   John Hutchinson, "Cultural Nationalism" in John Breuilly, ed., *The Oxford Handbook of the History of Nationalism*, Oxford: Oxford University Press, 2013: 75–94; Bob van der Linden, *Moral Languages from Colonial Punjab: The Singh Sabha, Arya Samaj and Ahmadiyahs*, New Delhi: Manohar, 2008.

13   Michael J. Franklin, *Orientalist Jones: Sir William Jones, Poet, Lawyer, and Linguist, 1746–1794*, New York: Oxford University Press, 2011.

Archaeological Survey of India (since 1861) was responsible for the research into and preservation of India's numerous historical monuments. These had suffered oblivion but were now re-consecrated into objects of contemplation and, moreover, besides numerous written sources, provided the basis for the writing of a historical narrative for India. Closely related was the establishment of museums throughout the subcontinent. The oldest one, Calcutta's Indian Museum, was founded in 1814 by the Asiatic Society of Bengal. A few other main ones were: Madras's Central Museum (1851), Lahore Museum (1865) and Bombay's Victory and Albert Museum (1872). The archeological and art objects displayed in these museums helped to cultivate the notion of India's classical heritage as a counterpart to the Greco-Roman one.

All this largely concerned colonial knowledge production, that is the mapping of land and people in the name of science. Yet, simultaneously, such initiatives were impossible without Indian assistance. Furthermore, its results unintendedly often proved fundamental to the making of (the) Indian nation(s). Colonial (historical) writings, research and collections became not only points of reference for Indian elites, but the latter themselves increasingly also took the lead in these processes of cultivation of culture. In congruence with what Romantic nationalists did in Europe, Indian intellectuals generally followed a 'salvage paradigm' and, for instance, collected and published ancient texts and wrote about 'authentic' (folk) traditions. Likewise, they organized themselves in voluntary associations and established learned institutions and journals (in both English and the vernaculars) dedicated to Indian literature, music and the arts. While thus claiming the nation's patrimony, they particularly adhered to the myth of a classical Golden Age, which was largely depicted as Hindu at the same time. Ultimately, it is this intriguing and complicated interaction between colonial/Orientalist knowledge production and Indian cultivation of culture that remains quintessential for the understanding of Indian Romantic nationalism.

More immediately, Romantic nationalism in India (and Asia) diverged from its European version because the last appeared within one civilization, although one that due to imperial expansion changed in many ways as well. Without any doubt, British rule was decisive to intellectual and emotional changes among Indians.[14] The humiliation of conquest, political elimination of their rulers and experience with European racism, either as govern-

---

14   Sudhir Chandra, *The Oppressive Present: Literature and Social Consciousness in Colonial India*, New Delhi: Oxford University Press, 1992; Margrit Pernau, *Emotions and Modernity in Colonial India: From Balance to Fervor, New Delhi*: Oxford University Press, 2019; Tapan Raychaudhuri, *Europe Reconsidered: Perceptions of the West in Nineteenth-Century Bengal*,

ment employee (as many elitist Indians were, at least temporarily) or otherwise, afflicted Indian thinkers with melancholy. Similar to what happened
in Europe, a sense of self-alienation and, closely related, processes of cultivation of culture led to the emergence of the idea of the Indian nation as
a moral community. Yet, the Indian encounter with British power was certainly different from, for example, the European national responses to French
Napoleonic hegemony because Indians simultaneously had to deal with the
modern thoughts and practices of a different civilization. Despite the many
parallels, therefore, Indian Romantic nationalism was more confrontational
than its European counterparts because its protagonists were painfully aware
of the fact that the cultural ground was shifting under their feet. It sometimes
also was 'an emotionally charged reply to the ruler's allegation that India never
was and never could be a nation'.[15]

Most significantly, Indian Romantic nationalists to a large extent understood modern ideas – including that so-difficult-to-define concept 'nation' –
in the light of their own cultural and intellectual traditions, institutions and,
indeed, feelings and emotions. 'Glorification of the land and people itself was
deeply rooted in the thought and literature of the subcontinent': the royal
lineage histories and ballads of the region currently known as Rajasthan, for
instance, poetically depicted 'the brave acts of kings, nobles and commoners
in defense of land and honour against neighbours, as well as other pre-colonial
outsiders'.[16] Following the ancient Sanskrit scriptures and mythologies, Hindus, Jains and Buddhists had a sacred geographical knowledge of (parts of)
the land that they called *Bharat* (still the official name of the Republic of India
today),[17] upon which they enacted with fervor through an innumerable number of pilgrim routes. Until the early nineteenth century, trade routes followed
the notion of five linked territories within the subcontinent, whereby from the
midland (the area between and around Lahore-Agra), four ways (*pathas*) led
like wheel spokes to the north (*Uttarpatha*), the south (*Dakshinapatta*), the

---

New Delhi: Oxford University Press, 2002 (second edition; first published in 1988) and *Perceptions, Emotions, Sensibilities: Essays on India's Colonial and Post-Colonial Experiences*,
New Delhi: Oxford University Press, 1999.
15   Raychaudhuri, *Perceptions, Emotions, Sensibilities*: 18.
16   C. A. Bayly, *Origins of Nationality in South Asia: Patriotism and Ethical Government in the
Making of Modern India*, New Delhi: Oxford University Press, 1998: 11, 27. See also: Sumit
Guha, *History and Collective Memory in South Asia, 1200–2000*, Seattle: University of Washington Press, 2019.
17   'Bharat' is an abbreviation of the Sanskrit 'Bharatvarsa', the land of the Bharata clan of the
Mahabharata epic. Hence, the term directly refers to the subcontinent's pre-Islamic past,
which since the nineteenth century was increasingly celebrated by Hindu nationalists.

east (*Pracya*) and the west (*Aparanta*). Conversely, the (north Indian) Muslim heirs of a composite Indo-Islamic culture of at least six centuries old had a clear sense of and emotional attachment to what they called 'Hindustan'. To different degrees, emergent ideas about (the) Indian nation(s) built further upon these pre-colonial 'patriotic' notions and, in result, the concerns of Indian Romantic nationalists repeatedly were different from what the colonial rulers had in mind for India.

In chorus, speeches and writings that proclaimed the Indian nation were often more about regional 'nations' such as Bengal and Punjab. Likewise, for instance, nineteenth century Bengali writers used the word 'Bengali' in a blurred manner, as synonymous with 'Indian', 'Hindu' and 'Aryan'. Regional patriotisms were thus more or less lifted out of their local base to back up an emerging national Indian one. In combination with a growing adherence to modern knowledge, then, Indian Romantic nationalist thoughts and emotions imaginatively spurred existing traditions into new intellectual, moral and increasingly political, if not revolutionary, directions. Indian thinkers appropriated not only European Enlightenment and liberal ideas in their own distinctive ways, but instantaneously turned to India's (mythological) past, in which tradition supposedly was still predominant. In these and other ways, they cultivated their traditions into a domain in which (the) nation(s) already was/were sovereign even though the state officially was in foreign hands, and so made Indian culture the source from where Indian nationalism(s) subsequently gained 'their basic moral strength both to stir the public mind and to infiltrate state institutions'.[18]

Romanticism, Indian Tradition and the Nation

The narrative begins in Calcutta (figure 2), which by the beginning of the nineteenth century was not only the capital of the British EIC, the largest clearing-house of trade in Asia and the hub for British expansion into Asia and the Pacific, but also an important place of scientific knowledge production.[19] What happened among the nineteenth century Bengali intelligentsia, 'the first Asian social group of any size whose mental world was transformed

18   Linden, *Moral Languages*: 231.
19   Kapil Raj, *Relocating Modern Science: Circulation and the Construction of Knowledge in South Asia and Europe, 1650–1900*, New York: Palgrave Macmillan, 2007 and "The Historical Anatomy of a Contact Zone: Calcutta in the Eighteenth Century", *Indian Economic and Social History Review*, 48, 1, 2011: 55–82.

through its interactions with the West',[20] remains to a great extent comparable to the intellectual and emotional scrimmages one usually associates with
Romantic nationalism in, for instance, Russia – between Slavophiles and West-
ernizers, conservatives and liberals – and the great social impact of men (and
some women) of letters at large.[21] The first generations of mostly English-
educated Bengalis wrestled not only with the results of modern science and
ideas of European Enlightenment thinkers such as Rousseau, Montesquieu,
Locke, Hume, Kant and Hegel, but also with the Romantic literature of Byron,
Goethe, Keats, Scott, Shelley, Wordsworth and so on.

The 'father of the Bengal Renaissance' Ram Mohan Roy, who died in Bristol
in 1833, explicitly seized Enlightenment and liberal ideas in the light of the
Iberian and Latin American constitutional revolutions, the movement for free
trade and parliamentary reform in Britain.[22] He wrote with feeling 'about the
fate of Italian and Spanish revolutionaries in the 1810s and supported the Irish
against the British'.[23] At the same time, nonetheless, he and other leading Bengali intellectuals remained steeped in their traditions. Thus, on the one hand,
Ram Mohan Roy contrasted Hindu culture with Christian Europe, whereby
he invoked scientific thinking and Christian morality against what he considered the anomalies of the Hindu tradition. Yet, on the other, he negatively
positioned Christianity versus the wisdom and spirituality of the Vedas and
Upanishads. Overall, Roy argued that culturally and morally Indians 'were the
equals of Europeans'.[24] While he repeatedly referred to India as a nation and
imagined freedom for India over a hundred years, however, he simultaneously
hoped 'that the day would not come too soon for his countrymen to learn from
contact with Europe'.[25]

At Calcutta's Hindu College, founded by Ram Mohan Roy in 1817, the charismatic Henry Derozio was particularly attracted to Western ideas and, in contrast to Roy, he largely dismissed Indian traditional ideas and practices. He

---

20   Raychaudhuri, *Europe Reconsidered*: xxi.
21   Although Calcutta is generally taken as a starting point to discuss modern Indian intel-
      lectual history, Bombay soon also emerged as a city of cosmopolitan ideas, in which
      (trading) communities of Indo-Portuguese, Parsi, Muslim Shia (Ismaili, Bohra, Khoja
      and Memon), Gujarati, Marathi and other backgrounds interacted with the British and
      amongst each other.
22   David Kopf, *British Orientalism and the Bengal Renaissance*, Berkeley, CA: University of
      California Press, 1969; Lynn Zastoupil, *Rammohun Roy and the Making of Victorian Britain*,
      New York: Palgrave Macmillan, 2010.
23   Mishra, *From the Ruins of Empire*: 168.
24   C. A. Bayly, *Recovering Liberties: Indian Thought in the Age of Liberalism and Empire*, Cam-
      bridge: Cambridge University Press, 2012: 60.
25   Raychaudhuri, *Europe Reconsidered*: 351.

FIGURE 2   Old Court House Street, Calcutta, photographer unknown, c. 1850s–60s
COURTESY OF THE RIJKSMUSEUM, AMSTERDAM

taught English literature and lectured on Hume and Kant. Also, he was a devotee of the English American Thomas Paine, whose thoughts had been crucial
to the American Revolution and reflected the Enlightenment rhetoric of global
human rights. He wrote numerous poems on Greek themes in the style of
Byron that were combined 'with verses on India as a once-great nation, fallen
on evil times', but like Greece in Ottoman times 'capable of recovering her former grandeur'.[26] No doubt, Derozio's heart lay in the country where he was
born to a Portuguese Indian father and an English mother. In his *To India–My
Native Land* (1828), for instance, he lamented that India was under British rule:

> My country! in thy day of glory past
> A beauteous halo circled round thy brow,
> And worshipped as a deity thou wast.
> Where is that glory, where that reverence now?

---

26   Bayly, *Recovering Liberties*: 48.

Thy eagle pinion is chained down at last,
And grovelling in the lowly dust art thou;
Thy minstrel hath no wreath to weave for thee
Save the sad story of thy misery!
Well–let me dive into the depths of time,
And bring from out the ages that have rolled
A few small fragments of those wrecks sublime,
Which human eyes may never more behold;
And let the guerdon of my labour be
My fallen country! one kind wish from thee![27]

Derozio encouraged his students to think for themselves and, following his premature death in 1831, a group of radical anglophile free thinkers, known as Derozians, established the Young Bengal movement as a non-subversive version of Giuseppe Mazzini's democratic nationalist association Young Italy.

Indeed, from the 1840s until the first decade of the twentieth century, Mazzini was 'the most truly admired foreign public moralist and political thinker in South Asia'.[28] Numerous (biographical) articles and booklets were written about him, including by such dissimilar nationalists as Surendranath Banerjee, Lala Lajpat Rai, Mahatma Gandhi and Vinayak Damodar Savarkar, who in 1907 translated the Italian's autobiography in Marathi. Mazzini's *The Duties of Man* (1860) was translated into various Indian languages and its Hindi version sold hundreds of thousands of copies.[29] In particular, Indian intellectuals were drawn to Mazzini's Romantic nationalist message that nations were human communities rather than mere territories: 'the country is the sentiment of love, the sense of fellowship that binds together all the sons of that territory'.[30] Thus, Surendranath Banerjee wrote in 1876:

> Mazzini lived and died for Italian unity. He rightly judged that Italy would never be great, unless the different peoples of Italy were united

---

27   H. L. V. Derozio, *Poems of Henry Louis Vivian Derozio: A Forgotten Anglo-Indian Poet*, introduced by F. B. Bradley-Birt and with a new foreword by R. K. Dasgupta, Calcutta: Oxford University Press, 1980 (second edition; first published in 1923): 2.

28   C. A. Bayly, "Liberalism at Large: Mazzini and Nineteenth-Century Indian Thought" in C. A. Bayly and E. F. Biagini, eds., *Guiseppe Mazzini and the Globalization of Democratic Nationalism, 1830–1920*, Oxford: Oxford University Press, 2008: 355.

29   Gita Srivastava, *Mazzini and His Impact on the Indian Nationalist Movement*, Allahabad: Chugh Publications, 1982.

30   As cited in Bayly, "Liberalism at Large": 372.

together by the bonds of a common nationality and common institutions. Might we not see in this much to guide and to instruct us? Is Indian
greatness possible unless we are thoroughly welded together into a com-
pact mass? [...] Are not Bengalis, Madrasis, Mahrattas, the people of the
Punjab, of Oudh, of Central India, all brothers?[31]

Moreover, he continued, Mazzini taught that 'moral regeneration, which in
most cases is synonymous with spiritual regeneration, must precede political
regeneration, and must precede the accomplishment of national greatness'.[32]
According to Banerjee, this process was not only similar to the way 'the purely
spiritual reformation' of the first Sikh Guru, Nanak, paved the way for 'the
political generation of the Sikh people',[33] but it also accounted, as he believed
history would prove, for 'one of the most powerful agencies of Indian progress
and Indian civilization', namely the Brahmo Samaj,[34] the monotheistic reform
movement established by Ram Mohan Roy in 1828.[35] In the end, nonetheless,
the image of Italy as 'a fallen nation rising up as India would rise' was more
important for Indians than any particular component of Mazzini's thought.[36]

Still, Indian Romantic nationalism developed originally alongside a great
enthusiasm for British rule: 'The colonial projection that the British conquest
was the best thing that had ever happened to India was widely accepted until
the 1890s'.[37] In general, elitist Indians since Ram Mohan Roy praised the worth
of modern education. Also, they believed in the efficacy of constitutional
agitation and reform. To different degrees, they trusted their rulers to foster
Indian representation in government and, hence, they saw British rule as a
necessary evil until they themselves were ready to take charge of their own
affairs. Guided by notions about freedom and rights, however, Indian intellectuals petitioned and disconcerted their rulers to bring them to a sense of
their responsibilities as caretakers or, at least, as rulers in partnership. They
mainly did so through organizations such as the British Indian Association –

31   Surendranath Banerjea, "Joseph Mazzini", delivered at a meeting of the Calcutta Utter-
      para Hitakari Sabha, 2 April 1876, in Surendranath Banerjea, *Speeches and Writings of the
      Hon. Surendranath Banerjea: Selected by Himself*, Madras: G. A. Natesan & Co, 1918: 413.
32   Ibid.: 400.
33   More in Chapter Two about the incorporation of Sikh Guru Nanak into the canon of
      Indian national heroes.
34   David Kopf, *The Brahmo Samaj and the Shaping of the Modern Indian Mind*, Princeton, NJ:
      Princeton University Press, 1979.
35   Banerjea, "Joseph Mazzini": 401.
36   Bayly, "Liberalism at Large": 359.
37   Raychaudhuri, *Perceptions, Emotions, Sensibilities*: 19.

set up in Calcutta in 1851 without a single British member – and above all, of course, the Indian National Congress (INC), founded in Bombay in 1885 (British India's first avowed nationalist organization, the Indian National Association, founded in 1876 by Surendranath Banerjee, merged with the INC). It was only towards the end of the nineteenth century, and especially in the wake of the infamous partition of Bengal by the British in 1905, that a growing number of Indian nationalists thought that British rule was no longer providential. This resulted into a division within the INC between 'moderates' led by Gopal Krishna Gokhale, who promoted reforms by working with existing government institutions and, hence, downplayed public agitation, and 'extremists' led by Bal Gangadhar Tilak, who advocated confrontation, if not the ejection of the British by force, and regarded the pursuit of social reform as a distraction from the road to *swaraj* (self-rule).

Significantly, this change in attitude towards British rule was congruent with a growing pride in the Hindu heritage. The generations after Derozio ever more ridiculed their own Anglicization and instead developed modern identities based on reinterpreted Hindu texts and traditions. For a long time, nineteenth century India's most famous and successful modern novelist Bankim Chandra Chatterjee considered modern European civilization the highest level of progress ever attained by man. Yet, later in his life, he self-consciously defined himself as a Hindu and was 'convinced of India's superiority over Europe on many points'.[38] He had become particularly critical about European science and materialism. As rephrased by Tapan Raychaudhuri:

> Now science was a monster stinking of human blood and bedecked with the weapons of destruction. With one hand it ran the machines producing goods and with the other it brushed away 'all that was ancient and pure, the cherished treasures of many millennia'. The Europeans wrongly accused the Hindus of worshipping inanimate objects. In fact they themselves had become the worshippers of lifeless things. They had harnessed the forces of nature but never stopped to think that these were permeated by the Divine consciousness. Nor did they enquire into God's purpose as revealed in nature. To play around with natural forces without such knowledge was a mortal sin. [...] Science had become a handmaiden to the intense materialism of nineteenth-century Europe, 'deadliest moral poison'.[39]

---

38   Raychaudhuri, *Europe Reconsidered*: 196.
39   Ibid.: 198.

Of course, similar ideas about progress and reconciliation with the natural world were common among European Romantics too. Yet, while the latter looked everywhere for models uncorrupted by capitalism – among other things, to the medieval guilds, the cities of ancient Greece, the 'noble savages' of Tahiti, the clans of Scotland and, of course, India –, nineteenth century Indian intellectuals basically reinterpreted, albeit rather idiosyncratically, the (ancient) Hindu heritage in view of European (Romantic) thought and literature. Despite the coeval influences of Buddhist, Jain and devotional (*bhakti*) traditions, and of Islamic (sufi) thought, Indian tradition in the modern period was almost exclusively seen as synonymous – and partially so in dialogue with European Orientalists – with Hindu texts, mythologies and practices. Furthermore, because of a newly found dignity in their past, Hindu thinkers increasingly felt the need to assert the moral and spiritual superiority of the Hindu tradition over materialist European culture.

At the same time, it should be underlined that numerous leading Hindus – from Ram Mohan Roy to India's most important propagator of the doctrine of Hindu spirituality in the West, Swami Vivekananda–[40] found a certain pride in the Indo-Islamic heritage of the subcontinent. The ever-growing focus on things Hindu did certainly not lead to an immediate and conscious anti-Muslim attitude among Hindu intellectuals. Modern Indian intellectual history is more complicated than that. Cultural identities and boundaries were defined, but rather intuitively and without any definite view of the future in mind. In fact, the idea of a homogenous Hindu community or Hinduism, as increasingly propagated by Hindu nationalists, was to a great extent introduced by European missionaries and scholars. The term 'Hindu' was first used only in the ninth century by people living outside India to describe the inhabitants of the subcontinent. It originates from the Persian Sindh, meaning the land on the banks of the Sindhu (the Indus River). Early Muslims used the Arabic 'Al-Hind' and later 'Hindustan' became the common geographical term for the northern parts of the subcontinent. The ancient texts that Hindus today claim their roots from (such as the Vedas, Ramayana, Mahabharata and Upanishads), do not ever use the terms Hindu. For centuries, Hindus did not call themselves Hindus but largely identified themselves as followers of Vishnu, Shiva and so on.

But why was the nineteenth century Indian intelligentsia attracted to European Romantic literature and thought in the first place? This question is

---

40   Ruth Harris, *Guru to the World: The Life and Legacy of Vivekananda*, Cambridge, Mass.: The Belknap Press of Harvard University Press, 2022.

especially interesting because most Romantic writings, such as Walter Scott's Waverley novels, were frowned upon by British educationists in India and they largely therefore were read outside of (missionary) school and college syllabi.[41] Did the European Romantic sensibility and the Indian sensibility share a common ground? At least, the accusations raised by leading (orthodox) Bengali Hindus at Derozio and the members of the Young Bengal movement (about their immorality, atheism and what not) were strikingly like those brought against Romantics in Britain at the time. On the other hand, India had strongly reinforced or directly inspired the European Romantic imagination since the late eighteenth century. In 1950, Raymond Schwab believed that this 'Oriental Renaissance' was as radical as the 'first' Renaissance.[42] After reading translations of Sanskrit texts such as the Bhagavad Gita, *Shakuntala*, Gita Govinda and the Upanishads, European Romantic thinkers glorified India as the country of origins, primeval revelations and innocent childhood. While realizing that Sanskrit collections of fables such as the *Panchatantra* and *Hitopadesha*, known as Bidpai's Tales in Islamic countries, had reached Europe along medieval trade routes, nineteenth century philologists regarded India as the ultimate source of many European folk stories. Over time, Europeans repeatedly also invoked Indian spirituality against modern European materialism and rationalism.[43]

Without any doubt, Indians felt much attracted to European Romantic (Orientalist) reinterpretations of their own literature because these texts generally set India in a positive light – both historically and spiritually – and thus strengthened their own sense of worth. While they must have been equally pleased by the Romantics' celebration of the sacredness and transcendence of all forms of life and nature, Indians were especially drawn to the revolutionary sympathies of some European Romantics, as well as their overall privileging of emotion over reason. For some time, Lord Byron achieved a cult status among the Bengali intelligentsia, as the 'friend of the oppressed, enemy of the oppressor, repository of love, youth embodied, intrepid, forever restless, and inimical

---

41   Priya Joshi, *In Another Country: Colonialism, Culture, and the English Novel in India*, New York: Columbia University Press, 2002.

42   Raymond Schwab, *The Oriental Renaissance: Europe's Rediscovery of India and the East, 1680–1880*, with an introduction by Edward W. Said, New York: Columbia University Press, 1984 (first published in French in 1950).

43   Wilhelm Halbfass, *India and Europe: An Essay in Understanding*, New Delhi: Motilal Banarsidass, 1990 (first published in 1988); Ronald Inden, *Imagining India*, Bloomington, IN: Indiana University Press, 2000 (second edition; first published in 1990); Schwab, *The Oriental Renaissance*.

to lethargy and the high-handedness of the society'.[44] Yet, similar to the way European Romantics understood India, Indians carefully selected what they liked best from European Romantic texts and thoughts. Moreover, they often compared these materials cross-culturally to Indian ideas and provided new meaning to Indian concepts, which they nonetheless continued to understand as being traditional.

Romantic Nationalism and the Global Circulation of Ideas

All in all, Indian Romantic nationalist thought emerged as part of a global con-junctural phenomenon rather than simply a lineage or influence diffused from Europe. The nineteenth century Indian intelligentsia actively, independently and creatively participated in the production of modern knowledge. The fact that they had quickly embraced the English language and print culture was critical. Books and articles were discussed passionately and translated from English (or other European languages) into different Indian languages or from one vernacular into another, whereby it evidently helped that many Indian intellectuals were at least bilingual. Ram Mohan Roy was proficient in Bengali, Sanskrit and Persian, as well as Greek, Latin, Hebrew and English. Also, the role of business interactions should not be underestimated in the circulation and production of ideas. From the 1820s onwards, Dwarkanath Tagore, the grand-father of the Bengali polymath and Asia's first Nobel Laureate Rabindranath Tagore, played a pioneering role in setting up a string of commercial ven-tures – such as banking, insurance and shipping companies – in partnership with British traders. In particular, Parsi businessmen did the same in Bombay. Soon, Indian entrepreneurs opened offices elsewhere in Asia and in Britain. As trade routes changed, Indian merchants from Shekhawati (today's Rajasthan) or other regions that earlier catered to the 'silk road' and/or Ganges River trade moved to the economically more important colonial port cities of Calcutta and Bombay. Yet, simultaneously, through investments in their native regions, they made their relatives at home somewhat familiar with novel ideas and practices. To a lesser extent, the same accounts for the Indian soldiers in the British Indian army, particularly those serving in the British Empire overseas, and Indian seamen. Alternately, the oral and written reports of Indian rulers or their envoys about their visits to Europe had an intellectual impact.

---

44   Abhishek Sarkar, "The Scottish 'Ploughman Poet' Among the Bengali Intelligentsia: Appreciating Robert Burns in Colonial Bengal", *Scottish Literary Review*, 11, 2, 2019: 113.

Fundamental to the emergence of Romantic nationalist thought was the ever-growing number of elitist Indians who went (for studies) to Britain, Europe and beyond. In 1868, Surendranath Banerjee, Romesh Chunder Dutt and Behari Lal Gupta travelled to England together and successfully completed their Indian Civil Service examinations. In comparison, during the nineteenth century, almost no indigenous intelligentsia from the Dutch East Indies departed to the Netherlands for studies or, in fact, were allowed in the colonial civil service in the first place. After the Parsi scholar, trader and politician Dadabhai Naoroji (figure 3) moved to England from Bombay, he became the first Asian to be elected as a British member of parliament between 1892 and 1895 and a central point of contact for Indians in Britain. Known as the 'Grand Old Man of India', he was president of the INC in 1886 and 1906. For decades and ultimately through his *Poverty and Un-British Rule in India* (1902), he familiarized audiences in India and Britain (and seemingly also Karl Marx) with his influential theory of the Indian 'wealth drain' into Britain.[45] By the end of the nineteenth century, London had become an important meeting place for radical Indian nationalists to discuss modern ideas and India's future. They particularly established links with their Irish nationalist counterparts, investigating strategies of both parliamentary pressure and armed insurrection.[46]

India House (1905–1910), a student residence in London's Highgate, was central to the development of nationalist revolutionary ideas. It was inaugurated, amongst others, by Dadabhai Naoroji, Lala Lajpat Rai and the nationalist lawyer and journalist Shyamji Krishnavarma. Under the patronage of the last, India House became a hub for Indian revolutionaries, who referred to themselves, again after Mazzini, as the Young India Party. Earlier, Krishnavarma participated in the Hindu reformer Swami Dayanand Saraswati's Arya Samaj (see further Chapter Three) and the Theosophical Society. Being a gifted linguist, he became the assistant of the Oxford Sanskritist Monier Monier-Williams.[47] India House served as the headquarters for Krishnavarma's Indian Home Rule

45   Dinyar Patel, *Naoroji: Pioneer of Indian Nationalism*, Harvard: Harvard University Press, 2020.

46   C. A. Bayly, "Ireland, India and the Empire: 1780–1914", *Transactions of the Royal Historical Society*, 10, 2000: 377–397; Elleke Boehmer, *Empire, the National, and the Postcolonial 1890–1920: Resistance in Interaction*, Oxford: Oxford University Press, 2002; Michael Silvestri, *Ireland and India: Nationalism, Empire and Memory*, Basingstoke: Palgrave Macmillan, 2009.

47   Harald Fischer-Tiné, *Shyamji Krishnavarma: Sanskrit, Sociology and anti-Imperialism*, New Delhi: Routledge, 2014; Nicholas Owen, "The Soft Heart of the British Empire: Indian Radicals in London", *Past and Present*, 220, 1, 2013: 143–184.

FIGURE 3   Dadabhai Naoroji by Lock & Whitfield, published by W. H. Allen & Co, 1889
COURTESY OF THE NATIONAL PORTRAIT GALLERY, LONDON

Society and the anti-colonial weekly newspaper *The Indian Sociologist* which reached global audiences beyond Britain and India. Numerous Indian intellectuals passed by or lived temporarily in India House, including Gopal Krishna Gokhale, Bal Gangadhar Tilak, Lala Har Dayal, V. V. S. Aiyar and Mohandas Karamchand Gandhi. Also, Krishnavarma offered scholarships to Indian students if they promised not to work for the colonial government thereafter. In 1907, however, he moved to Paris to avoid prosecution. Here, he worked closely together with S. R. Rana, the vice-president of the Home Rule Society in London and the founder of the Paris Indian Society in 1905, and Madame (Bhikaiji Rustom) Cama.[48] In general, he ended up in the circles of 'French

---

48   Ole Birk Laursen, "'I have only One Country, it is the World': Madame Cama, Anticolonialism, and Indian-Russian Revolutionary Networks in Paris, 1907–17", *History Workshop Journal*, 90, 2020: 96–114.

socialists, Chinese and Javanese pan-Asians, Egyptian nationalists, English suf-
fragists, Russian anarchists and Irish Fenians'.[49]

Meanwhile, the extreme nationalist Vinayak Damodar Savarkar emerged as
the main figure at the London India House. Through his Free India Society, he
taught Indian students the arts of revolutionary organization, bomb-making
and the underground press in preparation for an armed struggle in India. All
this culminated in July 1909, when the Indian student Madan Lal Dhingra,
probably on Savarkar's instructions, shot and killed the Political Aide-de-
Camp to the Secretary of State for India Sir William Curzon Wyllie. After his
arrest and before his execution, Dhingra made the following statement:

> As a Hindu I feel that the slavery of my nation is an insult to my God
> [Mother India]. Her cause is the cause of freedom. Her service is the
> service of Sri Krishna. Neither rich nor able, a poor son like myself can
> offer nothing but his blood on the altar of Mother's deliverance and so I
> rejoice at the prospect of my martyrdom.[50]

Soon thereafter Savarkar was arrested for his revolutionary activities and
imprisoned in India until 1937. During his imprisonment, however, he was
allowed to meet influential nationalists such as Gandhi and Bhimrao Ramji
Ambedkar, as well as Nathuram Godse, who later in his life assassinated
Gandhi. Moreover, he kept in contact with his followers through his writings, especially his most influential *Essentials of Hindutva* (1923), which in 1928
was reprinted as *Hindutva: Who is a Hindu?* In this book, Savarkar articulated
the political ideology of Hindutva ('Hindu-ness') as the essence of India. The
idea was championed by the Hindu Mahasabha political party (since 1921),
of which Savarkar became the president after his release, and the Rashtriya
Swayamsevak Sangh (RSS), a Hindu nationalist volunteer organization established by K. B. Hedgewar in 1925, a former member of the Mahasabha. In fact,
the leaders of the RSS took not only Hitler and Mussolini as heroic role models, but they also declared that Indian Muslims were the equivalent of the Jews
in Europe. Speech after speech, Savarkar supported Hitler's anti-Jewish policy
and, in 1938, he suggested the following solution for the Muslim 'problem' in
India: 'A nation is formed by a majority living therein. What did the Jews do in
Germany? They being in minority were driven out from Germany'.[51]

---

49   Fischer-Tiné, *Shyamji Krishnavarma*: 226.
50   As cited in Tilak Raj Sareen, *Indian Revolutionary Movement Abroad (1905–1921)*, New
      Delhi: Sterling, 1979: Appendix II, explanation added.
51   Marzia Casolari, "Hindutva's Foreign Tie-Up in the 1930s: Archival Evidence", *Economic
      and Political Weekly*, 35, 4, 2000: 223.

Besides with Irish nationalists, Indian intellectuals in Britain networked with a wide range of European anti-establishment figures (Fabian socialists, anarchists and so on) and 'black' nationalists from the British colonies in Africa and the Caribbean. In connection to the making of Indian Romantic nationalist thought, however, the Theosophical Society became particularly significant for them.[52] This especially so when the society moved its headquarters to Adyar, near Madras, six years after its foundation by Madame Helena Blavatsky and Henry Steel Olcott in 1875 in New York. Overall, Theosophists claimed to bring a new enlightenment based on the ancient wisdom of spiritual India. Mainly based on Blavatsky's writings, often as expanded by later writers, and Orientalist interpretations of Buddhist and Hindu sources, Theosophists investigated the spiritual element in human beings and the world, to promote 'universal brotherhood of man', irrespective of race, creed, color or sex. Contradictorily, they leaned toward the unity of the Indo-European tradition (Aryanism) and overall followed a hierarchical and racial worldview. They often advanced their ideas in a polarizing manner as being superior to Western rational science and, generally, as an international movement, it had a role in the development of radical anti-establishment and anti-colonial politics at once in metropoles and colonies.

Indian reformers and nationalists were attracted to the Theosophists because they judged British imperial rule negatively and, to the contrary, praised the Brahminical tradition (Sanskrit, Vedas and caste system) of a Hindu Golden Age and reinterpreted it in scientific evolutionary terms. In this way, Theosophists stood in line with English-educated Indians who claimed the same Aryan origin as that of the British and so morally questioned colonial rule. Typical for the global circulation of ideas, Gandhi and other Indian thinkers generally became more interested in the Hindu tradition through Theosophy. In turn, some leading Theosophists became great supporters of the Indian nationalist movement. During the 1880s, Allen Octavian Hume was instrumental in organizing the first meetings of the INC. Best known, however, remains the Irish Annie Besant, who in 1907 was appointed as the Theosophical Society's president. On the whole, she became much involved in the revival and dissemination of the Hindu tradition. She founded Central Hindu College (1898), being the forerunner of Benares Hindu University, learned Sanskrit, and published a translation of the Bhagavad Gita in 1895. During the First

---

52   Linden, *Music and Empire*: 15–20; Peter van der Veer, *Imperial Encounters: Religion and Modernity in India and Britain*, Princeton, NJ: Princeton University Press, 2001: Chapter Three.

World War, Besant modeled a Home Rule League on the Irish example and, in 1917, she was elected president of the INC.

The Irish couple James and Margaret Cousins should also be mentioned. Both were Theosophists and actively involved in all aspects of Irish political and literary life. Among other things, Margaret had founded the Irish Women's Franchise League and supported Irish independence. James was a writer, critic, and Irish nationalist, who published widely on Theosophy and was part of the Irish Literary Revival, nicknamed 'the Celtic Twilight', that included William Butler Yeats and James Joyce. In 1915, at the behest of Annie Besant, the couple left for India, where the two anti-imperial internationalists became much involved in Indian nationalist activities and, amongst others, worked closely together with Rabindranath Tagore.

As a follower of the Arts and Crafts Movement, James Cousins generally took up the cause of Indian ideals in the fields of art, literature and education.[53] This was not so much to promote nationalism but because he believed that India, as 'the mother of Asian culture', was the key to the spiritual survival of the world. In a formulation borrowed from the famous axiom of the Japanese art critic Okakura Kakuzo's declaration that 'Asia is one' (see further below), Cousins wrote: 'In Asia all roads lead to India – or rather, all roads lead *from* India'.[54] Moreover, he firmly and romantically believed that the supposedly shared Aryan origins and sensibilities of Indians and Celts had led to the Irish Literary Revival:

> So subtly, however, had the Aryan influence intermingled with the culture of Ireland that when, once again, at the beginning of the twentieth century, the ancient Asian spirit touched Ireland through the philosophy of India, as conveyed through the works of Edwin Arnold and the Theosophical Society, there was an immediate response. Two poets (AE and Yeats) found their inmost nature expressed in the Indian modes. They found also the spiritual truths that Asia had given to the world reflected in the old myths and legends of Ireland; and out of their illuminations and enthusiastic response arose the Irish Literary and Dramatic Revival whose influence at its height was purely spiritual.[55]

On the other hand, Margaret Cousins became not only a crucial fighter for women's rights in India but, being a musician herself, she generally also under-

---

53   James H. Cousins, *The Renaissance in India*, Madras: Ganesh & Co, 1918.

54   James H. Cousins, *The Cultural Unity of Asia*, Madras: Theosophical Publishing House, 1922: 122 (italics in original).

55   Ibid.: 7–8 (AE is the pseudonym of George William Russell).

lined the value of Indian music for the spiritual revival of the nation and played a role in the institutionalization of the modern education in south Indian 'Karnatak' art music.[56]

At the same time, Indian (Romantic) nationalists participated in Asian networks.[57] During the 1870s, the idea of the 'Muslim world' emerged as a conscious political concept,[58] partially through efforts of Jamal al-Din al-Afghani, who during his restless travels through Muslim countries spent several years in India propagating pan-Islamist thought as well.[59] In India, pan-Islamism ultimately led to the Khilafat Movement (1919–1924), which temporarily – and with the support of Mahatma Gandhi – united Muslims and Hindus in an anti-imperial struggle.[60] Of greater importance was pan-Asianism, which likewise appeared during the 1870s – as a matter of fact, 'Asia', understood as an umbrella term, is a European concept (since the ancient Greeks) and Asians adopted it only in response to the imperial encounter. Both Swami Vivekananda (figure 4), who visited Japan in 1893 while on his way to the World's Parliament of Religions, which was held in that same year as a side show of the Columbian Exposition in Chicago, and Rabindranath Tagore, who visited Japan for the first time in 1916 (figure 34), identified Asia, and above all India, by its inherent spirituality as the antithesis to Western materialism.[61]

Most significant to the global circulation of ideas remains the fact that the notion of spiritual India/Asia, which became imperative to Asian nationalisms, had its origins in the West. Since the seventeenth century, European travelers, missionaries, Orientalists and (Romantic) philosophers had constructed Asia as the spiritual counterpart of Europe. In the decades around the turn of the nineteenth and twentieth centuries, Theosophists popularized

---

56   Margaret E. Cousins, *The Music of Orient and Occident: Essays Towards Mutual Under-standing*, Madras: B. G. Paul & Co, 1935; James H. Cousins and Margaret E. Cousins, *We Two Together*, Madras: Ganesh & Co, 1950.

57   Aydin, *The Politics of Anti-Westernism in Asia*; Tim Harper, *Underground Asia: Global Revolutionaries and the Assault on Empire*, London: Allen Lane, 2020; Mishra, *From the Ruins of Empire*; Carolien Stolte and Harald Fischer-Tiné, "Imagining Asia in India: Nationalism and Internationalism (ca. 1905–1940)", *Comparative Studies in Society and History*, 54, 1, 2012: 65–92.

58   Cemil Aydin, *The Idea of the Muslim World: A Global Intellectual History*, Cambridge, Mass.: Harvard University Press, 2017.

59   On al-Afghani: Mishra, *From the Ruins*: Chapter Two.

60   Gail Minault, *The Khilafat Movement: Religious Symbolism and Political Mobilization in India*, New York: Columbia University Press, 1982.

61   Stephen N. Hay, *Asian Ideas of East and West: Tagore and His Critics in Japan, China, and India*, Cambridge, MA: Harvard University Press, 1970.

FIGURE 4   Swami Vivekananda by Sudhir Chowdhury, publisher unknown, mid-20th century
             COURTESY OF PRIYA PAUL, NEW DELHI

this idea. In chorus, the spiritual-material polarity had a precedent in European Romanticism, which thrived on the opposition between emotion and
reason. Furthermore, as more or less Romantic ideologies, pan-Islamism and
pan-Asianism emerged in binary opposition to that of the idea of 'the West' as
the ultimate standard for universal progress. This led to the following ambiguous position. On the one hand, the West was admired as something to be
achieved in the future and it therefore made one think about the necessity
of reforming one's own tradition. Yet, on the other, this situation equally led to
anti-Western ideologies, whereby Asian thinkers overall employed the universal standards of the Enlightenment to condemn European imperialists of their
(racist) hypocrisy in violating the very ideals they claimed to uphold in their
civilizing mission.

     A great influence on the pan-Asianist ideas of Rabindranath Tagore and
other Bengalis was Okakura Kakuzo (alias Tenshin), a leading scholar in the
nationalist Japanese art scene who had acquired some international fame

because of his design for the interior of the Japanese pavilion at the Columbian Exposition in Chicago in 1893.[62] At this occasion, this Japanese pioneer in pan-Asianism probably also heard about Vivekananda. In any case, he came to India a few years later to invite the Swami to come to Tokyo for another conference on world religions, albeit without result because the leading Godman of that time died in 1902. Even so, the two met and travelled together to the Buddhist pilgrimage places of Bodhgaya, Benares and Sarnath. Altogether Okakura spent around nine months in India, mostly at the Tagore family home in Calcutta. During this period, he wrote *The Ideals of the East with Special Reference to the Art of Japan* (1903), of which the opening paragraph became famous as manifesto for pan-Asianism:

> Asia is one. The Himalayas divide, only to accentuate, two mighty civilizations, the Chinese with its communism of Confucius, and the Indian with its individualism of the Vedas. But not even the snowy barriers can interrupt for one moment that broad expanse of love for the Ultimate and Universal, which is the common thought-inheritance of every Asiatic race, enabling them to produce all the great religions of the world, and distinguishing them from those maritime peoples of the Mediterranean and the Baltic, who dwell on the Particular, and to search out the means, not the end, of life.[63]

In the footsteps of his American teacher Ernest Fenollosa, an art historian and philosopher, Okakura saw spirituality as an exclusively Asian virtue and believed that it was Asia's destiny to spiritualize the West, especially through its art. Simultaneously, the oneness of the declaration that 'Asia is one' owes part of its inspiration to Vivekananda's Hindu neo-Vedanta universalism.[64] After his return to Japan in 1903, Okakura sent his two favourite students Yokoyama Taikan and Hishida Shunso to Calcutta. While Rabindranath had

---

62   In 1904, Okakura was invited to catalogue the collection of Chinese and Japanese paintings, which was begun by his mentor Ernest Fenollosa, at the newly established Museum of Arts in Boston, where he became the first curator of the department of Chinese and Japanese art in 1910. Soon the museum became interested in Indian art as well and, at the advice of Okakura, it appointed Ananda Coomaraswamy as curator in 1917.

63   Okakura Kakuzo, *The Ideals of the East with Special Reference to the Art of Japan*, London: John Murray, 1903: 1.

64   By and large, neo-Vedanta refers to modern Hindu thought that reinterpreted the tradition in the light of Western concepts and which became criticized for its universalism. Besides Swami Vivekananda, two other famous neo-Vedanta proponents were Aurobindo Ghosh and Sarvepalli Radhakrishnan.

a specific pan-Asianist bond with Okakura,[65] these two Japanese artists particularly influenced the work of his nephew Abanindranath Tagore, the leading figure of the nationalist Bengal School of Art.

Pan-Asianist ideas were undoubtedly strengthened by the Japanese victory over Russia in 1905, being the first time that an Asian nation defeated a Western one. Now Japan was seen as being as modern as the West and, hence, the country attracted a great number of intellectuals and students from all over Asia, including from the Islamic world and India, but especially from China and Korea. Asian nationalists used the Japanese victory to question earlier assumptions about white-race supremacy and Asian backwardness. Although Gandhi rejected the Japanese model of development (and indeed, under the influence of John Ruskin, Henry David Thoreau, Lev Tolstoy and others, Western progress and civilization at large), he too was much impressed by 'the epic heroism' shown by the Japanese in 1905. The secret of their victory, he argued, was:

> [...] unity, patriotism and the resolve to do or die. All the Japanese are animated by the same spirit. No one is considered greater than the other, and there is no rift of any kind between them. They think nothing else but service to the nation [...] This unity and patriotic spirit together with a heroic indifference to life (or death) have created an atmosphere in Japan the like of which is nowhere to be found in the world.[66]

The Irish Margaret Noble, better known as Sister Nivedita, was typical for the era as a broker between different global intellectual networks. In Ireland and Britain, she was involved in the Fabian Society, the Irish Literary Revival, the Arts and Crafts Movement and the Theosophical Society. In 1892, she spoke out fearlessly in favour of the Home Rule Bill. Also, she wrote enthusiastically about the social and political ideas of her friend Prince Peter Kropotkin, the Russian anarchist, and was an admirer of Mazzini's Young Italy movement.[67] Yet, after meeting Vivekananda in London, her life took a spiritual turn. In 1898, she moved to India and became a disciple of the swami, who renamed her Sister Nivedita ('Dedicated One').[68] After her guru's death, nonetheless,

65   Rustom Barucha, *Another Asia: Rabindranath Tagore and Okakura Tenshin*, New Delhi: Oxford University Press, 2006: 16–17.
66   As cited in M. K. Gandhi, *'Hind Swaraj' and Other Writings*, edited by Anthony J. Parel, Cambridge: Cambridge University Press, 1997: 27–28.
67   Boehmer, *Empire, the National*: 45.
68   About the relationship between Vivekananda and Nivedita: Harris, *Guru to the World*, chapters 13, 14 and 15.

her revolutionary spirit boiled up again. She became increasingly involved in Indian nationalist activities, advocating Vivekananda's 'aggressive Hinduism', while working closely together with Aurobindo Ghosh and others. In addition, she forged contacts with nationalists such as Surendranath Banerjee, Annie Besant, Gopal Krishna Gokhale and the Tagore family, and exerted a great influence on the Tamil nationalist and literary figure Subramania Bharati. Nivedita was a prolific writer and extensively toured India to deliver lectures on Indian culture and nationalism. Under the spell of Okakura, she became a pan-Asianist and basically the co-author of his *The Ideals of the East*, for she not only helped him rewriting the book, but she also facilitated the publication and contributed a lengthy introduction in which she argued that Hinduism was the source of the underlying unity of Asia.[69] The last years of her life she mainly devoted to supporting the creation of a nationalist Indian art, while working together with, amongst others, Abanindranath Tagore and Ananda Coomaraswamy.

All in all, these global intellectual interactions reveal that the history of Indian Romantic nationalism cannot be characterized as merely the story of a unitary oppositional ideology competing with Western universalism, but it must equally acknowledge a repeatedly surfacing cosmopolitanism. This cosmopolitan moment not only demonstrates 'the complex, multidirectional, and hybrid nature of imperialism' but, ironically, also shows how the increasing global circulation of ideas led to 'a way of thinking that challenged imperialism more fundamentally than any other nationalist ideology'.[70] Thus, as Indian Romantic nationalism was based upon both the idea of a territorial homeland and extraterritorial global connections, it has little use to territorialize Indian intellectuals either through a teleology of (the Indian) nation or wider territorializations such as pan-Asianism or pan-Islamism. Although these categories are understandable, and sometimes unavoidable, Indians generally of course thought, in manifold and often contradictory ways, beyond the categories to which their lives and work was subsequently connected. Also, ideas do not circulate unchanged and Indian thinkers continually adjusted their intellectual horizons and practices to changed circumstances, audiences and projects. Thus, for instance, pan-Asianism and pan-Islamism came about in part through anti-Western internationalist solidarities. Ultimately, elitist Indians had anything but consistent imaginings about both the making of the

---

69   Nivedita, "Introduction" in Okakura, *The Ideals of the East*: xv.
70   Louise Blakeney Williams, "Overcoming the 'Contagion of Mimicry': The Cosmopolitan Nationalism and Modernist History of Rabindranath Tagore and W. B. Yeats", *American Historical Review*, 112, 1, 2007: 72.

(independent Indian) nation (-state) and the meaning of anti-colonialism. But it is for these reasons that the history of Indian Romantic nationalist thought remains so intriguing and, moreover, of continuing importance for an understanding of the global age.

CHAPTER 1

Hail to the Mother[land]!

Cultivation of Language: the Historical Novel and the Motherland

Just as in Europe, language and historical awareness lay at the heart of Romantic nationalist thought in India. Since the late nineteenth century, for instance, the Bengali and Tamil languages and scripts became identity markers of corresponding nations with distinct histories. Similarly, Punjabi in the *Gurmukhi* script was adopted as the language of the Sikh nation. Moreover, in the north, Hindu nationalists propagated Hindi in the *Devanagari* script as national language and, simultaneously, ascribed Urdu in the *Nastaliq* script – that was widely used by Muslims, Hindus and Sikhs alike – to be a symbol of Islam. Undeniably important to these developments was the modernization of Indian languages and scripts. Firstly, because the introduction of printing presses, type fonts, grammars and dictionaries – all of which were often initiated by European Christian missionaries – led to different degrees of standardization. Secondly, because Indian intellectuals explored new formats of writing: newspapers, periodicals, history books, novels and so on. In addition, the emergence of the vernacular languages as channels for education and literature – and consequently of cultivation of culture and collective self-awareness – was closely linked to the use of historical materials and themes. Again, comparable to Europe, historical novels and dramas contributed to a popular interest in the Indian past. Walter Scott, who was formative to the making of the historical novel in Europe, had also a great influence on Indian novelists, first in Bengal and later elsewhere, including on Hari Narayan Apte in Marathi, C. V. Raman Pillai in Malayam, Abdul Halim Sharar in Urdu and Bhai Vir Singh in Punjabi. Although Scott's poetry was much more admired than his novels, works such as *Ivanhoe, The Lady of the Lake, The Bride of Lammermoor, Kenilworth, The Lay of the Last Minstrel* and *Marmion* were translated into at least three Indian languages.[1]

Besides Persian, which was used by the East India Company (EIC) as official language until it was replaced with English in 1835, the British in Bengal learned the local language, mainly to communicate with clerks and to spread

---

1 Priya Joshi, *In Another Country: Colonialism, Culture, and the English Novel in India*, New York: Columbia University Press, 2002: 70, 72.

the word of the Gospel. For this reason, Bengali teachers were employed to produce educational works in the vernacular. Ramram Basu worked as a scribe with different British officials and missionaries. In 1801, he was appointed as a teacher of Sanskrit at Fort William College and one year later he wrote his *Raja Pratapaditya Charita* (Life of King Pratapaditya), the first 'exercise in modern, rationalist historiography' in Bengali.[2] As the ruler of a Bengali Hindu kingdom, Pratapaditya (1561–1611) had fought against the Mughals and subsequently his bravery and heroism became the subject of many ballads. By the beginning of the twentieth century, his story motivated several Bengalis to produce historical romances and plays. For indeed, since the 1850s, lively public theatre scenes developed in Calcutta and the western Indian cities of Bombay (Parsi theatre) and Poona (Marathi theatre) that were crucial to the national cultivation of culture. In particular, the plays printed and performed by Calcutta's National Theatre (since 1872) adopted a political tone and, accordingly, the British introduced the Dramatic Performances Act (1876) to police seditious Indian theatre.

Bankim Chandra Chatterjee became the best known and most successful author of historical novels in the subcontinent. Through his numerous writings and as the founder-editor of the literary magazine *Bangadarshan*, he was pivotal to the cultivation of modern Bengali language and culture, as well as Indian Romantic nationalist thought at large. According to the major Indian National Congress (INC) leader Bipin Chandra Pal Pal: 'The "Bangadarshan" School did for contemporary Bengalee thought and literature what the French Encyclopaedists did for the eighteenth century European thought and French literature'.[3] Chatterjee's historical novels, which were often first serialized in *Bangadarshan*, were translated into English and the main Indian languages, as well as reprinted several times.[4] He was infatuated by the writings of Walter Scott, especially his Waverley novels.[5] As Bipin Chandra Pal wrote: '[...] Walter Scott was a favourite of our generation. [...] we devoured literally many of his Waverley novels. His "Ivanhoe" was most popular with us. And in Bankim Chandra's "Durgeshnandini" we found a strange similitude with Ivanhoe. Bankim Chandra at once rose in our estimation as Sir Walter Scott of

---

2   Ranajit Guha, *History at the Limit of World-History*, New York: Columbia University Press, 2002: 11.

3   Bipin Chandra Pal, *Memories of My Life and Times*, Calcutta: Modern Book Agency, 1932: 226.

4   The main ones are *Durgeshnandini* (1865), *Mrinalini* (1869), *Chandrasekhar* (1874), *Anandamath* (1882), *Sitaram* (1887) and *Rajsingha* (1893).

5   Tapan Raychaudhuri, *Europe Reconsidered: Perceptions of the West in Nineteenth-Century Bengal*, New Delhi: Oxford University Press, 2002 (second edition; first published in 1988): 173.

Bengal'.[6] Chatterjee himself thought that the Scotsman was 'one of the great literary figures of all time': 'He bracketed him with Kalidasa [of *Shakuntala* fame and generally regarded to be the greatest poet of Sanskrit lyrical poetry] and compared him, favourably, with Shakespeare for his insights in human nature'.[7]

Like other Bengali literary figures, Chatterjee admired Shakespeare and Byron, but he was dismissive about Émile Zola, Jane Austen and especially Charles Dickens.[8] Rather than historical or realist novels, however, nineteenth century Indians, including Chatterjee, preferred to read Victorian melodrama. G. W. M. Reynolds's *The Mysteries of London* (1844) was most popular, as it was in England at the time. This presumably so because the heroic archetypes in this genre reminded Indians of their traditional epics and folk stories. Regardless, as a reflection of their own cultural ideas, emotions and experiences, Indian authors indigenized the historical novel in different ways. For instance, as emphasized by Priya Joshi, Chatterjee drew from the Indian epic tradition by introducing an omniscient narrator – who raises his voice and asserts his judgement over all matters, '*especially* those involving moral issues (an area in which Scott was decisively silent)' – and larger than life heroes – 'not to reflect upon a settled history but to shape and inspire an unfolding one'.[9] In contrast, she continues: 'Through the presence of a relatively weak and passive hero, Scott's narrator helps to explain a history that is already settled and "at peace"'.[10]

Principally, Chatterjee created 'imaginary pasts in which his characters portrayed a range of values desirable in the contemporary world'.[11] In chorus, he wrote his historical essays and novels to counter the European claim that Hindus, unlike Muslims, wrote no history. In accordance with the times, he generally adhered to the idea of a pre-Muslim Hindu Golden Age. In this, he was influenced by the European search for the Indo-European past, which among nationalist Hindus led to the equalization of the terms 'Aryan' and 'Hindu' (more about this in Chapter Three). Closely related, Bankim believed

---

6   Pal, *Memories*: 228.
7   Raychaudhuri, *Europe Reconsidered*: 128, explanation mine.
8   Ibid.: 19.
9   Joshi, *In Another Country*: 155–156, emphasis in original.
10   Ibid.: 155. Cf. Nilanjana Dutta, "'Scott of Bengal': Examining the European Legacy in the Historical Novels of Bankimchandra Chatterjee", Unpublished PhD: University of North Carolina, Chapel Hill, 2009: 142 and Joep Leerssen, "Introduction" in Joep Leerssen, ed., *Encyclopedia of Romantic Nationalism in Europe*, volume one, Amsterdam: Amsterdam University Press, 2018: 35.
11   Joshi, *In Another Country*: 162.

that Muslim rule in India had been a period of decline. A viewpoint that to a great extent originated from the work of European Orientalists and historians, who generally bolstered the idea that Muslims were foreign conquerors.

Besides in English (first in 1905), Chatterjee's most famous, albeit controversial,[12] historical novel *Anandamath* or 'The Sacred Brotherhood' (1882) was initially translated in Marathi (1897), Kannada (1897), Gujarati (1901), Tamil (1905), Hindi (1906), Telugu (1907) and Malayalam (1909).[13] The action of the book takes place in the 1770s during the period of the Sannyasi Rebellion, the declining power of the Muslim ruler of Bengal and the rise of the EIC. For basic historical information, Chatterjee relied upon William Wilson Hunter's *Annals of Rural Bengal* (1860) and G. R. Gleig's *Memoirs of the Life of the Right Hon. Warren Hastings, First Governor-General of Bengal, Compiled from Original papers* (1841). For local cultural knowledge and natural descriptions, he drew from his experiences as a civil service officer stationed in different Bengali districts. More importantly, *Anandamath* is 'replete with hymns, quotations from scriptures, and evocations of scenes of divine exploits'.[14]

The novel concerns a troupe of Hindu religious ascetics (*sannyasis*) who call themselves *santans* or children of the Mother. They live in the jungle in an abandoned monastery, in which the focus of their worship is enshrined, namely, three images of the Mother Goddess (in her past, present and future form). Her present form is identified with an image of Kali (figure 5), the fearsome Mother with her protruding tongue and necklace of human skulls, who dances on the corpse of Shiva and can both take and give life. Her future form is represented as the ten-armed Mother Goddess, the symbol of power with all her shining weapons, being a description that no doubt is reminiscent of the Goddess of War, Durga, slayer of demons and protectress. Yet most significant remains the fact that Chatterjee describes the past Mother Goddess as the one that nurtures the motherland. Thus, the *santans* are dedicated to the service of both the Mother and the motherland, to whom they vow celibacy till her freedom is attained.

Against the background of a severe famine caused by successive yearly droughts, unfair land taxes and administrative mismanagement, the *santans*

---

12   Chatterjee's attitude towards Muslims remains ambiguous. Although he certainly became a Hindu revivalist towards the end of his life, Julius Lipner has soothed Chatterjee's anti-Muslimness in: Bankimcandra Chatterji, *Anandamath, or The Sacred Brotherhood*, translated and with an introduction and critical apparatus by Julius J. Lipner, New York: Oxford University Press, 2005.

13   Sabyasachi Bhattacharya, *Vande Mataram: The Biography of a Song*, New Delhi: Penguin, 2003: 19.

14   Dutta, "'Scott of Bengal'": 139.

FIGURE 5   Advertisement Kali Cigarettes, lithograph by unknown artist, published by The
Calcutta Art Studio, ca. 1885–1895
COURTESY OF THE METROPOLITAN MUSEUM OF ART, NEW YORK

decide to fight against the armies of the Muslim rulers and their British allies.
Although they are on the winning side, they do not press their advantage and
under the leadership of their guru Satyananda leave the field following the
advice of a mysterious seer who suddenly appears in the final scene. The latter
tells Satyananda that British rule is necessary for the return of the true 'inner'

Hindu spirit, but that this is only possible by learning the 'outward' lessons of the Europeans:

> The English are very knowledgeable in the outward knowledge, and they're very good at instructing people. Therefore we'll make them king. And when by this teaching our people are well instructed about external things, they'll be ready to understand the inner. Then no longer will there be any obstacles to spreading the Eternal Code, and the true Code will shine forth by itself again. And till that day English rule will remain intact. Their subjects will be happy under the English, and they will be free to follow their religion. Therefore wise one, refrain from fighting the English, and follow me.[15]

Chatterjee apparently adheres here to the common idea amongst elitist Bengalis that British rule was providential. But, considering his official position, it remains difficult to decide today whether he did so out of conviction or expediency. Because of colonial censorship and like other Hindu novelists and dramatists, he might also have channelized his anti-colonial emotions by writing about Hindu resistance against Muslim rule as a stand-in. In any case, by reconstructing the past in the format of a modern historical novel, Chatterjee took an intuitive leap towards an imagined future for the Bengal nation, and this certainly had little to do with inherited tradition.

The scholar and educationist Bhudev Mukherjee is generally seen as the first writer of historical fiction in Bengali. The two stories in his *Aitihasik Upanyas* or Historical Novels (1857) follow similar ones in Hobart Caunter's *The Romance of History: India* (three volumes, 1836), whereby 'Anguriya Binimay', based upon Caunter's 'The Mahratta Chief', 'projects Shivaji as the ideal Hindu hero' (see also the next chapter).[16] Much more interesting, however, is Mukherjee's *Svapnalabadha Bharatbarsher Itihas* or the 'History of India as Revealed in a Dream' (1862). In this alternative history of India, he imagines what India could have been when the Marathas would not have lost the Third Battle of Panipat and when the British had subsequently not come to rule the subcontinent.[17] Accordingly, he envisions 'a prosperous India under a wise Hindu emperor, its ideology combining quintessentially Hindu virtues with Western

15   Chatterji, *Anandamath*: 229.
16   Raychaudhuri, *Europe Reconsidered*: 40.
17   The Third Battle of Panipat took place north of Delhi in 1761, between the Marathas, supported by four Indian allies, and the invading Afghan army of Ahmad Shah Durrani.

science and technology, *dharma* [right way of living, eternal law] with the rights of the people'.[18]

Conversely, in connection to the idea of the motherland, Mukherjee gave new meaning to the Hindu myth that the body of Shiva's dead spouse, Sati, cut into pieces by Vishnu's disc, was scattered all over the subcontinent and thus created fifty-one pilgrimage sites sacred to all Hindus:

> When I was a student of Hindu college, a European teacher told [us] that patriotism was unknown to the Hindus, for no Indian language had any word to express the idea. I believed his word and was deeply distressed by the thought. I knew then [...] the mythical account of [...] Sati's death, but that knowledge did not help me refute the teacher's statement or console myself. Now I know that to the descendants of the Aryans the entire motherland with its fifty-two places of pilgrimage is in truth the person of the Deity.[19]

Since ancient times, and comparable to what happened in many other places in the pre-modern world, Hindus approached the created world as feminine: natural sites (caves, rivers, mountains and so on) were associated with the divine power (*shakti*) of the great Goddess and generally represented by numerous local goddesses. Obviously, Mukherjee, Chatterjee and other Indian writers drew on this rich mythology which linked the body of the Goddess with the body of the earth.

Swadeshi and the Soul of the Nation

In 1905, ostensibly for administrative reasons, yet equally to 'dampen radical nationalism in the process',[20] the British decided to cut Bengal, officially known at the time as the Bengal Presidency, into two. As a result, Calcutta's Hindu elite would be a Bengali-speaking minority in a province that also included Bihar and Orissa, while Eastern Bengal and Assam would be a Muslim majority province with Dacca as its capital. For Mother-Goddess-worshipping Bengali Hindus this was nothing less than the vivisection of their motherland. Hence, they began to advocate *swadeshi* or the boycotting of British goods and

---

18   Raychaudhuri, *Europe Reconsidered*: 40, translation mine.
19   Ibid.
20   C. A. Bayly, *Origins of Nationality in South Asia: Patriotism and Ethical Government in the Making of Modern India*, New Delhi: Oxford University Press, 1998: 198.

the development of an indigenous economy instead. Besides mass protests, the Bengal partition triggered militant bombings and shootings. Shocked by the British' disregard for Indian opinion, nationalists throughout India supported the *swadeshi* movement and protested locally. In 1906, then, the INC first articulated the demand for *swaraj* (self-rule), which soon would become the most popular mantra of Indian nationalism. Instantaneously, however, at the first meeting of the Muslim League in Dacca, Bengali Muslims condemned the *swadeshi* movement and supported the partition of Bengal. This without result because the British reversed the partition in 1911. The Bengali speaking districts were once again unified and Assam, Bihar and Orissa separated. All this to the dislike of Bengali Muslims, who as a minority community felt betrayed by the colonial government.

During the *swadeshi* period, Bankim Chandra Chatterjee's poem 'Vande Mataram' or 'Hail to the Mother[land]', which was repeatedly sung in *Anandamath* and specifically identified Bengal as Mother Goddess, was adopted as nationalist slogan and attained mass popularity. As Mohandas Karamchand Gandhi commented from South Africa: 'The song, it is said, has proved so popular that it has come to be our National Anthem. [...] Just as we worship our mother, so is this song a passionate prayer to India'.[21] A few years later, Ananda Coomaraswamy wrote that Vande Mataram expressed 'the aims and the power of the awakened nation, as the Marseillaise embodied the ideal of awakened France, or as those of Ireland are expressed in the songs of Ethna Carberry'.[22] As a matter of fact, while the Irish nationalist movement Sinn Féin had a great impact on nationalist thinking in Bengal, Irish nationalists in turn found inspiration in India's new spirit of self-assertion and published Vande Mataram in the inaugural issue of the *United Irishman* (1906), although of course with the motherland praised as a Mother Goddess replaced with 'Ireland, land of martyrs, "Gaelic heights", and heroic "Celts" in the making'.[23]

The British officially forbade the public use of the words Vande Mataram during *swadeshi* actions. Nonetheless, the slogan was heard at gatherings throughout the subcontinent. It also appeared (sometimes as part of the whole poem, which was not banned) in journals and pamphlets. Bipin Chandra Pal, one of the leading figures of the *swadeshi* movement, began a newspaper entitled *Vande Mataram*. With Lala Lajpat Rai and Bal Gangadhar Tilak, he was part of the 'Lal-Bal-Pal' triumvirate of assertive nationalists (figure 6).

21   As cited in Bhattacharya, *Vande Mataram*: 24.
22   Ananda K. Coomaraswamy, *Essays in National Idealism*, New Delhi: Munshiram Manoharlal, 1981 (first published in 1909): 13.
23   Elleke Boehmer, *Empire, the National, and the Postcolonial 1890–1920: Resistance in Interaction*, Oxford: Oxford University Press, 2002: 32.

FIGURE 6   'Mother India in Chains' (with national leaders Lala Lajpat Rai, Bal Gangadhar
            Tilak, Motilal Nehru (perhaps) and Bipin Chandra Pal) by D. Banerjee, publisher
            unknown, 1930s
            COURTESY OF PRIYA PAUL, NEW DELHI

Characteristic for them was a change in mood, from reason to emotion, which largely resulted from decades of accumulated political frustrations and racial humiliations.[24] While the earlier two generations of Indian intellectuals generally favoured social reforms in cooperation with the British, *swadeshi* leaders now increasingly perceived colonial rule as 'the root evil in Indian life' and its extermination as 'the most important task facing the nation'.[25]

The Cambridge-educated nationalist and neo-Hindu sage Aurobindo Ghosh became more militant than the Lal-Bal-Pal triumvirate, with which he worked closely together at first. From Pal, in fact, he soon took over the editorship of *Vande Mataram*. Aurobindo was the driving force behind the popularization of Vande Mataram as a nationalist slogan. He produced several powerful translations of the song into English, including the following one in prose from 1909:

> I bow to thee, Mother,
> richly-watered, richly-fruited,
> cool with the winds of the south,
> dark with the crops of the harvests,
> The Mother!
> Her nights rejoicing in the glory of the moonlight,
> her lands clothed beautifully with her trees in flowering bloom,
> sweet of laughter, sweet of speech,
> the Mother, giver of boons, giver of bliss!
>
> Terrible with the clamorous shouts of seventy million throats,
> and the sharpness of swords raised in twice seventy million hands,
> who sayeth to thee, Mother, that thou art weak?
> Holder of multitudinous strength,
> I bow to her who saves,
> to her who drives from her the armies of her foemen,
> the Mother!
>
> Thou art knowledge, thou art conduct,
> thou our heart, thou our soul,

24   Mimasha Pandit, *Performing Nationhood: The Emotional Roots of Swadeshi Nationhood in Bengal, 1905–12*, New Delhi: Oxford University Press, 2019 and Tapan Raychaudhuri, *Perceptions, Emotions, Sensibilities: Essays on India's Colonial and Post-Colonial Experiences*, New Delhi: Oxford University Press, 1999.
25   Raychaudhuri, *Perceptions, Emotions, Sensibilities*: 63.

for thou art the life in our body.
In the arm thou art might, O Mother,
in the heart, O Mother, thou art love and faith,
it is thy image we raise in every temple.

For thou art Durga holding her ten weapons of war,
Kamala [an incarnation of Lakshmi] at play in the lotuses,
and Speech, the goddess, giver of all lore,
to thee I bow!
I bow to thee, goddess of wealth,
pure and peerless,
richly-watered, richly-fruited,
the Mother!
I bow to thee, Mother,
dark-hued, candid,
sweetly smiling, jewelled and adorned,
the holder of wealth, the lady of plenty,
the Mother![26]

Aurobindo was much inspired by the Irish and Italian nationalist movements as well as the French and American Revolutions. While in public he largely followed the Lal-Bal-Pal political stance (non-cooperation, passive resistance and so on), he simultaneously took up secret revolutionary activity as a preparation for open revolt against the British. In this, Sister Nivedita became his closest collaborator.

As already remarked in the Introduction, Nivedita was a disciple of the Hindu revivalist Swami Vivekananda, who successfully launched Hindu neo-Vedanta universalism, with yoga as an Indian 'Vedic' science at its spiritual core, in the West. Or as he said himself: 'I give them spirituality, and they give me money'.[27] Both Aurobindo and Nivedita especially admired him because he self-assertively propagated the spiritual superiority of the Hindu tradition. The Swami was the most famous devotee of the charismatic Ramakrishna Parama-hamsa, an illiterate Tantric priest and medium of the Mother Goddess Kali at Calcutta's Dakshineshwar Kali Temple who gained a large following among

---

26   Bhattacharya, *Vande Mataram*: 71–72, explanation added.

27   As cited in Karl Baier, "Swami Vivekananda: Reform Hinduism, Nationalism and Sci-entistic Yoga", *Interdisciplinary Journal for Religion and Transformation in Contemporary Society*, 5, 2019: 233.

Bengalis.[28] Over time, nonetheless, he wholly reinterpreted his guru's Tantric devotion to the Goddess Kali as the Universal Mother by replacing Kali with the notion of Mother India and Tantric devotion with ascetic dedication to the nation.[29] In her 'last will and testament', the pamphlet *Aggressive Hinduism* (1905), Nivedita explicitly wrote that Vivekananda always talked about making Hinduism aggressive. After his death, she infused her guru's ideas into her own nativist Hindu politics to counter British imperialism. 'India should evict its colonial "robbers"', she wrote, and 'go back to where she was before [...] Anything else will do little good and much harm'.[30] Rabindranath Tagore's novel *Gora* (1907) is clearly intended as a respectful, but critical, tribute to Nivedita. 'Gora' means 'white' and the protagonist is described as a Kali-dedicated traditionalist of Irish origin. In the novel, Tagore dramatizes how a European may paradoxically become more orthodox than a born-Hindu, while believing that 'a strict adherence to doctrine will provide an effective resistance to colonial denigration'.[31]

Aurobindo greatly appreciated Nivedita's *Kali, The Mother* (1900) and, after meeting her in 1902, he increasingly invoked the vengeful divine Mother Kali, that defining figure in Bengali revolutionary thought, in his political writings. In his anonymously written pamphlet, *Bhawani Mandir* (1905), which he essentially wrote under the influence of Chatterjee's *Anandamath* and Nivedita's *Kali, The Mother*, he developed his idea of a small group of revolutionaries dedicated to Mother India. Indeed, while most leading Indian nationalists still thought that violent agitational tactics were too disruptive, to the contrary, Aurobindo and Nivedita argued that the use of (terrorist) violence was not only acceptable, but also natural to the Mother, who in the form of Kali was ugly, brutal and chaotic. The two nationalists together extensively travelled and lectured throughout the subcontinent but especially in Bengal, and among other things they told young Indians to read Mazzini's biography and the Bhagavad Gita (about which more in the next chapter).

Khudiram Bose heard Aurobindo and Nivedita during one of their tours through the Bengali countryside and was heavily inspired by them. Subsequently, he was sentenced to death in 1908 for an attempt to assassinate

---

28   About Ramakrishna and his relationship with Vivekananda: Ruth Harris, *Guru to the World: The Life and Legacy of Vivekananda*, Cambridge, Mass.: The Belknap Press of Harvard University Press, 2022, Chapters Two and Three.

29   Peter van der Veer, *Imperial Encounters: Religion and Modernity in India and Britain*, Princeton, NJ: Princeton University Press, 2001: 72.

30   As cited in Boehmer, *Empire, the National*: 52.

31   Boehmer, *Empire, the National*: 41.

a British judge, but whereby he killed two English women instead. 'Vande Mataram', wrote Khudiram, as a statement before dying. His death made Bal Gangadhar Tilak call for immediate *swaraj*, for which the British jailed him for six years in Mandalay, Burma. In 1910, a five-yards-long *dhoti* (loincloth) became available for sale in Calcutta. It was soon forfeited by the British because it had the following poem, titled 'Farewell Mother', printed upon it in praise of Khudiram:

> Mother, farewell
> I shall go to the gallows with a smile.
> The people of India will see this.
> One bomb can kill a man.
> There are lakhs[32] of bombs in our homes.
> Mother, what can the English do? If I come back,
> Do not forget, Mother
> Your foolish child, Khudiram.
> See that I get your sacred feet at the end.
> When shall I call you again 'Mother' with the ease of my mind?
> Mother, do not keep this sinner in another country.
> It is written that you have 36 crores[33] of sons and daughters.
> Mother, Khudiram's name vanishes now.
> He is now turned to dust.
> See that, Mother, I sit on your lap again.
> In this kingdom of Bhisma, who else is there like you?
> You are unparalleled, Mother.
> When shall I depart from this world with a shout of Vande Mataram?[34]

By this time, Aurobindo and Nivedita had taken distance from their aggressive Hindu politics. Though a self-professed Hindu, Nivedita remained a white woman under the Raj, and it would be dangerous for her to take a frontline position. For the last five years of her life, therefore, she devoted herself to her writing and work for what Aurobindo called 'the revival of the aesthetic mind of India'. Parallel to the Irish art revival, she argued that 'art needed to grow out of a national struggle, and in turn had the power to give wing to the "free spirit" of the nation'.[35] Obviously, the British saw this as a much less

---

32   One lakh is 100,000.

33   One crore is 10,000,000.

34   Sumathi Ramaswamy, *The Goddess and the Nation: Mapping Mother India*, Durham, NC: Duke University Press, 2010: 145.

35   As cited in Boehmer, *Empire, the National*: 103–104.

threatening activity. In 1910, Aurobindo fled from the British to the French colonial enclave Pondicherry in south India, where he established an *ashram* (spiritual retreat). Before that, he had already urged his followers to refrain from terrorist activities and to stick to British laws. While in exile, Aurobindo devoted himself to the development of a system of yoga for the benefit of the unity and fulfilment of the whole divine being of man. In doing so, he aimed to continue Swami Vivekananda's conquest of the world on the grounds of India's spiritual supremacy. Although Aurobindo and Nivedita had prepared some ideological groundwork for the succeeding Indian freedom movement, they thus ultimately engrossed themselves in Hindu spirituality, while believing that freedom in the first place was a quality of the human soul, as ideally to be perfected within the manifested soul of the nation.

Mother India: Patriotic Songs and Visual Representations

One important way in which the invocation of the Bengali/Indian nation as a Mother Goddess reached wider audiences was through *swadeshi* songs, of which recordings were made that soon proved highly successful. Rabindranath Tagore sang Vande Mataram for the first time in a political context at the 1896 session of the INC. During the *swadeshi* period, he took not only a leading role in public protests with fiery speeches, but he also composed several protest songs that invoked the image of a once-whole Mother whose very body was now endangered. Among them was 'Amar Sonar Bangla' (My Golden Bengal), which he composed in 1905 and around 70 years later would become the national anthem of Bangladesh, the latter-day incarnation of colonial East Bengal. The Golden Bengal to whom the song is dedicated is addressed as 'Ma' (mother) and ultimately this is a song of mourning, an elegy for the idyllic pastoral scene of the 'authentic' Bengal: her mango groves, paddy fields, riverbanks and banyan trees. By writing it, Tagore had hoped that the divisive violence between Hindus and Muslims that accompanied the partition of Bengal was temporary and that it would promote the need for united anti-colonial strategies instead.

Tagore also composed the Indian unity song 'Jana Gana Mana', of which the first stanza was eventually adopted as the national anthem of independent India. In 1911, it was publicly recited for the first time at the annual session of the INC in Calcutta. During a 1919 visit to the Theosophical College in Madanappale (south India), where James Cousins was the principal, Tagore himself translated Jana Gana Mana into English as 'The Morning Song of India' and, with the help of Margaret Cousins, he set down the notation which is followed till this day. Interestingly, in its first stanza, Tagore puts language-based regions (Punjab, Gujarat, Maratha, Orissa and Bengal) and the Indian geographical landscape (the Vindhyas and the Himalayas, the Ganges and Yamuna Rivers, and the Indian Ocean) side by side:

> Thou art the ruler of the minds of all people,
> dispenser of India's destiny.
> Thy name rouses the hearts of Punjab, Sindh, Gujarat and Maratha,
> of the Dravida and Orissa and Bengal;
> It echoes in the hills of Vindhya and the Himalayas,
> mingles in the music of Ganga [sic] and Yamuna
> and is chanted by the waves of the Indian Sea [sic].
> They pray for thy blessings and sing thy praise.
> The saving of all people waits in thy hand,
> thou dispenser of India's destiny.
> Victory, Victory, Victory to thee.[36]

Thus, Tagore bequeathed linguistic regions with a naturalness that is as primeval as the national landscape and, basically, he demarcates them as territorial domains of local nations. Although the respective languages of these regions were not considered their most dominant feature then, they surely gained in cultural and political significance over time, especially after Indian independence.

Like Rabindranath, the poet, playwright and musician Dwijendralal Ray composed patriotic *swadeshi* songs that described the beauty of rural Bengal, including the popular 'Banga Amar, Janani Amar' (Bengal of mine, my motherland) and 'Dhanadhyanya Puspabhara' ([My land], abounding with wealth and grain). Well known too during the *swadeshi* period were the lines written by Rajanikanta Sen in reply to the complaint by some Indians that India-manufactured clothes were not so fine in comparison to the boycotted British ones:

> The Mother has given us this simple cloth, wear it with pride,
> She is poor and destitute today, and cannot afford no more.[37]

---

36   https://en.wikipedia.org/wiki/Jana_Gana_Mana.

37   As cited in Sugata Bose, "Nation as Mother: Representations and Contestations of 'India' in Bengali Literature and Culture" in Sugata Bose and Ayesha Jalal, eds., *Nationalism, Democracy, and Development: State and Politics in India*, New Delhi: Oxford University Press, 1997: 61.

His devotion to the nation was even more explicit in 'We may be poor, we may be small':

> We may be poor, we may be small,
> But we are a nation of seven crores; brothers, wake up.
> Defend your homes, protect your shops,
> Don't let the grain from our barns be looted abroad.
> We will eat our own coarse grain and wear the rough, home-spun cloth,
> What do we care for lavender and imported trinkets.
> Foreigners drain away our Mother's milk,
> Will we simply stand and watch?
> Don't lose this opportunity, brothers,
> Come and congregate at the feet of the Mother.
> Giving away from our own homes and begging from foreigners,
> We will not buy the fragile glass, it breaks so easily,
> We will rather be poor and live our simple lives,
> No one can then rob us of our self-respect.
> Don't lose this opportunity, brothers,
> Come and congregate at the feet of the Mother.[38]

Some Bengali intellectuals argued that they themselves, as modern city dwellers, had lost contact with the soil, unlike the rural people, who they saw as the true embodiment of the soul of India.[39] According to Aurobindo Ghosh, therefore, *swadeshi* songs were a reflection of the fact that Bengali literature had returned to its essential and eternal self:

> The lyric and the lyrical spirit, the spirit of simple, direct and poignant expression, of deep, passionate, straightforward emotion, of a frank and exalted enthusiasm, the dominant note of love and *bhakti* (sentimental devotionalism), of a mingled sweetness and strength, the potent intellect dominated by the self-illuminated heart, a mystical exaltation of feeling and spiritual insight expressing itself with plain concreteness and practicality – this is the soul of Bengal.[40]

---

38   Ibid.: 62.
39   Bipin Chandra Pal, *The Soul of India: A Constructive Study of Indian Thoughts and Ideals*, Calcutta: Choudhury and Choudhury, 1911: 146–147.
40   As cited in Dipesh Chakrabarty, "Romantic Archives: Literature and the Politics of Identity in Bengal", *Critical Inquiry*, 30, 3, 2004: 659.

Like Romantic nationalists in Europe, Bengalis were interested in their own folk literature and culture since the late nineteenth century. Inspired by the work of Richard Carnac Temple and other British folklorists, Reverend and Professor of English Lal Behari Day wrote *Folktales of Bengal* (1883), the first collection of Indian folk tales written by an Indian. Day 'knew the Grimm's work and duly sought to express the Aryan origins of the Bengali stories'.[41] After scouring the Bengali countryside for old manuscripts, Dinesh Chandra Sen, who was another great admirer of Byron, Scott and other European Romantic writers, published two books on the history of Bengali (oral) literature: *Bangabhasha o Shahitya* or Bengali Language and Literature (1896) and *History of Bengali Language and Literature* (1911). According to Sen, Bengali folk literature was 'read and admired by millions – the illiterate masses forming by far the most devoted of their admirers' and it therefore expressed 'the poetry of the race'.[42] In his literary research, he sought a pure Bengali essence unscathed by foreign influence. Simultaneously, he underlined the important contribution of Muslims, and particularly of his guru, the poet Jasimuddin. Rabindranath Tagore welcomed Sen's *Bangabhasha o Shahitya* because it showed that there was a path of friendship between Hindus and Muslims 'in spite of many troubles and disturbances'.[43]

In his writings, songs and lectures, Tagore most firmly stressed the spiritual importance for Bengalis to reacquaint themselves with the language and literature of rural Bengal. He himself became preoccupied with Bengali folk music, especially the songs of love, mysticism and universal brotherhood of the Bauls, the wandering minstrels and mystics recruited from both the Bengali Hindu and Muslim communities. He emphasized that Baul poems were important because of their universal appeal, and he rebuked those elitist Bengalis who used English themes and idioms in their writings, or others who tried to counteract British influences 'by "purifying" Bengali with stilted Sanskritisms'.[44] In his 1896-lecture on national literature, given at the annual meeting of the Bangiya Sahitya Parishad or Bengali Literary Academy, which was founded in 1893, Tagore expressed the hope that Bengali literature would act as 'the live umbilical cord' that would unite the past, the present of the future of the Bengali people.[45] In 1897 and 1898, he published two volumes

---

41   Partha Mitter, *Art and Nationalism in Colonial India, 1850–1922: Occidental Orientations*, Cambridge: Cambridge University Press, 1994: 127.

42   Chakrabarty, "Romantic Archives": 660.

43   Ibid.: 662–663.

44   Bob van der Linden, *Arnold Bake: A Life with South Asian Music*, London: Routledge, 2018: 51.

45   Chakrabarty, "Romantic Archives": 661.

of Bengali folk stories, mostly from oral sources. Over time, nonetheless, the project of creating a Bengali national literature got increasingly communal. Muslim intellectuals in Calcutta thought that the Bengali Literary Academy was too Hindu focused and, in 1911, they therefore set up the Muslim Literary Association (Bangiya Mussalman Sahitya Samiti).

Even so, following the popularity of Vande Mataram and a growing emotional attachment to the idea of the Indian nation, Mother India (*Bharat Mata*) was increasingly represented as a national symbol in visual forms. Herein, of course, she was reminiscent of Britannia, Columbia, Erin or Hibernia, Germania, Marianne, Guadalupe and other female figures who came to embody the country as motherland around the world. Among the earliest known visual representations of Mother India is the celebrated watercolour painting *Bharat Mata* (1905) by Abanindranath Tagore (figure 7), a nephew of Rabindranath. He personified Mother India as a Bengali lady holding four symbolic objects in the fashion of Hindu deities, but which themselves were emblems of nationalist *swadeshi* aspiration: food (rice), white clothing (homespun cotton), knowledge (manuscripts) and 'spirituality' (prayer bead). Apparently, he first titled her *Bangla Mata* (Mother Bengal) and only later changed this into *Bharat Mata*. Yet, Abanindranath's painting did not become the iconic image of Mother India as an actual Goddess. Instead, she was initially depicted as being rather belligerent and, in this, she no doubt benefitted from the Goddess Durga, from whom she generally adopted an accompanying lion too.

Mother India's simultaneous association with Kali, the Goddess of death and destruction (as propagated by Aurobindo and Indian revolutionaries), proved more problematic for both the British and Indian nationalists. For some time already, the wild Kali was the morbid focus of British fascination, fear and wrath. Throughout the nineteenth century, they campaigned against the infamous 'thuggees' with their allegedly twin penchant for highway robbery and human sacrifice in devotion to Kali. Hence, for them, a lithographed advertisement for Kali Cigarettes linked an item of middle-class consumption to *swadeshi* and to an image of the power that the national struggle could unleash (figure 5). According to Partha Mitter, the lithograph might have had a hidden anti-colonial message 'in its colour symbolism of the black goddess dominating a supine, white-skinned Siva'.[46] On the other hand, modernizing Hindus were embarrassed by the uncontrollable Kali in view of their reformist ideology of bourgeois motherhood. Although images of Mother India sometimes retained martial traces, especially during the *swadeshi* period, she ulti-

---

46   Mitter, *Art and Nationalism*: caption to colour plate 12.

FIGURE 7   *Bharat Mata*, watercolour painting by Abanindranath Tagore, 1905
SOURCE: WIKICOMMONS

mately became shaped, both in writings and visual representations, as a dominantly nurturing and compassionate Mother: tender, pacific and asexual. Indeed, all this was generally in accordance with the Victorian idea of the woman as 'the angel of the house', which was a point of recognition shared by the British and Indian reformers.

FIGURE 8   *Hind Devi*, Advertisement Ahmedabad Textiles Mills Co., artist unknown, original
            printed on textile, c. 1930
            COLLECTION MAP, BANGALORE: COURTESY CIVIC VISUAL ARCHIVE, NEW
            DELHI

In addition, Mother India was imagined as the embodiment of the mapped form of the territory of the Indian nation, of which images were soon to be seen on paintings, calendars, posters and so on (figure 8; book cover). In a country with myriad languages and varied literacy levels, such visual representation was most important because it provided a unifying, culturally resonant all-Indian nationalist reference point. The joining of Mother India with the modern map of the nation, as well as the flag that comes to be increasingly associated with her realm, not only signaled a novel way of relating to land, but also enlivened in the popular mind the image of a motherland worth protecting and dying for. Thus, Mother India emerged as a modern novel territorial deity rather than a nonspecific earth (*shakti*), warrior (Kali) or Mother Goddess, although for some at times undeniably she came to represent all of this. In unison, however, Indian nationalists argued that the motherland transcended the map of India created by the British. As Bipin Chandra Pal wrote in *The Soul of India* (1911):

> This Mother is the spirit of India. This geographical habitat of ours is only the outer body of our Mother. The earth we tread on is not a mere bit geological structure. It is the physical embodiment of the Mother [...] Our history is the sacred biography of the Mother. Our philosophies are the revelations of the Mother's mind. Our arts–our poetry and our painting, our music and our drama, our architecture and our sculpture, all these are the outflow of the Mother's diverse emotional moods and experiences. Our religion is the organized expression of the soul of the Mother. The outside knows her as India [...] It is, I know, exceedingly difficult, if it be not absolutely impossible, for the European or American to clearly understand or fully appreciate this strange idealization of our land, which has given birth to this cult of the Mother among us.[47]

In 1901, Rabindranath Tagore published two articles in *Bangadarshan* in which he summarized and discussed Ernest Renan's famous tract *What is a Nation?* (1882). While the title of the second article, 'Hindutva', makes clear that he imagined the Indian nation as a Hindu one, his appropriation of Renan's thesis that the nation is a soul, a spiritual principle, remains more intriguing. According to Tagore, the ancient Hindu nation was not defined by geographical boundaries or linguistic unity. To the contrary, it was to be found in an intuitively recognized and interiorized unifying civilization. In other words, it rested in the soul instead of the soil or political institutions:

---

47   Pal, *The Soul of India*: 187–189.

> A nation is not built on [the basis of] geography, race and language. A battlefield and a place of work can be laid out on a piece of land, but a piece of land does not create the soul of nation. Only human beings are the principal constituents of the sacred thing I call the community of people. The nation born of deep historical stirrings is a mental thing, a mental family, it is not determined by the shape of the land.[48]

Closely related, one of the protagonists in Tagore's anti-nationalist novel *The Home and the World* (1919; first published in Bengali as *Ghaire Baire* in 1916), in which Vande Mataram played a crucial role, proclaims that he is willing to become a martyr for the nation, but that 'Geography is not a truth' and 'One can't lay down one's life for a map'.[49]

The prominent Tamil literary figure Subramania Bharati was much influenced by English Romantic poets – for some time he even used the pen name 'Shelley-*dasan*' (Shelley's disciple) – and a great admirer of Mazzini. Through his numerous publications he brought the ideas of *swadeshi* and Mother India to south India. Because of his travels and the fact that he knew different languages, including Tamil, English and Hindi, he was pivotal to a network of nationalists that connected north and south. He considered Sister Nivedita as his guru and, among many other things, wrote odes to Tilak, Lala Lajpat Rai and Gandhi, and translated speeches of Tilak, Vivekananda and Aurobindo.[50] In 1905, he rendered Vande Mataram into Tamil, using the prosody of the Shaivite devotional (*bhakti*) poets. Typical for the times, however, Bharati combined a pride in Tamil culture with a devotion to the Indian nation, as exemplified by the following famous Tamil poem:

> Long live glorious Tamil, long live the fine Tamil people!
> Long live the auspicious precious Bharata country!
> The troubles that plague us today, may they vanish!
> May goodness gather among us! All that is evil should wither!
> Virtue should grow among us! All that is sinful should disappear!
> The manly efforts of the noble inhabitants of this country, may they excel

---

48   As cited in Victor A. van Bijlert, "Tagore's Vision of the Indian Nation: 1900–1917" in Kathleen M. O'Connell and Joseph T. O'Connell, eds., *Rabindranath Tagore: Reclaiming a Cultural Icon*, Kolkata: Visva-Bharati, 2009: 50.

49   Rabindranath Tagore, *The Home and the World*, New Delhi: Penguin, 2005 (first published in English in 1919): 71.

50   In 2000, the biographical film *Bharati* was released and won the National Film Award for Best Feature Film in Tamil.

day by day!
May my fellow citizens flourish forever!
Vande Mataram! *Vande Mataram*![51]

The cover page of a 1909 issue of the Tamil daily magazine *Vijaya*, which
Bharati published first from Madras and then from Pondicherry (where he
went in exile in 1908 to escape British persecution, like Aurobindo Ghosh did),
shows *Bharat Mata* – written in the *Devanagari* script – as a four-armed Goddess with her diverse offspring occupying a map of the subcontinent.[52] The
image confirms Bharati's 'pluralistic vision of Indian national territory as the
patrimony of the several communities that occupy it'.[53] At Mother India's feet
are the figures of four men who stand embracing each other in elaborately
carved boats with banners. From their clothing, they can be recognized as
Hindu and Muslim; the banners declare, in Tamil and Telugu respectively, that
disunity had to be resisted. Distinctive for Bharati's vision also are the two
slogans at either side of Mother India: 'Allahu Akbar' (God is Great) in the
Nastaliq script and Vande Mataram in *Devanagari*. Leading Hindus, including
Bharati, at the time wanted the latter to become the national script. Supposedly for that reason in the picture, then, the Urdu, Tamil and Telugu scripts
altogether are subordinate to the larger written *Devanagari* script as used for
both *Bharat Mata* and Vande Mataram.

In Pondicherry, Bharati spent many hours discussing Sanskrit literature
with Aurobindo Ghosh. Bharati himself translated Vedic hymns, Patanjali's
Yoga Sutra and the Bhagavad Gita into Tamil. Moreover, in 1912, he wrote an
allegorical ode to Mother India, *Panchali Sabadham* (Panchali's Pledge), based
upon a pivotal game of dice incident in the Mahabharata, the great epic of
which the Bhagavad Gita is part.[54] In it, he represents not only the Pandavas
as the Indians, the Kauravas as the British and the battle of Kurukshetra as
that of the Indian freedom struggle, but also portrays the main female character Draupadi, a pawn in the conflict between the Pandava and Kaurava clans,
as Mother India as well as a manifestation of the Mother Goddess Shakti. As
Usha Rajagopalan wrote:

---

51   As cited in Ramaswamy, *The Goddess and the Nation*: 19 (italics in original).
52   See the image at: https://en.wikipedia.org/wiki/Subramania_Bharati.
53   Ramaswamy, *The Goddess and the Nation*: 21.
54   The core of the Mahabharata was composed around 300–200 BCE, but some sections are
      much older. Various episodes, stories and even whole texts, including the Bhagavad Gita,
      have been inserted sometime around 400 CE. Although the text is generally attributed to
      Vyasa, it is the result of oral composition and, accordingly, there is no original version,
      and many versions circulate instead.

FIGURE 9   Vande Mataram paintings by K. Tejendra Kumar Mitra
            SOURCE: ANONYMOUS, BANDE MATARAM ALBUM, CAWNPORE: PRAKASH
            PUSTAKALAYA, 1923: N.P.

The figure of Draupadi is symbolic of Mother India robbed of her freedom and also of the Indian woman who suffers indignity and oppression in the name of tradition. Draupadi is also the manifestation of the
Mother Goddess, Shakti, come to vanquish evil and establish good. By
invoking the name of Shakti, all crises can be resolved. Just as the Pandava queen will win freedom for herself and her husbands, citizens of
India will unite and win freedom for their country and women will break
the shackles imposed by patriarchy and seek liberation for themselves.[55]

All in all, the *swadeshi* movement, first in Bengal and then elsewhere in
the subcontinent, led to literary, aural and visual representations of Mother
India that reflected the assertion of Romantic nationalist emotions in the
Indian public sphere. Since the symbol of a Goddess as the motherland was
culturally rooted, it reached people's hearts easily. Furthermore, rather than
through print media, among the wider population both India's history and the
idea of the nation became major topics of discussion through dramas, songs
and visual representations (paintings, advertisements, calendars and so on).
In this context, I end this chapter with an intriguing image, namely, a series

55   Subramani Bharati, *Panchali's Pledge (Panchali Sabadham)*, translated by Usha
      Rajagopalan, Gurgaon: Hachette India, 2012 (first published in 1912): 16.

FIGURE 10   'Mother India' from Vande Mataram paintings by K. Tejendra Kumar Mitra
SOURCE: ANONYMOUS, BANDE MATARAM ALBUM, CAWNPORE: PRAKASH
PUSTAKALAYA, 1923: N.P.

of 13 paintings created by K. Tejendra Kumar Mitra in a 1923-booklet with an
English translation of Vande Mataram by Aurobindo Ghosh (figure 9).[56]

While the first 12 paintings are representations of the first two verses
of Vande Mataram, the last painting is most noteworthy because it depicts
Mother India rising out of the middle of the subcontinent with some national

---

56   Anonymous, *Bande Mataram Album*, Cawnpore: Prakash Pustakalaya, 1923.

heroes at her feet (figure 10).[57] During the early twentieth century, numerous of such paintings appeared and together created a canon of 'freedom fighters' who came to be known throughout the subcontinent.[58] Obviously this process had begun earlier. For instance, the Calcutta Art Studio produced portrait images of nationalist leaders like Bankim Chandra Chatterjee and Surendranath Banerjee, and the Ravi Varma Fine Art Lithographic Press printed portraits of Tilak and Mahadev Govind Ranade, one of the founding members of the INC. Rather than on these nationalist leaders, however, the next chapter's focus is on legendary national heroes because these ultimately are more distinctive to Romantic nationalism.

---

57   As the image is unclear, it remains difficult to identify the people and I am thankful to Kama Maclean and Jim Masselos for providing some suggestions here. The person on the far left looks like a Muslim (Khilafatists Muhammed Ali Jauhar or Shaukat Ali?) and the one next to him might be Motilal Nehru, President of INC and the father of India's first prime minister Jawaharlal Nehru. The man in black with the hat most likely is a Parsi (Pherozesha Mehta, although he is generally depicted with glasses, Dadabhai Naoroji or Dinshaw Edulji Wacha?). Aside him is maybe Chandra Shekar Azad because of the moustache. On the far right seems to be Bal Gangadhar Tilak because of the headgear. Is the person next to him V. O. Chidambaram Pillai (see below) or is he Subramania Bharati instead, or yet again, Lala Lajpat Rai? The man in front might also be from south India: the scholar U. V. Swaminatha Iyer (about whom more in Chapter Three)? The combination of north and south Indians, if true at all, would make Mitra's painting rather unique. The presence of the boat in the background is intriguing too. Does it refer to the Swadeshi Steam Navigation Company founded in 1906 by the south Indian INC leader V. O. Chidambaram Pillai to break the British monopoly over maritime trade? Or is it the Japanese steamship Komagata Maru, on which 376 Punjabis (mostly Sikhs) in 1914 attempted to immigrate to Canada, but were denied entry in Vancouver and forced to return to Calcutta?

58   Mitter, *Art and Nationalism*; Christopher Pinney, *'Photos of the Gods': The Printed Image and Political Struggle in India*, London: Reaktion Books, 2004; Ramaswamy, *The Goddess and the Nation*.

CHAPTER 2

Legendary National Heroes

James Tod's Rajput Heroes

Since the late nineteenth century, Rajasthan ('Land of Kings'), formerly known as Rajputana ('Land of Rajputs'),[1] has been famous for its romantic (ruined) forts and palaces as well as love and war stories. The city of Udaipur, with its imposing multi-storied fortress-palace picturesquely set at the man-made Pichola lake, is one of its best-known sights. Located at the highest level of the fortress-palace, in what nowadays is the City Palace Museum, is Badi Chatur Chowk, a small open and airy courtyard with pavilions on three sides. Through the openings in the wall on the fourth side one has a wonderful view of Pichola lake and the surrounding hills. The wall itself contains a glass mosaic from 1712, with faces of Portuguese men admiring flowers, while Indian ladies are depicted standing nearby. The main pavilion, on the opposite side, contains Dutch blue ceramic tiles covering the columns, the ceiling and the projecting balcony. In another pavilion some priceless locally made historical miniature paintings are exhibited, yet it is the third pavilion that is of greatest interest to the discussion of Indian Romantic nationalism. It shows an Indian writing desk with a matrass and cushion behind it for someone to work, while sitting cross-legged. The desk is sided to its left by a standing fan and to its right by a Western-style table and chair. The pavilion is dedicated to Lieutenant-Colonel James Tod, the English-born officer of the East India Company (EIC) and author of the *Annals and Antiquities of Rajasthan or the Central and Western Rajput States of India* (two volumes, successively published in 1829 and 1832), of which a boxed three volume copy of the 1920 edition is laying on the table. At the back of the wall there are three photographs that feature Tod, namely, besides a miniature that shows a meeting between him and the Maharana of Udaipur, a photograph of a painting (from the *Annals*) of Tod and his

---

1 'Rajput' (from the Sanskrit 'rajaputra' or 'son of a king') denotes a large multi-component cluster of castes, kin bodies and local groups originating mostly from peasant or pastoral communities. Rajputs are historically associated with warriorhood and, over time, they became landed aristocrats and transformed into a ruling class. Before 1949, Rajputana was the name coined by the British for the region that, besides the Indian state of Rajasthan, included parts of present-day Madhya Pradesh, Gujarat and some adjoining areas in Sindh, Pakistan.

© BOB VAN DER LINDEN, 2024 | DOI:10.1163/9789004694804_004

Jain guru Yati Gyanchandra, with whom he worked extensively on relevant written sources, as well as a close-up of Tod from that very same painting.

Since 1997, the Maharana of Mewar Charitable Foundation annually honours a foreign individual, 'who, like Colonel Tod, has produced a work of permanent value, and has contributed through his works an understanding of the spirit and values of Mewar' (the region of which Udaipur is the capital) with the Lieutenant-Colonel James Tod Award. In 2020, the prize was given to the British scholar Norbert Peabody, author of the companion volume to the bicentenary and lavishly produced 2023 limited edition re-issue of the *Annals* commissioned by the Royal Asiatic Society. Earlier recipients were Richard Attenborough (some scenes of his *Gandhi* were filmed in Udaipur) and M. M. Kaye, the author of *The Far Pavilions*. But who was James Tod, why is he still remembered in Rajasthan and, indeed, what does he have to do with the subject of Romantic nationalism in India?

Tod arrived in Calcutta in 1799 and served the EIC until 1822. After the rulers of the kingdoms of Rajputana acknowledged the suzerainty of the EIC by treaties in 1818, he became the Company's first political agent to the western states of Rajputana, which during the preceding half century had been plundered and pauperized by Maratha and Pindari armies. In the following four years, Tod explored the region extensively and learned a great deal about the local language and culture. Furthermore, he did much to bring the Rajput rulers back in power and, through his intelligence service, he generally played a key role in the military and political history of the region. In all this, Tod adhered to Romantic ideas. For instance, he believed that the social system of the Rajputs was like the feudal system of medieval Europe, and that their traditions of remembering history over time by bards (on whom, typical for a Romanticist, he relied much for his historical writing) was comparable to that of the clan poets of the Scottish Highlanders. Tod's main source of inspiration for his viewpoints was the English Whig historian Henry Hallam's *View of the State of Europe during the Middle Ages* (1818), although his comparative argument about Europe and India simultaneously contested the book's conclusions. According to Tod, the feudal affinity between Europe and India could be explained by the fact that the tribes of Europe and the Rajputs had a common Scythian origin in Central Asia. Civilizational progress, therefore, he continued, perhaps would enable Britons and Rajputs to realize a common brotherhood.[2] Undoubtedly, Tod's identification with the Rajputs, and

---

2 Lloyd I. Rudolph and Susanne Hoeber Rudolph, *Romanticism's Child: An Intellectual History of James Tod's Influence on Indian History and Historiography*, New Delhi: Oxford University Press, 2017: 21.

the Mewar dynasty was counter cultural. He disliked modern European civilization and he saw himself as a 'modern Scythian'.[3] His views reflected Golden Age thinking and the Enlightenment search for the (racial) origins of man.

Of a renowned Scottish family and with an upbringing in Scotland, Tod was familiar with Walter Scott's historical novels. In general, he felt attracted to the writings of Byron, Shelley, Keats and so on, and especially to the Romantic notion that human beings achieved their highest fulfilment in their transcendent national identity. He celebrated the Greek struggle for national liberty against Ottoman rule. 'We are all Greeks. Our laws, our literature, our religion, our arts all have their roots in Greece', wrote Shelley, and Byron's death in 1824 in Greece during the war of independence undeniably 'symbolized the Romantics' passionate commitment to national sovereignty and freedom, terms whose career began a generation earlier in the aftermath of the French Revolution'.[4] Accordingly, Tod argued that the Rajputs were a nation, whereby he not only identified Mewar's struggle against the Mughals with the Greek fight against the Ottomans, but also compared the near victory of Mewar's Maharana Pratap Singh (figure 12) over the Mughals at the Battle of Haldighati (1576) with that of Sparta's resistance against the overwhelming Persian forces at Thermopylae. Afterwards, this comparison was repeatedly taken up by Indian nationalists to claim that Hindus were 'martial' rather than 'effeminate', as the British often argued at the time.

Again and again, for instance, Mahatma Gandhi made rhetorical use of Tod's Haldighati-Thermopylae comparison. At a Law College in Madras in 1920, five years after his return to India from 21 years in South Africa, he lectured about the problem of the unwillingness of Hindus to cooperate with Muslims because they were fearful of their martiality. Their fear, he told the students, was degrading to Hindus, 'whose land was dotted, as Col. Tod said, with a thousand of Thermopaelies [sic]. The death of a martyr is far more preferable to the death of a coward'.[5] Moreover, in 1931, during a meeting of the Federal Structure Committee in London to discuss the topic of Indian defence, Gandhi adopted the British theory of the Indian 'martial races', while arguing that India definitely could defend itself:

> After all, India is not a nation which has never known how to defend herself. There is all the material there. There are Mohammedans, standing in no dread of foreign invasion. The Sikhs will refuse to think they

3 Jason Freitag, *Serving Empire, Serving Nation: James Tod and the Rajputs of Rajasthan*, Leiden: Brill, 2009: 46.
4 Rudolph and Rudolph, *Romanticism's Child*: 142.
5 As cited in Freitag, *Serving Empire*: 127.

can be conquered by anybody. The Gurkha, immediately he develops the national mind, will say, 'I alone can defend India'. Then there are the Rajputs, who are supposed to be responsible for a thousand Thermopylaes, and not one little Thermopylae [as] in Greece. This is what the Englishman, Colonel Tod, told us. Colonel Tod has taught us to believe that every pass in Rajputana is a Thermopylae. Do these people stand in need of learning the art of defence?[6]

Although Tod wrote and published his *Annals and Antiquities of Rajasthan* in Britain after his departure from India, it has had a decisive impact on modern Rajasthani history and culture. To begin with, by reproducing, albeit in a rather uncritical manner, the genealogical records and heroic exploits of the Rajputs, as mostly supplied by themselves, he helped to invent the 'modern Rajput tradition'.[7] In doing so, he paved the way for Rajputs to negotiate their way into British India with their preferred identity and heritage intact. Against this background, Mewar's Maharana Fateh Singh (r. 1884–1930) spent much money on restoring the glorious Rajput forts of Chittorgarh and Kumbalgarh. Simultaneously, Tod's description of the Rajputs, Marathas and Mughals as distinct nations influenced the way in which the people belonging to these communities came to see themselves in relation to each other. In general, his *Annals* was crucial to the emergence of Maharana Pratap Singh, Prithviraj Chauhan (c. 1160–1192), whom Tod labelled 'the Last Hindu Emperor' (figure 11), and Padmini (the 13th–14th century legendary queen of Mewar) as iconic heroes of the Rajput nation, as well as for the popular Indian nationalist imaginary.[8]

After its initial publication in London, Tod's *Annals* went quickly out of print and it was only 70 years later, in 1873, that Higgenbotham & Co in Madras brought out a next edition. The best-known edition of the book, however, remains the three-volume 1920-set mentioned in the first paragraph, which was edited, introduced and annotated by William Crooke, a key figure in the study and documentation of Indian folklore. In addition, the *Annals* was translated and published in the major north Indian languages, especially in Bengali,

6   Ibid.: 128.
7   D. H. A. Kolff, *Naukar, Rajput, Sepoy: The Ethnohistory of the Military Labour Market in Hindustan, 1450–1850*, Cambridge: Cambridge University Press, 1990.
8   On the influence of Tod's *Annals* on the Indian nationalist, Hindu and Muslim imaginaries in relation to Prithviraj Chauhan and Padmini: Cynthia Talbot, *The Last Hindu Emperor: Prithviraj Chauhan and the Indian Past, 1200–2000*, Cambridge: Cambridge University Press, 2016 and Ramya Sreenivasan, *The Many Lives of a Rajput Queen: Heroic Pasts in India, c. 1500–1900*, Seattle: University of Washington Press, 2007.

FIGURE 11   'Prithviraj Chauhan', Advertisement calendar, artist unknown, published by
Dahyabhai Punamchand & Co, 1934

and at least from the following dates: Bengali (1872), Urdu (1877), Hindi (1906), Gujarati (1912) and Marathi (1908).[9] This publication history demonstrates that the book was widely available to educated (north) Indian audiences.

In an extraordinary afterlife, Tod's account of the heroic Rajput struggles inspired, besides a growing interest in history, a great number of novels, theatre performances and, as I will discuss later in this chapter, films. In 1896, Lala Lajpat Rai wrote: 'If every Hindu Raja or Maharaja gets a history of his family and kingdom written on the model of Tod's history, then it can be hoped that Hindu children will get an opportunity to read the accounts of bravery shown by their ancestors in resisting attacks by enemies'.[10] In line with his call, Abanindranath Tagore's children's book *Raj Kahini* (1905), a retelling of some of Tod's stories, has fed the imagination of Indian youth to this day. Earlier in Bengal (again, a most crucial region), Tod's *Annals* had instigated plays such as Michael Madhusudan Dutt's *Krishna Kumari* (1860), Jyotirindranath Tagore's *Sarojini ba Chittor Akraman* (1875) and Girishchandra Ghosh's *Ananda Raho* (1881), as well as historical novels like Romesh Chandra Dutt's *Rajput Jivansandhya* (1879), which had Maharana Pratap Singh as hero. Dwijendralal Ray wrote even four Rajput plays: *Tarabai* (1903), *Rana Pratapsingha* (1905), *Durgadas* (1906) and *Mewar Patan* (1908). The lines 'Who is there willing to live without freedom, willing to live like that? Who wants to wear fetters, ah wear fetters?' from Rangalal Banerjee's *Padmini Upakhyan* or 'The Sage of Padmini' (1858) were widely known during the *swadeshi* period. Rangalal was an admirer of Romanticists like Byron, Scott and Thomas Moore, and these lines essentially were a free translation of Thomas Campbell's 'From life without freedom – Oh who not fly? For one day of freedom – Oh who would not die?'

Bankim Chandra Chatterjee's *Rajsingha* (1893), should be mentioned too.[11] The novel's climax is a footnote in Indian history, which Chatterjee assumingly encountered in Tod's *Annals*, namely, the conflict between Mughal Emperor Aurangzeb and Rajput king Rajsingha. Nonetheless, Chatterjee elevates the status of battle between his ideal hero Rajsingha and Aurangzeb to that of 'the

---

9   See for a publication list, Freitag, *Serving Empire*: 174–179.
10   Lala Lajpat Rai, "Shivaji (1896)", excerpts translated from Urdu, in B. R. Nanda, ed., *The Collected Works of Lala Lajpat Rai*, volume one, New Delhi: Manohar, 2004: 341.
11   The first edition of *Rajsingha* (1882) had only 83 pages and its fourth edition (1893) 434 pages. In 1930 the book provided the basis for a silent Bengali movie and, in 1976, a volume on Rajsingha appeared in the famous comic books series *Amar Chitra Katha* (Immortal Picture Stories).

battles of Salamanca and Austerlitz' as well as the struggle between William of Orange and Philip II of Spain.[12] Like Tod's 'Battle of Thermopylae' comparison and similar to what Walter Scott had done for several relatively unknown events in Scottish history, he further titles the chapter on Rajsingha's fights in Rajasthan's mountain passes as 'Second Xerxes-Second Plataea'. In contrast to Tod and his pre-colonial local sources, however, most Bengali authors celebrated the upholding of Hindu Rajput honour by, amongst others, Maharana Pratap Singh and Padmini, as part of 'an exemplary history in which heroic Rajput warriors and sacrificing queens resisted "Muslim" conquest'.[13] Moreover, while Rajput bravery, loyalty and self-sacrifice thus came to be seen as essential values for the building of the ideal Hindu nation, these values implicitly also were emotional and indefinite calls for Indian resistance against the British.

Hero-Worship beyond Rajputana: from Shivaji to Krishna

Of course, James Tod was not the only British colonial officer in the subcontinent who became interested in, and wrote about, regional history and culture and so inspired Indians to do the same. James Grant Duff's *History of the Marathas* (three volumes, 1826) led to generations of Indian thinkers who wanted to prove that the power and role of the Marathas had been greater than the Scotsman thought.[14] In *Rise of the Maratha Power* (1900), Mahadev Govind Ranade argued not only that the Marathas as a people emerged from a seventeenth century political, social and religious renaissance, but also that the battles of the great Maratha leader Shivaji against the mighty Mughals were to be understood as the resistance of an emerging nation to foreign domination (figure 12).[15] Conversely, Ranade turned Shivaji into a hero of the Maratha nation by associating him with the local devotional (*bhakti*) movement, of which the followers acknowledge Vishnu as the supreme deity, although as a devotee of his family deity, Bhawani, Shivaji was a follower of Shiva.

---

12   Nilanjana Dutta, "'Scott of Bengal': Examining the European Legacy in the Historical Novels of Bankimchandra Chatterjee", Unpublished PhD: University of North Carolina, Chapel Hill, 2009: 172–173.

13   Sreenivasan, *The Many Lives of a Rajput Queen*: 204.

14   Sumit Guha, *History and Collective Memory in South Asia, 1200–2000*, Seattle: University of Washington Press, 2019, Chapter Three.

15   M. G. Ranade, *Rise of the Maratha Power*, Bombay: Punalekar, 1900.

FIGURE 12   'The Nation's Five Gems' (Shivaji, Guru Gobind Singh, Maharana Pratap Singh,
               Mattar Chattar Bal and Banda Bahadur) by Aryan, published by Kedar Nath
               Arya, Sialkot, 1930s–1940s
               COURTESY OF PRIYA PAUL, NEW DELHI

Over time, Shivaji became probably more known nationally than Tod's Rajput heroes. The Maratha leader was the subject of numerous plays and novels, including the earlier mentioned first historical novel in Bengali *Anguriya Binimay* (1857) by Bhudev Mukherjee and Romesh Chandra Dutt's *Maharastra Jivanprabhat* (1871). Partially based on Ranade's materials, Lala Lajpat Rai wrote *Shivaji, the Great Patriot* (1896) in Urdu. In Bombay, Bal Gangadhar Tilak reinterpreted Shivaji into a *swadeshi* hero by organizing a festival in his honour.[16] Ever since, it has not only been celebrated annually, but also worsened Hindu-Muslim relations – although Tilak himself proclaimed 'that had he been a north Indian he would himself have adopted [the third Mughal Emperor] Akbar as a hero for both Hindus and Muslims'.[17] As a matter of fact, although Shivaji became a champion of Hindu glory in popular perception, his use of Hindu symbols to legitimize his rule was aimed more at Hindu and Maratha competitors than at Muslim rulers, for whom his hostility was largely political instead of religious – the political and military rivalry between the Marathas and the Rajputs is a good example here. Likewise, as a marker of pre-colonial times, the language used at the Maratha court was heavily dominated by Persian, as it was the case at the early nineteenth century court of Sikh Maharaja Ranjit Singh in Lahore for example.

Rabindranath Tagore made his friend Sarat Kumar Ray write histories of the Marathas and the Sikhs, which he published in Bengali in 1908 and 1910 respectively, and with introductions by the poet himself, because he thought that 'a thorough study of the rise and fall of the Marathas and the Sikhs alone would illustrate how a nation would come to the forefront of history, what moral inspiration led to its success and how the decay of that moral power led inevitably to its decline'.[18] The case of Sikh hero-worship remains interesting, both inside and outside the Sikh tradition. While in pre-colonial times, Sikh identities often overlapped with those of other communities, Sikhism was defined during the Singh Sabha Reformation (c. 1875–1920) as a distinct

---

16   By this time, an increasing number of national Hindu festivals was emerging and partially so because modern means of transport and communication (railway, telegraph, print culture and so on) made it possible. In fact, the largest north Indian Hindu festival, the Kumbh Mela, was institutionalized as such only during this period. See: Kama Maclean, *Pilgrimage and Power: The Kumbh Mela in Allahabad, 1765–1954*, New York: Oxford University Press, 2008.

17   Peter Hardy, *The Muslims of British India*, Cambridge: Cambridge University Press, 1972: 142, explanation added.

18   Chanda Chatterjee, "Rabindranath Tagore's Use of Guru Gobind Singh as National Icon" in K. L. Tuteja and Kaustav Chakraborty, eds., *Tagore and Nationalism*, New Delhi: Springer, 2017: 258.

religion and nation.[19] In the context of a fast-changing Punjabi society under British colonial rule, Singh Sabhaites, among other things: standardized doctrine, conduct and ritual; wrote historical works and novels; mapped pilgrimage sites; and canonized their art and music. Besides hagiographies of the ten Sikh Gurus, an ever-growing canon of martyrs, who gave their life for the Sikh community, fed Sikh national thought. This hero-worship reached the wider Sikh community by itinerant singers, known as *dhadhis*, of ballads and narrators of the heroic Sikh tradition, as well as by popular writings, schoolbooks, Sikh art and so on. The historical novels of Bhai Vir Singh, such as *Sundari* (1889) and *Bijay Singh* (1899), which often were (and are) understood by many Sikhs to reflect real historical events, portray the brave struggles of Sikh heroes and heroines against the Afghan and Mughal rulers, who are of course negatively stereotyped. In writing them, Vir Singh was inspired by the work of Walter Scott.[20]

In addition, the first Sikh Guru, Nanak (1469–1539), and the tenth and last one, Gobind Singh (1666–1708) (figure 12), were canonized as national heroes, albeit to a lesser extent than, and in the case of Nanak in a different way from, Maharana Pratap Singh and Shivaji. After the region's annexation by the British in 1849, a good number of Bengalis (and Brahmo Samajis in particular) came to Punjab to work in the administration. They became generally fascinated with Sikh history, especially the Sikhs' resistance to the Mughals, the success of Maharaja Ranjit Singh in building an empire at a time when other Indian rulers were overruled by the EIC and the bravery of the Sikhs in the Anglo-Sikh Wars of 1845–1846 and 1848–1849. Above all, however, Bengalis were inspired by the life and teachings of Guru Gobind Singh.[21] Between 1885 and 1909, Rabindranath Tagore wrote several Sikh-related poems and essays, which except for one were all about the tenth Sikh Guru. Yet, while he initially described the latter as an ideal national hero, he subsequently projected his negative views about the increasing militancy in the *swadeshi* period by comparing it with Guru Gobind Singh's radicalization of the Sikh community through his establishing of the spiritual-military *Khalsa* order. At the

19   Bob van der Linden, *Moral Languages from Colonial Punjab: The Singh Sabha, Arya Samaj and Ahmadiyahs*, New Delhi: Manohar, 2008.

20   Sant Singh Sekhon and Kartar Singh Duggal, *A History of Punjabi Literature*, New Delhi: Sahitya Akademi, 1992: 237.

21   Himadri Banerjee, "Bengali Perceptions of the Sikhs: The Nineteenth and Twentieth Centuries" in Joseph T. O'Connell, Milton Israel, et al., eds., *Sikh History and Religion in the Twentieth Century*, Toronto: University of Toronto, Centre for South Asian Studies, 1988: 110–133.

same time, nonetheless, Tagore continued to praise Guru Nanak's liberalism towards different faiths and other aspects of the Sikh tradition, especially its attitude toward caste. Basically, he positioned Nanak within the idea of the *bhakti* movement as the true spirit of the emergent Indian nation, integrating Hindu, Muslim, Sikh and other communities through the songs of saint-poets (Chaitanya, Kabir, Mirabai, Nanak, Tulsidas, Tukuram and so on) who transcended communal boundaries. Rabindranath Tagore, Kshiti Mohan Sen and other Bengalis were very much responsible for the proliferation of this Romantic line of thinking.[22]

The Sikh Gurus were also worshipped as national heroes in south India. For instance, the nationalist and 'father of the modern Tamil short story', V. V. S. Aiyar, was much attracted to the Sikh Gurus' criticism of caste and the 'patriotism' of Guru Gobind Singh, of whom he wrote a biography in Tamil, as he did of Mazzini and Maharana Pratap Singh. Also, Aiyar made plans to reform Tamil society along the lines of the Sikh tradition. Subramania Bharati admired the Sikhs so much that, under the influence of a Sikh friend, he started to grow a beard and to wear a turban. In 1909, he wrote a poem about Guru Gobind Singh as an example for the nation in the Tamil weekly *India*, which he edited and had as its motto the slogan of the French Revolution 'Liberty, Equality and Fraternity'. In fact, Bharati's nationalist imagination generally too was shaped by *bhakti* poetry, albeit of the Tamil variety.

The 1857 Revolt, which Giuseppe Mazzini called an 'insurrection of the first magnitude',[23] was no doubt a critical event to the emergence of Indian Romantic nationalist thought. One of its results was that several heroes who fought against the British, instead of Muslim rulers, entered the Indian national imaginary. Most prominent was Rani Lakshmi Bai (born as Manakarnika), the Queen of Jhansi (figure 13), a widow and skilled warrior who defended her town against the British. A figure of loss but not of defeat, the Queen lost her family, her kingdom and died in battle in her twenties, but she nonetheless became a national symbol.[24] Her legend led to a rich oral and popular visual tradition. It was also transmitted in plays and writings in different languages, including Durga Prasad Mishra's *Jhansi ki Veer Rani Lakshmibai ka Jeevan Charitra* or 'The Life Story of the Brave Queen Lakshmibai of Jhansi' (1884) in

---

22   John Stratton Hawley, *A Storm of Songs: India and the Idea of the Bhakti Movement*, Cambridge, MA: Harvard University Press, 2015.

23   Gita Srivastava, *Mazzini and His Impact on the Indian Nationalist Movement*, Allahabad: Chugh Publications, 1982: 195.

24   Harleen Singh, *The Rani of Jhansi: Gender, History, and Fable in India*, Cambridge: Cambridge University Press, 2014.

FIGURE 13   Rani of Jhansi, artist unknown, published by Oriental Calendar Manufacturing
             Ltd., n.d.
             COURTESY OF PRIYA PAUL, NEW DELHI

Hindi.[25] Bankim Chandra Chatterjee 'admired the Rani of Jhansi as the great-est woman ever in human history and would have liked to write a novel about her heroic role'.[26] Subhadra Kumari Chauhan's poem 'Jhansi ki Rani' (1930) became one of the most recited and sung poems in Hindi literature, especially the line 'Like a man she fought, she was the Rani of Jhansi'. During the Second World War, Subhas Chandra Bose's Indian National Army had its all-female brigade, the Rani of Jhansi Regiment, fighting against the British in Burma. Besides to the idea of the defence of the Indian motherland, in popular per-ception the Rani of Jhansi legend to a certain extent connected also to the earlier mentioned diverse Hindu cultural traditions of the prehistoric Mother Goddess, the primal *Shakti* and the female avengers Kali and Durga.

Hero-worship of mythological gods was distinctive to Indian Romantic nationalist thought as well. Best known probably is Krishna, the protagonist of the central drama of the Mahabharata, the Bhagavad Gita. In this national epic, of which the content is known, albeit to different extents and through various interpretations, to members of all Indian communities, Krishna rouses Arjuna, the hero, to action in an apocalyptic battle that will mark the passing of an age by preaching him the doctrine of acting out of duty alone, with-out the desire for any particular result. Numerous modern Indian writers – like Bankim Chandra Chatterjee – and Hindu nationalists – including Bipin Chandra Pal, Bal Gangadhar Tilak, Aurobindo Ghosh and Gandhi – reinter-preted this spiritual message into a political activist one. In *The Message of the Bhagavad Gita* (1908), Lala Lajpat Rai underlined that a nation's prosper-ity and success depended 'upon wisdom like that of Krishna and on bravery like that of Arjuna' and, accordingly, that Indians would find salvation in the disinterested performance of their duty, without attachments to its fruits, at any cost and any risk: 'if ever any nation stood in need of a message like that of Krishna, it is the Indians of today' and so 'let them invoke his aid by act-ing up to the message'.[27] Repeatedly, Indian nationalists depicted Krishna as a far sighted statesman and national hero, 'a kind of indigenized Mazzini, while

---

25   As in the case of Tod's Rajput heroes, numerous English novels about the Queen of Jhansi as a brave example of Indian resistance to colonial rule also were published in Victorian Britain, including Michael White's *Lachmi Bai Rani of Jhansi: The Jeanne D'Arc of India* (1901).

26   Tapan Raychaudhuri, *Europe Reconsidered: Perceptions of the West in Nineteenth-Century Bengal*, New Delhi: Oxford University Press, 2002 (second edition: first published in 1988): 133.

27   Lala Lajpat Rai, "The Message of the Bhagavad Gita (1908)" in B. R. Nanda, ed., *The Collected Works*, volume three: 353.

the Gita became a divine Indian avatar of *The Duties of Man*.[28] Such thinking was similar to European Romantic cravings to seek the historical Jesus, 'who, through the concept of sacrifice, merged imperceptibly with great national heroes, such as Garibaldi, Gordon of Khartoum or Scott of the Antarctic'.[29]

Overall, the British felt anxious about Indian appropriations of mythological heroes. Or, as the British ethnographer and colonial administrator Herbert Hope Risley mournfully summed up in his speech that introduced the 1910 Indian Press Act (just after he had been appointed Permanent Secretary at the India Office in London):

> Everyday the Press proclaims, openly or by suggestion or allusion, that the only cure for the ills of India is independence from foreign rule, independence to be won by heroic deeds, self-sacrifice, martyrdom on the part of the young, in any case by some form of violence. Hindu mythology, ancient and modern history, and more especially the European literature of revolution, are ransacked to furnish examples that justify revolt and proclaim its inevitable success. The methods of guerilla warfare as practiced in Circassia, Spain and South Africa; Mazzini's gospel of political assassination; Kossuth's most violent doctrines; the doings of Russian Nihilists; the murder of the Marquis Ito; the dialogue between Arjuna and Krishna in the Gita, a book that is to Hindus what the *Imitation of Christ* is to emotional Christians – all these are pressed into the service of inflaming impressionable minds. The last instance is perhaps the worst. I can imagine no more wicked desecration than that the sacrilegious hand of the anarchist should be laid upon the Indian Song of Songs and that a masterpiece of transcendental philosophy and religious ecstasy should be perverted to the base uses of preaching political murder.[30]

Without any doubt, Risley was thus conscious of the significance of the Bhagavad Gita as a global moral and/or spiritual text. In translation, it was admired for different and often misleading reasons by numerous Western thinkers,

28   C. A. Bayly, "India, the Bhagavad Gita and the World", *Modern Intellectual History*, 7, 2, 2010: 286–287.
29   Ibid.
30   As cited in Christopher Pinney, "Iatrogenic Religion and Politics" in Raminder Kaur and William Mazzarella, eds., *Censorship in South Asia: Cultural Regulation from Sedition to Seduction*, Bloomington, IN: Indiana University Press, 2009: 31.

including the German philosophers Arthur Schopenhauer and Friedrich Nietzsche, the American Transcendentalists Henry David Thoreau and Ralph Waldo Emerson, the German Orientalist Friedrich Max Müller and, indeed, Giuseppe Mazzini.

In turn, European interpretations of the text became influential in India. Aurobindo Ghosh and Gandhi read the Gita for the first time in English translation, namely, the Victorian poet Edward Arnold's highly influential *The Song Celestial* (1885). Theosophists were particularly crucial to the diffusion and politicization of the Gita, both in India and around the world. For instance, Gandhi had come to know about Arnold's *The Song Celestial* through Theosophist friends. Afterwards, the Gita became his 'spiritual dictionary', and it is the book most Gandhi statues hold. Lala Lajpat Rai to a great extent based his reinterpretation of the work on Annie Besant's translation *The Bhagavad Gita or the Lord's Song* (1895), in which she cleverly constructed a parallel between the war in the Mahabharata and the Indian nationalist struggle.[31] It was Besant's allegorical reading also that fed the 'aggressive' neo-Hindu politics of Aurobindo and Sister Nivedita.[32]

Remediation in Indian Cinema

Although by the turn of the twentieth century modern print culture was widely spread in India, its impact was obviously constrained by limited literacy. At the same time, newly politicized popular practices such as Tilak's nationalist *Shiv Jayanti* festival were probably more powerful than print but remained limited to their performative setting. Hence, as in the case of Goddess Mother India, the emerging canon of reinterpreted historical and mythological national heroes was especially remediated into mass culture through different forms of visual representation.[33] Initially, the invention of lithography led to mass circulation of images of legendary national heroes. Raja Ravi Varma (1848–1906) won the hearts of the nation by romantically bringing to

---

31   Annie Besant, *The Bhagavad Gita or the Lord's Song*, London: Theosophical Publishing Society, 1895.

32   Elleke Boehmer, *Empire, the National, and the Postcolonial 1890–1920: Resistance in Interaction*, Oxford: Oxford University Press, 2002.

33   The term 'remediation' is generally understood, Ann Rigney writes, 'as the continuous translation of media content from older to newer media and from one platform to another, with a view to creating fresh effects of immediacy' in "Cultural Memory Studies: Mediation, Narrative, and the Aesthetic" in Anna Lisa Tota and Trevor Hagen, eds., *Routledge International Handbook of Memory Studies*, London: Routledge, 2016: 69.

life the ancient Hindu epics in his oil paintings,[34] which were subsequently mass produced as oleographs by his own Ravi Varma Fine Art Lithographic Press and to be found on posters, calendars, matchbox labels and so on (see for instance: figure 24). In fact, the paintings that Ravi Varma prepared to be lithographed remained very close to their German forerunners, which earlier monopolized the Indian market.[35] Lesser known, however, remains that his work inspired the pioneers of the Indian film industry, which united print culture with the physical appeal of theatrical and ritual performance. Indeed, commercial Indian cinema making was not only crucial to the development of Indian nationalism, but also rather exceptional in the colonial world because it was developed largely by local independent producers supplying a huge domestic market.

The Parsi Dadasaheb (Dhundiraj Govind) Phalke, 'the father of Indian cinema' who had worked for the Ravi Varma Press during the first decade of the twentieth century, can be seen as Ravi Varma's successor in the field of popular visuality. He largely modelled his films, which he produced in line with the nationalist call for *swadeshi* and were phenomenally successful, on episodes from the Ramayana and Mahabharata. His 'earliest mythological films are essentially animated Ravi Varma prints, and both were indebted to the aesthetics and make-up of the then popular Parsi and Marathi theatre'.[36] To be clear, although early Indian mythological films were silent ones and produced with regional audiences in mind, by using different languages in the intertitle frames, they simultaneously catered to an all-Indian market. In addition, the mythological, as an allegory of the present to avoid censorship, was sometimes used to criticize colonial rule and modern times, especially by underlining the moral and spiritual superiority of the Indian tradition. Ravi Varma had painted dramatic episodes from the life of the legendary king Harishchandra, which were printed and circulated by the Ravi Varma Press. Probably because of his familiarity with this material, Phalke decided to make his debut with *Raja Harishchandra* (1913), which was successfully marketed with Hindu nationalistic overtones, as the 'first film of Indian manufacture, specially prepared at enormous cost and sure to appeal to our Hindu patrons'.[37]

---

34   The Ravi Varma Press brought out portraits of Maharana Pratap Singh and Shivaji as well.
35   Erwin Neumayer and Christine Schelberger, eds., *Raja Ravi Varma: Portrait of an Artist* (*The Diary of C. Raja Raja Varma*), New Delhi: Oxford University Press, 2005: 268–269, 272–273.
36   Ibid.: 4–5.
37   As cited in Harald Fisher-Tiné, "Before Bollywood: Bombay Cinema and the Rise of the Film Industry in Late Colonial India" in Harald Fischer-Tiné and Maria Framke, eds.,

Harishchandra became a moral hero for Gandhi and many other Indians because of his absolute adherence to truth. Films about him continued to be made, including the first Marathi 'talkie' *Ayodhyecha Raja* (1932), of which a remade appeared in Hindi under the name *Ayodhya ka Raja* (1932), making it the first double-language film in the subcontinent. In 2008, the coloured version of the milestone in Kannada cinema *Satya Harishchandra* (1965) was a commercial success. *Bhakta Vidur* (1921) was a more direct anti-colonial production. It was released during the mounting nationalist agitation against the Anarchical and Revolutionary Crimes Act of 1919, popularly known as the Rowlatt Act, which brought Gandhi to the mainstream of the Indian nationalist struggle. The main character Vidur – who in the Mahabharata is the chief advisor to the Kauravas – was unambiguously modelled on Gandhi and the film featured contemporary political events as well. As the censor board concluded: 'We know what you are doing, it is not Vidur, it is Gandhiji, we won't allow it'.[38] Afraid that people would be incited to join Gandhi's non-cooperation movement, then, *Bhakta Vidur* was the first Indian film to be banned by the British in Karachi and Madras, amongst other places.

The introduction of sound technology in the 1930s largely reorganized Indian cinema into regional language-based industries. Yet, the incorporation of songs that conveyed nationalist messages connected the nation at the same time. For instance, in the first Tamil 'talkie' about the legendary ancient Sanskrit poet and dramatist *Kalidas* (1931), T. P. Rajalakshmi, the first Tamil and Telegu film heroine, female director and producer in the south Indian film industry, sang two nationalist songs that were unrelated to the story – one urging 'the need for unity among Indians' and the other commending 'the *charka* (spinning wheel), a nationalist symbol popularized by Gandhi' (see further Chapter Five).[39] These songs were originally written for the theatre stage by the nationalist and first lyricist in the Tamil film industry, Madurai Baskara Das, and already widely known and popular. Over time, the songs and poems of Subramania Bharati were repeatedly used in Tamil cinema as well.

Also, Phalke made films about the *bhakti* poet-saints Namdev, Mirabai and apparently Tukaram and, in general, mythological films were increas-

Routledge Handbook of the History of Colonialism in South Asia, London: Routledge, 2021: 359–372.

38   Jeannine Woods, *Visions of Empire and Other Imaginings: Cinema, Ireland and India 1910–1962*, Bern: Peter Lang, 2011: 98.

39   Stephen Putnam Hughes, "Tamil Mythological Cinema and the Politics of Secular Modernism" in Birgit Meyer, ed., *Aesthetic Formations: Media, Religion, and the Senses*, New York: Palgrave Macmillan, 2009: 105.

ingly joined by devotional (*bhakti*) ones, which presented 'historical figures rather than mythological, heroic or divine characters'.[40] Thus, the Tamil movie *Pattinathar* (1935) was advertised as: 'The soul stirring life of a miracle working saint of the tenth century known to every Tamilian', depicting 'The riches and life of Tamil Nad [*sic*] a thousand years ago'.[41] In order to distinguish the film from mythological ones, the producers prominently advertised it as being based on the 'True historical background designed by University Professors of Research'.[42] In this way, they aligned *Pattinathar* with the identity politics of the Tamil Renaissance, about which more in the next Chapter.

Although the film industry to different extents turned *bhakti* saints into national heroes, devotional films simultaneously strengthened regional national identities. In Bengal, *Chandidas* (1932) was the first of a long row of devotional films, often focused on the *bhakti* saint Chaitanya, that linked cinema with the making of a Bengali national identity, whereby the songs of Rabindranath Tagore and Vaishnavite *kirtan* (see also Chapter Four) were crucial in distinguishing the films produced in Calcutta from those elsewhere in the subcontinent.[43] Conversely, the popularity of devotional films was undeniably related to the personality of Gandhi. His 'experiments with truth', as he called his political and spiritual struggle, were not only closely aligned to *bhakti*, but most Indians saw him as a true saint.[44] In fact, advertisements of films regardless of their themes generally were accompanied by large photographs of Gandhi or by captions such as 'helper to the cause of Mahatma Gandhi'.[45]

Probably more than any other *bhakti* saint the sixteenth century north Indian Hindu poet-singer Mirabai, a devotee of Krishna, became a pan-Indian figure. Her songs are sung and known all the way to the southern-most tip of the subcontinent by people who otherwise have little command of Hindi. Mira's life story and songs soon caught the attention of European Orientalists, from James Tod to Annie Besant, who included her in *Children of the Motherland* (1905). Tagore, Gandhi and other Indian thinkers revered *bhakti* poetry because of its message of Hindu-Muslim unity. Gandhi even re-christened one of his disciples, the English Madeleine Slade, as Mira, while elevating himself

40   Rachel Dwyer, *Filming the Gods: Religion and Indian Cinema*, London: Routledge, 2006: 63.
41   Hughes, "Tamil Mythological Cinema": 110.
42   Ibid.
43   Sharmistha Gooptu, *Bengali Cinema: 'An Other Nation'*, London: Routledge, 2011.
44   Dwyer, *Filming the Gods*: 69.
45   As cited in: Woods, *Visions of Empire*: 99.

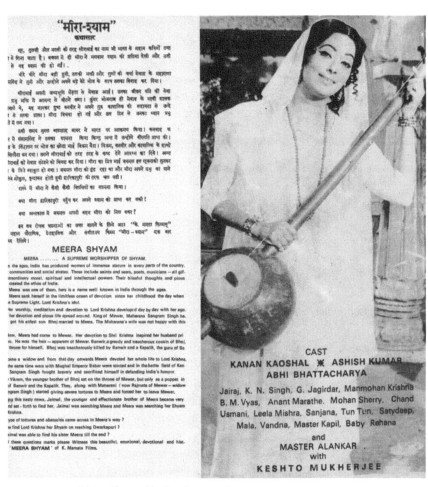

FIGURE 14   Meera Shyam, film brochure, 1976
               COURTESY OF PRIYA PAUL, NEW DELHI

to the position of Krishna on the way. Expectedly, as her songs were loved by
Hindus, Muslims, Sikhs and Christians, Mirabai became the subject of several
films (figure 14). Directed by the American Ellis Duncan, who made several
Tamil films without ever learning the language, the 1945 Tamil classic *Meera*
starred south India's most renowned vocalist M. S. Subbalakshmi as Mira and
singing in Hindi. In 1947, a Hindi version of the film appeared, which was
introduced by the female nationalist politician and poet Sarojini Naidu. Further, the original Tamil film was dubbed in other Indian languages, although
the songs continued to be sung in Hindi in all versions. The film brought Subbalakshmi to national prominence and produced some of the most popular
interpretations of Mira's song.

Three of James Tod's heroes were repeatedly remediated in Indian cinema. Following earlier movies like *Maharana Pratap* (1946) and *Chetak aur Rana Pratap* (1958), Maharana Pratap Singh was recently resuscitated as national hero, for example through the film *Maharana Pratap: The First Freedom Fighter* (2012) and popular TV-series such as *Bharat ka Veer: Maharana Pratap* (2013–2015). Prithviraj Chauhan and Padmini experienced similar revivals. The Hindi TV-series *Dharti ka Veer Yodha Prithviraj Chauhan* ran successfully on prime time between 2006 and 2009. Interestingly, the Tamil film *Prithvirajan* (1942) featured Subramania Bharati's 1920-song 'Bharata Samudayam Vazhgave' or 'Long Live the People of India', although his name is not credited because his songs were banned. Among the movies and TV-series about Padmini are: *Chitor Rani Padmini* (1963), *Maharani Padmini* (1964), *Padmaavat* (2018) and the historical drama tv-series *Chittod ki Rani Padmini ka Johur* (2009). Even more films and TV-series were made about Shivaji and Rani Lakshmi Bai. To mention just a few about the first: *Sinhagad* (1933), *Chhatrapati Shivaji Maharaj* (1952), *Farzand* (2018), *Fatteshikast* (2019) and the popular TV-series *Veer Shivaji* (2011–2012). India's first technicolour film *Jhansi ki Rani* (1953), of which an English version appeared as *The Tiger and the Flame* (1956), featured the song 'Hamara Pyara Hindustan' (Our Beloved Hindusthan) sung by Muhammed Rafi, with the lines: 'Whether we gain victory or defeat, let the future generations remember that the first sword against British injustice was raised by the Queen of Jhansi, Rani Lakshmi Bai'. Alternately, the Queen's last words in the film, 'Azadi mar ho' (Freedom is Immortal), are whispered with the India's national anthem Jana Gana Mana sounding softly in the background, connecting the 1857 Revolt to the imminent independence of the nation. In this century, *Jhansi ki Rani* (TV-series, 2009) and *Manikarnika: The Queen of Jhansi* (2019) were very popular.

Over time, all above mentioned national historical heroes ended up in the public sphere, for instance as statues, street-names and on stamps. Since the late 1960s, they also received their own volumes in the enormously successful 'educational' comic series *Amar Chitra Katha* (Immortal Picture Stories), which carries the subtitle 'The Glorious Heritage of India'.[46] In addition, the series has numerous volumes on mythological heroes, including about Krishna, as well on episodes from the Mahabharata and the Ramayana.[47] In fact, following the large-scale expansion of television in India and the rise of

---

46   Karline McLain, *India's Immortal Comic Books: Gods, Kings, and Other Heroes*, Bloomington, IN: Indian University Press, 2009.

47   As in the case of the Mahabharata, there is no original version of the Ramayana. Numerous tellings exist in South Asia among Hindus, Buddhists and Jains, as well as in Southeast

extreme right wing Hindutva politics in the 1990s, these epics have become more popular than ever before. Most important to this was their serialization, during the late 1980s and early 1990s respectively, by India's national television broadcaster, *Doordarshan*, which at the time still had no competitors. No doubt, this was a crucial event towards the national homogenization of the diverse narrative traditions of both epics. For Hindus in particular, their weekly watching became something of a collective national ritual and the series not only strengthened the traditional hero worship of Krishna as a wise ruler and moral example, but especially also of the God Rama as muscular and aggressive rather than in the more traditional style as benign and loving, with a smooth and almost flabby body. Ever since, Hindu nationalists increasingly invoked the Ramayana and its hero to mobilize Hindus, including during the demolition of the Babri Masjid ('Mosque of Mughal Emperor Babur') in Ayodhya, which led to widespread violence between Hindus and Muslims and the call among Hindu nationalists for the return of the Golden Age when Rama supposedly ruled in Ayodhya (*Ramraj*). Earlier, in fact, Gandhi had already argued that, instead of Western representative institutions, the Ramayana's kingdom of Rama, a patriarchy in which the ruler, the embodiment of moral virtue, always gave voice to the collective will, should be the model for India's future.

In this context it remains intriguing that, for the greater part of the twentieth century, Bombay's Hindi cinema was pervasively influenced by Muslim culture. This, on the one hand, because of the great number of Muslim writers, lyricists, directors and actors. And, on the other, because of its use of colloquial Urdu ('Hindustani'), mainly to reach the maximum audience but also because of its poetic quality. As a matter of fact, Urdu film songs (*ghazals*), often with loss, nostalgia and sadness as a theme, continue to be popular or at least permeate the Hindi film lyric.[48] At the same time, stereotypes about Muslims were inherent to Hindi cinema. In line with the British view of Indian history, Muslims were repeatedly depicted as invaders (the enemy of Marathas, Rajputs, Sikhs and so on) and the Islamic period as one of decline. Following the idea of Hindu-Muslim harmony as dominantly promulgated by the Indian National Congress (INC), however, several historical movies about the Mughal court appeared to promote national unity. *Pukar* (1939), *Tansen* (1943), *Humayun* (1945), *Shah Jahan* (1946), *Anarkali* (1953), *Malika-e-Alam Noor Jahan*

Asia. Some of the most important versions in India are Valmiki's Ramayana in Sanskrit (c. 200 BCE–200 ACE), Kampan's *Iramavataram* in Tamil from the ninth century and Tulsidas's *Ramcharitmanas* in Hindi from the sixteenth century.

48   Dwyer, *Filming the Gods*: Chapter Three.

FIGURE 15   Noor Jahan, still from *Malika-e-Alam Noor Jahan*, 1954
COURTESY OF PRIYA PAUL, NEW DELHI

(1954) (figure 15) and *Noor Jahan* (1967) are only a few examples. The heroes of these films, however, 'were those seen in Nehru's *The Discovery of India* (1946), such as Akbar, rather than the heroes of the Muslim community, such as Aurangzeb, Chenghis Khan and Mahmud of Ghazni'.[49] They generally confirm the idea of India's 'unity in diversity' as expressed by Nehru in *The Discovery of India* and subsequently propagated by the Indian government during the Nehruvian era (1947–1964). In this context, Mughal Emperor Akbar was particularly projected as a national hero because of his religious and cultural tolerance. Thus, for instance, *Mughal-e-Azam* (1960) opens with a map of India which rises behind a shot of an archetypical Indian village, accompanied by a male voiceover which declares:

I am India. I was plundered by barbarism and saved by the merciful. The unwise tied me in chains, those who loved me have freed me. Jalul-ud-Din Mohammed Akbar transcended barriers of religion and tradition [...] and taught man to love his fellow man. Thus he embraced this country.

49   Ibid.: 116.

Then again, from the very first historical films onward, Muslim elites were exoticized as representatives of a lost aristocratic world, as exemplified by extravagant sets, captivating court dances and Persianized Urdu dialogues. Satyajit Ray's classics *Jalsaghar* or 'The Music Room' (1958) and *Shatranj ke Khilari* or 'The Chess Players' (1977) are two famous examples. For a period, then, Muslims were cast for limited roles like the Imam, the courtesan or a stereotypical occupation such as the Muslim tailor (*darzi*). Yet, with the rise of Hindutva, they were particularly demonized, for example in recent historical films such as *Bajirao Mastani* (2015), *Padmaavat, Manikarnika, Panipat* (2019) and *Tanhaji* (2020).[50] Obviously, such movies especially catered to Hindu audiences in northern India. But what about south India, where there are much fewer Muslims? Since the late nineteenth century, Tamils became aware of their own Dravidian identity. Subsequently, resistance against the Aryan north grew and became partially based upon a Romantic call for a revival of a Tamil Golden Age. The next chapter looks at this call from a comparative perspective with the simultaneous appeals for Aryan/Hindu and Muslim Golden Ages.

---

50   Kalyani Chadha and Anandam P. Kavoori, "Exoticized, Marginalized, Demonized: The Muslim Other in Indian Cinema" in Anandam P. Kavoori and Ashwin Punathakbekar, eds., *Global Bollywood*, New York: New York University Press, 2008: 131–145.

CHAPTER 3

Aryan, Tamil and Muslim Golden Ages

Sanskrit, the Vedas and Aryanism

Although European (missionary) scholars in India had perceived similarities between European languages and Sanskrit since the sixteenth century, the following famous 'philologer passage' from the 'Third Anniversary Discourse', also known as 'On the Hindus', delivered by William Jones to Calcutta's Asiatic Society of Bengal on 2 February 1786 (published in 1788) is often cited as the beginning of comparative-historical linguistics (the work of Franz Bopp, Rasmus Rask, Jacob Grimm and so on):[1]

> The *Sanscrit* language, whatever be its antiquity, is of a wonderful structure; more perfect than the *Greek*, more copious than the *Latin*, and more exquisitely refined than either, yet bearing to both of them a stronger affinity, both in the roots of verbs and the forms of grammar, than could possibly have been produced by accident; so strong indeed, that no philologer could examine them all three, without believing them to have sprung from some common source, which, perhaps, no longer exists: there is a similar reason, though not quite so forcible, for supposing that both the *Gothick* and the *Celtick*, though blended with a very different idiom, had the same origin with *Sanscrit*; and the old *Persian* might be added to the same family, if this were the place for discussing any question concerning the antiquities of *Persia*.[2]

In 1813, the term 'Indo-European' was coined for this common original language 'which, perhaps, no longer exists'.

Intriguingly, Jones's research had its roots in a belief in the Old Testament genealogy of the 'Tree of Nations'. According to this Mosaic ethnology, which is a rationalized version of the Tower of Babel narrative and a common heritage of Jews, Christians and Muslims, Jones believed that the world's popu-

---

1   The nineteenth century study of Sanskrit phonetics and grammar lay not only the basis of comparative-historical linguistics, but it also anticipated the formation of the International Phonetic Alphabet and computer programming.
2   As cited in Thomas R. Trautmann, *Aryans and British India*, Berkeley, CA: University of California Press, 1997: 38.

© BOB VAN DER LINDEN, 2024 | DOI:10.1163/9789004694804_005

lation descended as nations with specific languages from Noah's three sons, Ham, Japhet and Shem, and their wives, after they survived the Deluge. For Jones, therefore, his linguistic discoveries were above all proof of the common ancestry of Indians and Europeans as descendants of Ham, rather than Japhet as most of his contemporaries believed. To a large extent, his interpretation followed Jacob Bryant's *A New System, or an Analysis of Ancient Mythology* (1774–1776) and it was also the one that he encountered among Indian Muslims. The idea is captured too in the colossal statue of Jones in toga, while leaning with one arm on his translation of the 'Laws of Manu',[3] in St. Paul's Cathedral, London. The scene from the Puranic story of the churning of the milk ocean by the gods and demons on the pedestal depicts nothing more than Jones's desire to endorse the truth of the Biblical narrative of the Deluge in Sanskrit literature.

In Jones's footsteps, nineteenth century European scholars continued to be more interested in India's ancient past than in its present. Henry Thomas Colebrooke specifically identified Sanskrit as the cradle of Indian civilization. In general, he and Jones contrasted contemporary Hinduism with a Vedic Golden Age, which the two classicists undoubtedly believed to be like that of ancient Greece and Rome. Most significant, however, became the theory of Sanskrit-speaking Aryans invading the subcontinent.[4] The *Rig Veda* (c. 1500–1200 BCE)[5] mentions the arrival of pastoralists who identified themselves as 'Arya' (literally 'noble'). After their encounter and intermingling with the local population, Arya continued to function 'both as a marker of community and as an evaluation of cultural sophistication'.[6] Until colonial times, nonetheless, the term was solely used in India as a descriptive term for the descendants of the Aryans. Europeans were not seen as Aryan but labelled *faringi* (a word derived from the Persian term for Franks), *mleccha* (Sanskrit for barbarian) or *yavana* (Sanskrit for Greek or Westerner). In the end, European Orientalists defined

---

3 In 1776, Jones translated this Sanskrit text, generally known as *Manu Smriti* or *Dharma Sastra* (c. 200 BCE–300 CE), which was wrongly identified by the British as the sacred law book of the Hindus.

4 Nowadays, the idea of a mass migration of Aryans invading the subcontinent has fallen out of favour among scholars, who to the contrary assume that successively small groups trickled in and much intermingled with the local population.

5 In the Hindu tradition, the four Vedas (*Rig Veda*, *Sama Veda*, *Yajur Veda* and *Atharva Veda*) are regarded as *shruti* ('what is heard') in contrast to *smriti* ('what is remembered') texts such as the Mahabharata and Ramayana.

6 Tony Ballantyne, *Orientalism and Race: Aryanism in the British Empire*, Basingstoke: Palgrave Macmillan, 2002: 5.

the Aryans as the founders of Indian civilization and the Vedas as recordings of the beginning of Indian history. Simultaneously, they propounded the
idea that the Sanskrit-speaking Aryans subjugated the local population of the
subcontinent, partially by imposing a caste system with Brahmins at the top,
followed by Kshatriyas and Vaishyas, and Shudras even lower, and the exclu-
sion of the untouchables. Furthermore, they described Hindus as belonging to
the first three castes of this system and Shudras and the untouchables as the
descendants of the original population of India.

Fundamental to the spread of the term Arya and knowledge about the
Aryan invasion theory as well as the *Rig Veda* in Europe and India was the work
of the German Friedrich Max Müller (figure 16),[7] who lived and worked in
Britain for most of his life, since 1868 as Oxford's first Professor of Comparative
Philology. He was a pioneer in Sanskrit philology as well as in the comparative study of language, mythology and religion. He never visited India but
since his early youth, when one of his schoolbooks had a picture of Benares
on the cover, he had a great interest in the country and, over the decades, he
met numerous, often eminent, Indians in Europe.[8] With a sceptical attitude
towards industrialization and the belief in progress at large, Max Müller generally discovered spiritual India as the opposite pole of the materialistic West, as
was common at the time among both counter-cultural Westerners and nationalist Indians. In 1896, he met Swami Vivekananda and two years later, to the
great delight of the latter, he published *Ramakrishna: His Life and Sayings*, in
which the Indian guru was represented as 'the embodiment of "pure" Hinduism'.[9]

From 1849 to 1874, the East India Company and, after its abolishment in
1858, the British government sponsored Max Müller's translation of the *Rig
Veda*, which he believed to be the most ancient literature in the world. This was
a most decisive event for the interaction between European Orientalist knowledge and Indian Romantic national thought. For until that time knowledge
of the Vedas was not codified. To the contrary, it was embodied knowledge,
transmitted orally by highly specialized Brahmins, sometimes with the help of

---

7   His father, the Romantic poet Wilhelm Müller – best known as the author of *Die Schöne
    Müllerin* and *Winterreise* from the famous Franz Schubert song cycles – became a great sup-
    porter of the Greek struggle against the Ottoman Empire by writing poems on the subject
    and therefore was nicknamed 'The Greek'.
8   Friedrich Max Müller, *Auld Lang Syne, volume two: My Indian Friends*, New York: C. Scribner's
    Sons, 1899.
9   Ruth Harris, *Guru to the World: The Life and Legacy of Vivekananda*, Cambridge, Mass.: The
    Belknap Press of Harvard University Press, 2022: 208.

FIGURE 16   Friedrich Max Müller, photographer unknown
                   SOURCE: *Cassell's Universal Portrait Gallery*, LONDON: CASSELL AND
                   COMPANY, 1895: 319

manuscripts, of which the earliest probably date from the sixteenth century –
much like the Iliad and Odyssey in Greece, which were composed several hundred years later in another early Indo-European language. It was only due to
Max Müller and later European and Indian Orientalists that the Vedas became
available for reference to Hindu intellectuals. By translating the *Rig Veda* into
English, Max Müller hoped that educated Indians would be inspired by his
image of a Vedic Golden Age and accordingly reform Hindu society to recap-
ture something of this lost glory. To be clear, however, the lengthy and obscure
Vedas are riddled with contradictions and are therefore anything but authoritative guidebooks for human behaviour.

In addition, Max Müller strongly promoted the Aryan race theory. He asserted that there was an original Aryan homeland in Central Asia. He described the Aryans who entered India as upper caste and 'fair-skinned' in opposition to the lower caste and untouchable 'dark skinned' original inhabitants of the subcontinent, whom he believed to be Turanians of Scythian origins.[10] In his later years, nonetheless, Max Müller was deeply saddened by the fact that Aryan was used in racist terms because for him it was strictly related to language. As he wrote in *Biographies of Words and the Home of the Aryas* (1888): 'An ethnologist who speaks of Aryan race, Aryan blood, Aryan eyes and hair, is as great a sinner as a linguist who speaks of a dolichocephalic dictionary or a brachycephalic grammar' and 'the blackest Hindus represent an earlier stage of Aryan speech and thought than the fairest Scandinavians'.[11] Even so, Max Müller's ideas about the Aryan race, and his writings in general, were enthusiastically received in India. The term Arya began to feature in the names of books, journals and societies, as well as in the names of street corner shops. Increasingly, Indian thinkers used the terms 'Aryan' and 'Hindu' as substitutable. Also, the Aryan theory provided some Indians with status and self-esteem in relation to the colonial ruler. As a Bengali correspondent wrote in 1874 in the *Indian Mirror*: 'We were niggers at one time. We now become brethren'.[12] Moreover, Hindu thinkers began to argue that an Aryan 'Hindu' Golden Age, dominated by Sanskrit-speaking Brahmins, who revered the Vedas and the caste system, had been corrupted because of the inclusion of the meaningless idolatry (including 'phallic worship') and rituals of the original inhabitants of the subcontinent, as well as Muslim tyranny afterwards.

One of the most influential Indian reinterpretations of Aryanism was made by Dayanand Saraswati, who in 1875 founded the influential Hindu reform movement the Arya Samaj ('Noble Society').[13] After many years of traditional education, he became acquainted with modern ideas in Calcutta, where he met numerous Bengali intellectuals. He was familiar with the writings of Max Müller and other European Orientalist scholars as well. Probably more than any other Indian before him, he played off the antiquity and divine inspiration (*shruti*) of the Vedas and a few other selected ancient Sanskrit texts

10   Romila Thapar, "The Theory of Aryan Race and India: History and Politics", *Social Scientist*, 24, 1–3, 1996: 5–6.

11   Friedrich Max Müller, *Biographies of Words and the Home of the Aryas*, London: Longmans, Green, and Co., 1888: 120.

12   As cited in Ballantyne, *Orientalism and Race*: 44.

13   Bob van der Linden, *Moral Languages from Colonial Punjab: The Singh Sabha, Arya Samaj and Ahmadiyahs*, New Delhi: Manohar, 2008.

against Hindu orthodox positions. Furthermore, Dayanand used this argument to assert the superiority of the Hindu tradition over Christianity, Islam and other traditions. He came up with the slogan 'Back to the Vedas' to propagate the revival of the Golden Age of *Aryavarta* (the name for Aryan land of roughly today's Punjab, Rajasthan and the Gangetic plains of north India), *dharma* and the Sanskrit language. In his view, the Vedas contained complete human knowledge. Even modern inventions such as the railway and the telegraph, he argued, had already been known to Vedic poets. However odd these claims may seem, in Dayanand footsteps, Hindu nationalists often continued to argue in this way.

In opposition to the Aryan invasion theory, Dayanand argued that the Aryans originally came from Tibet, where according to him all humanity lived at that time. In his view, only upper castes were Aryans, although untouchables could be incorporated once they had gone through a purification ritual. Further, he presented Hinduism as a religion of the book, which it never was, and contemporaries called him the 'Luther of India' because he brought the Vedas to the people by translating them into Hindi. Much along the lines of the activities of Protestant missionaries in Punjab, he embraced vernacular preaching, founded schools and used the printing press as a weapon for his crusade. On the whole, Dayanand's ideas were important to the emergence of Hindu Romantic nationalist thought because he did much for the self-identification of Hindus as Aryans and, closely related, a homogenous Hindu nation. In 1898, Lala Lajpat Rai portrayed Dayanand as a 'saviour of the Vedic religion' who had 'infused new life into a dying race', lifted a great religion 'from the pit of darkness', brought out a great language – Sanskrit – from oblivion, and inspired the Hindus to come out of their 'hidebound orthodoxy'.[14]

Numerous Indian intellectuals appropriated Aryanism to define the Hindu nation. Bal Gangadhar Tilak projected this modern idea back to Vedic times and he believed that it was the duty of Indian leaders to revive that period when India was united as a great and self-contained nation. In *Orion or Researches into the Antiquity of the Vedas* (1893), he endorsed the antiquity of the *Rig Veda*, by taking it back to 4500 BCE, much earlier than the 1500 BCE suggested by Max Müller, while constructing his argument on what he interpreted as references to planetary positions.[15] In *The Arctic Home in the Vedas* (1903), Tilak argued that the Aryans had migrated from the Arctic regions in

---

14   Lala Lajpat Rai, "Swami Dayanand (1898)", excerpts translated from Urdu, in B. R. Nanda, ed., *The Collected Works of Lala Lajpat Rai*, volume one, New Delhi: Manohar, 2004: 371–418.

15   B. G. Tilak, *Orion or Researches into the Antiquity of the Vedas*, Bombay: Mrs. Radhabdi Atmaram Sagoon, 1893.

the post-glacial age and then branched off, with one group going to Europe and another coming to India.[16] Subsequently, he continued, the European Aryans relapsed into barbarism, while the Indo-Aryans retained their original, superior civilization which they re-established after conquering the non-Aryans of India. According to Tilak, the superiority of the Indo-Aryans was particularly manifest in the *Devanagari* script used for Sanskrit, and later Hindi, which was repeatedly praised by European scholars as being the most perfect in the world. Like many other leading Hindus at the time, he wanted it to become the national script for India.

To the contrary, Swami Vivekananda claimed that Aryans had always lived in northern India and had shaped the flourishing Brahminical tradition of the ancient Indian nation. Hence, he argued, it was this identity that needed to be re-established: 'Just as Sanskrit has been the linguistic solution, so the Arya the racial solution. So the Brahminhood is the solution of the varying degrees of progress and culture as well as that of all social and political problems'.[17] Vivekananda took this idea from the Mahabharata, in which the Brahmin caste was the only one that existed in the Golden Age of *satya yuga* ('age of truth'). In his view, the diverse Hindu traditions had to unite themselves under Brahminical leadership and the banner of neo-Vedanta philosophy to revive that great Aryan nation of the past. Hindu spirituality and race were inherent to his 'aggressive Hinduism':

> There may be a nation whose theme of life is political supremacy; religion and everything else must become subordinate to that great theme of its life. But there is another nation whose great theme of life is spirituality and renunciation [...]. The secret of a true Hindu's character lies in the subordination of his knowledge of European science and learning, of his wealth, position and name, to that one principal theme which is born in every Hindu child – the spirituality and purity of the race.[18]

While Vivekananda proclaimed in the West – including in his famous speech before the World's Parliament of Religions in Chicago – that all religions were true and Hinduism was a tolerant and inclusive 'world religion', he ultimately

---

16   B. G. Tilak, *The Arctic Home in the Vedas*, Poona City: Messrs. Tilak Bros. Gaikwar Waida, 1925 (first published in 1903).

17   Karl Baier, "Swami Vivekananda: Reform Hinduism, Nationalism and Scientist Yoga", *Interdisciplinary Journal for Religion and Transformation in Contemporary Society*, 5, 2019: 237.

18   Ibid.: 236.

believed that religions were only a different stage in the journey, 'the aim of which is the perfect conception of the Vedas'.[19] Partially influenced by Theosophist thought, then, he became one of the founding fathers of Vedic science.

Aryanism became important in other ways too. North Indian upper castes sometimes legitimized their status and identity by way of their Aryan descent. In doing so, they effectively marginalized lower castes and non-Hindus, above all Muslims. Aurobindo Ghosh and Sister Nivedita argued that Indians had not only to recover 'the Aryan strength, the Aryan discipline, the Aryan character, the Aryan life' to produce the true expression of 'the undying soul of the nation', but they also hoped that 'aggressive Hinduism' – being the highest form of homage to the Divine Mother, the Bhagavad Gita's warrior devotion to Kali – would eventually create a stage for a global Hindu spiritual imperialism or Aryanization.[20] In west India, the low caste social reformer Jyotirao Phule (1827–1890), who was greatly influenced by Thomas Paine's *Rights of Man*, appropriated the Aryan theory to his own advantage. He argued that upper caste leaders as descendants of Aryan conquerors were foreigners. Their culture, including the caste system, therefore, was alien to India's original inhabitants, of whom the low castes were the successors and, indeed, inheritors of a distinct Golden Age. Phule remained aloof of the Indian National Congress (INC) because he regarded it as a Brahminical organization. In general, he thought that nationalism was an illusion created by upper caste manipulation to conceal inner divisions of Indian society. Accordingly, he founded his own movement, the Sathyashodhak Samaj or Society of the Seekers of Truth, to strengthen solidarity among the lower castes.[21] Most significant, however, remains the fact that Aryanism complicated the making of the Indian nation because it created a linguistic and racial divide between the Aryan north and Dravidian/Tamil south.

Tamil and the Origins of Man

The Ganges, though flowing from the foot of Vishnu and through Siva's hair, is not an ancient stream. Geology, looking further than

---

19   Ibid.: 239.

20   Elleke Boehmer, *Empire, the National, and the Postcolonial 1890–1920: Resistance in Inter-action*, Oxford: Oxford University Press, 2002: 108, 112.

21   Rosalind O'Hanlon, *Caste, Conflict and Ideology: Mahatma Jotirao Phule and Low-Caste Protest in Nineteenth-Century Western India*, Cambridge: Cambridge University Press, 1985.

religion, knows of a time when neither the river nor the Himalayas that nourish it existed, and an ocean flowed over the holy places of Hindustan. The mountains rose, their debris silted up the ocean, the gods took their seats on them and contrived the river, and the India we call immemorial came into being. But India is really far older. In the days of the prehistoric ocean the southern part of the peninsula already existed, and the high places of Dravidia have been land since land began, and have seen on the one side the sinking of a continent that joined them to Africa, and on the other the upheaval of the Himalayas from a sea. They are older than anything in the world.[22]

E. M. FORSTER, A Passage to India (1924)[23]

The Aryan invasion theory shaped research into the linguistic differences between Sanskrit and the south Indian languages or what came to be known as the 'Dravidian proof'.[24] Francis Whyte Ellis, a British civil servant in the Madras Presidency and a scholar of Tamil and Sanskrit, was the first to question the conclusion of British Orientalist scholars in Calcutta, such as William Carey, Henry Thomas Colebrooke and Charles Wilkens, that all Indian languages had derived from Sanskrit. In his 'Note to the Introduction' of Alexander Duncan Campbell's *A Grammar of the Teloogoo Language, commonly termed the Gentoo, peculiar to the Hindoos inhabiting the North Eastern provinces of the Indian Peninsula* (1816), he underlined that the core of the south Indian languages (he did not use the term Dravidian) was the same and unrelated to Sanskrit. Forty years later, Reverend Robert Caldwell, a Scottish missionary from the Society for the Propagation of the Gospel, argued in *A Comparative Grammar of the Dravidian or South-Indian Family of Languages* (1857) that Tamil, Telugu, Kannada and Malayalam formed a distinct 'Dravidian' language family.[25] In addition, he emphasized that south India had been the victim of a racial conquest of original Dravidian peoples by Brahminical Aryans, who had brought Sanskrit, Hindu rituals and an alien caste system with them. Caldwell was

---

22 In the *Imperial Gazetteer of India* (1909) and elsewhere, the British even divided the geology of the subcontinent racially into Dravidian and Aryan periods.
23 E. M. Forster, *A Passage to India*, London: Penguin, 1979 (first published in 1924): 109.
24 Thomas R. Trautmann, *Languages and Nations: Conversations in Colonial South India*, Berkeley, CA: University of California Press, 2006.
25 The origin of the Sanskrit word 'dravida' is Tamil and in the Sanskrit tradition it was used to denote the geographical region of south India.

much impressed by Tamil, the 'most highly cultivated *ab intra* of all Dravidian idioms', and he underlined that it could do without 'its Sanskrit, if need be, and not only stand alone, but flourish, without its aid'.[26] Thus, he challenged the accepted view of the time that Sanskrit was the primal source of Indian civilization. Furthermore, he helped to draw attention to the unique identity of the Dravidian, and especially Tamil, peoples of the peninsula.

Since the beginning of the nineteenth century, British officials and their Tamil-speaking assistants at the College of Fort St. George in Madras had published works in Tamil (grammars, editions of ancient literary works, prose translations and so on). Soon Tamil intellectuals also dedicated themselves to the modern study of Tamil and the recovery of their past. In this, they were particularly inspired by the idea that Tamil was a second classical language besides Sanskrit and, moreover, the only living Indian language with a continuous documented tradition of more than two thousand years. Fundamental to this 'Tamil Renaissance' was the work of U. V. Swaminathan Iyer (figure 17) and C. W. Thamotharampillai, who salvaged and subsequently edited and published many long-forgotten (palm leaf) Tamil manuscripts. Tamil associations were established, and the Tamil language was generally modernized, historicized and canonized. The principal source for Tamil Romantic nationalist thought became the so-called Sangam literature era (c. 300 BCE to c. 300 CE). Tamil intellectuals nostalgically portrayed an ancient, adventurous and heroic Tamil people roaming the high seas (towards southeast Asia) in pursuit of gold and glory. From the early twentieth century onward, the Pure Tamil Movement (*Thani Tamil Iyakkam*) began to cleanse Tamil of words of Sanskrit origin, although over time, for instance, Sanskritic phraseology and rules of compounding and suffixes remained.[27] Subramania Bharati did not enter the Aryan-Dravidian controversy because he favoured Hindi as national language.[28] Yet, by writing in Tamil and through his overall dedication to the Tamil nation he gave 'a dimension and stature to Tamil literature and culture that was quite as important as scholarly defences'.[29]

Two mythological heroes were specifically defined as 'founding fathers' of the ancient Tamil tradition. Due to his mythical origins, the Vedic sage Agastya,

---

26   As cited in Eugene F. Irschick, *Politics and Social Conflict in South Asia: the Non-Brahman Movement and Tamil Separatism 1916–1929*, Berkeley, CA: University of California Press, 1969: 278, italics in original.

27   Sumathi Ramaswamy, *Passions of the Tongue: Language Devotion in Tamil India, 1891–1970*, Berkeley, CA: University of California Press, 1997: 146.

28   Ibid.: 58.

29   Irschick, *Politics and Social Conflict*: 285.

FIGURE 17   U. V. Swaminatha Iyer studying palm leaf manuscripts, photographer
                 unknown, n.d.
                 SOURCE: WIKICOMMONS

who appears in numerous Sanskrit works, including the Mahabharata and the
Ramayana, was appropriated in different ways in north and south India. While
in the north he is credited with bringing the Sanskrit language to the south,
paradoxically in the south he came to be seen as the father of Tamil language
and the compiler of the first Tamil grammar, although some Tamil intellectuals – including K. N. Sivaraja Pillai in *Agastya in the Tamil Land* (1930) –
countered such claims as pure fiction. Conversely, the poet-saint Thiruvalluvar
was sanctified as the father of Tamil literature, south India's champion in the
face of advancing Sanskritization from the north. Moreover, as there was a con-
vergence between a pre-colonial Tamil reading of Thiruvalluvar as a low caste
and a European (missionary) desire to accept that version, his legend came
to emphasize the conflict between Brahmins and non-Brahmins. The prime
work credited to him is *Thirukkural* (c. 500 CE), one of the most revered texts
in the Tamil language and one which from the beginning of the eighteenth
century onward caught the attention of European Orientalists. Currently, a
huge statue of Thiruvalluvar is standing at Kanyakumari, the most southern
tip of the peninsula (and a small one in front of London's School of Oriental
and African Studies).

Like Lal Behari Day in Bengal, the polymath S. M. Natesa Sastri was inspired by British folklorists working in India. Believing that folklore was national literature that had to be rescued from oblivion, he wrote *The Folklore of Southern India* (1884–1893), a four-volume collection of Tamil folk tales. He was familiar with the work of European folklorists, including the Grimm brothers, and his own writings were well received in Europe, especially at the Folklore Society in London.[30] In fact, Sastri collaborated with Alexander William Clouston, who devoted his life to the study of the migration of Asian folklore to Europe. The Scottish folklorist wrote a detailed comparative note to Sastri's translation of the ancient folk tale *Alekesa Katha* ('Story of King Alekesa') from Tamil into *The King and His Four Ministers* (1889). Also, he used one of his folktales 'for the missing link in a chain of transmission of a humorous tale that had its final destination in far-away Norway'.[31] Interestingly, Sastri wrote *Dinadayalu* (1900), his first Tamil novel of six, under the pseudonym 'Swadesamitran' ('Friend of *swadeshi*'), which was also the name of a Tamil nationalist newspaper. Despite Sastri's efforts, nonetheless, Tamil folklore was overshadowed by the Sangam literature as the essence of the Tamil nation, although Subramania Bharati continued to rely much on folk metres and forms for his poetry – as Rabindranath Tagore did in Bengal. Following Samuel Vedanayagam Pillai's *Prathapa Mudaliar Charithram* or The Life of Prathapa Mudaliar (1879), the modern (historical) novel became crucial to the cultivation of Tamil culture as well. Yet, to gain acceptance within the Tamil textual tradition (of mainly poetry), early Tamil novels contained numerous references to proverbs from ancient texts, folk tales and songs, and so on. In result, they became compendiums of Tamil literature.[32] Subsequently, the popular historical novels by Ramaswamy Krishnamurti, better known by his pen name 'Kalki', glorified the south Indian past of the Chola and Pallava dynasties.

By the beginning of the twentieth century, non-Brahmin Tamil revivalists began to question Caldwell's assumption that the 'higher civilization' of the Tamils was derived from Aryan culture and Sanskrit. To the contrary, for example, the Tamil scholar S. Somasundara Bharati argued that Aryans were provided with a ready-made civilization:

> The special features, idiosyncracies and peculiar genius of Tamil literature so much attracted the Aryan scholars and kings; the almost primitive

---

30 Stuart Blackburn, *Print, Folklore, and Nationalism in Colonial South India*, New Delhi: Permanent Black, 2003: 165–174.

31 Ibid.: 187.

32 Sascha Ebeling, *Colonizing the Realm of Words: The Transformation of Tamil Literature in Nineteenth-Century South India*, Albany: State University of New York Press, 2010.

innocence and natural morality that characterised the Tamil people so far interested them, that they seriously set about studying the Tamils and their country.[33]

In addition, Tamil national reformers defined a 'neo-Shaivism' not only as the religion of ancient non-Aryan Brahmin Tamils, but also for the present, that is, 'the monotheistic "rational" worship of Shiva using pure Tamil rituals based on Tamil scriptures performed by Tamil ("non-Brahmin") priests through the liturgical medium of divine Tamil'.[34] As a matter of fact, the *Rig Veda* does not mention Shiva and specifically condemns the worship of the *lingam* or Shiva in his prime form.

In works such as *Some Early Sovereigns of Travancore* (1894) and *Some Milestones in the History of Tamil Literature* (1895), P. Sundaram Pillai historicized Tamil society and literature before the coming of the Aryans. His famous historical drama *Manonmaniam* (1891) was based upon Lord Bulwer Lytton's *The Secret Way: A Lost Tale of Miletus* (1889). It became an influential text in the development of Tamil nationalism, mainly because of its invocatory verse to the Goddess Tamil at the beginning, which in 1970 was adopted as the official prayer song of the Indian (linguistic) state of Tamil Nadu ('Tamil country'), the name given one year earlier to the area that had remained of the earlier Madras State (1950–1969). Explicitly, Pillai believed that Valmiki's Ramayana was solely written 'to proclaim the powers of the Aryans, and to represent their rivals and enemies the Dravidians, who had attained a high degree of civilization at that period, in the worst possible colour'.[35] Ideas like this were eagerly seized upon by low caste reformers, like Iyothee Thass, who in a similar way as Jyotirao Phule in west India, argued that the lower castes were the proponents of India's oldest civilization, the Dravidian one.

E. V. Ramaswamy, commonly known as 'Periyar', emerged as the prime mover of non-Brahmin Dravidianism. Disillusioned with the INC and Mahatma Gandhi, he founded the anti-Brahmin Self-Respect Movement, while arguing that the concept of 'self-respect', based on social equality, was unique to Tamil culture and could be traced back to the Sangam period. During the 1920s, members of the movement had the *Manu Smriti* ('Laws of Manu') burned repeatedly and later the Ramayana and the Mahabharata would share the same fate. Like Iyothee Thass, Periyar presented the lower castes as having descended from the first Buddhists. With the help of the Theosophist leader

---

33   As cited in Irschick, *Politics and Social Conflict*: 285.

34   Ramaswamy, *Passions of the Tongue*: 25.

35   As cited in Irschick, *Politics and Social Conflict*: 283.

Henry Steel Olcott, Thass himself had become a Buddhist and called upon lower castes to do the same. In 1898, he established the Sakya Buddhist Society, which soon had branches throughout the peninsula. Both Olcott and Iyothee Thass had a fundamental influence on Ceylon's Buddhist revivalist Anagarika Dharmapala, who like Vivekananda spoke at the World's Parliament of Religions in Chicago. Indeed, ironically, although the two Chicago-speakers promoted Asian spirituality to the world, they are mainly remembered today as inspirators of Hindu nationalism and Ceylonese Buddhist nationalism respectively.

Eventually, the question of the origin of Tamil civilization was answered in a rather unexpected way, but one which shows the importance of the global circulation of ideas at the same time. In 1864, the British zoologist Philip Sclater came up with the theory of a great continent located south of the Indian peninsula that had formed a land-bridge linking India, Madagascar and Africa. He coined it 'Lemuria' after the existence of lemur-like primates on these three disconnected lands. Subsequently, the German evolutionary biologist Ernst Haeckel proposed in *History of Creation* (1876) that Lemuria was 'the probable cradle of the human race', the original 'paradise' (figure 18) from which humans had emerged to populate the Earth by way of Indian and Africa.[36] While Theosophists were the initial promotors of the Lemuria theory in south India, Charles D. Maclean was the first British official who theorized Lemuria on the basis of Haeckel's work as the proto-Dravidian homeland. In *The Manual of the Administration of the Madras Presidency* (1885), he suggested that 'southern India was once the passage-ground by which the ancient progenitors of northern and Mediterranean races proceeded to the parts of the globe which they now inhabit' from Lemuria.[37] Later, Lemuria was cursorily discussed by Edgar Thurston, Herbert Hope Risley and other colonial officials.

Unlike European authors, however, Tamil revivalists from the late nineteenth century onward began to describe Lemuria as the Tamil homeland. They saw it as the birthplace of Tamil language and the cradle of Tamil civilization, whereby they generally misquoted or reinterpreted the work of European scholars to give scientific credibility to their assertions. As S. Somasundara Bharati wrote in his *Tamil Classics and Tamilakam* (1912):

> Progressive geological research is ready and willing to shake hands with the primeval poems of the Tamil country and establish that the ances-

---

36   Sumathi Ramaswamy, *The Lost Land of Lemuria: Fabulous Geographies, Catastrophic Histories*, Berkeley, CA: University of California Press, 2004: 35–38.

37   As cited in Ibid.: 101.

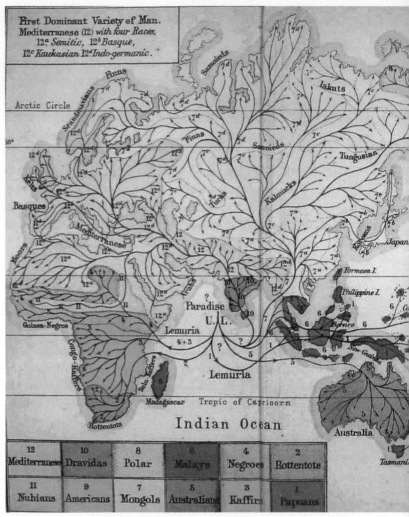

First Dominant Variety of Man.
Mediterranese (12) *with four Races,*
12ᵃ *Semitic,* 12ᵇ *Basque,*
12ᶜ *Kaukasian* 12ᵈ *Indo-germanic*.

12 Mediterranese	10 Dravidas	8 Polar	6 Malays	4 Negroes	2 Hottentots
11 Nubians	9 Americans	7 Mongols	5 Australians	3 Kaffirs	1 Papuans

FIGURE 18   'Hypothetical Sketch of the Monophyletic Origin and of the
                   Extension of the 12 Races of Man from Lemuria over the Earth'
                   SOURCE: ERNST HAECKEL, *The History of Creation,* VOLUME TWO,
                   NEW YORK: D. APPLETON AND COMPANY, 1880: FRONTISPIECE

tral home of the Tamils was in the far south of the Indian subcontinent
now under the sea and not above the snow-clad Himalayan heights, or in
the land of the celestials, or in the country of the Hebrews before their
dispersion.[38]

---

38   Ibid.: 109.

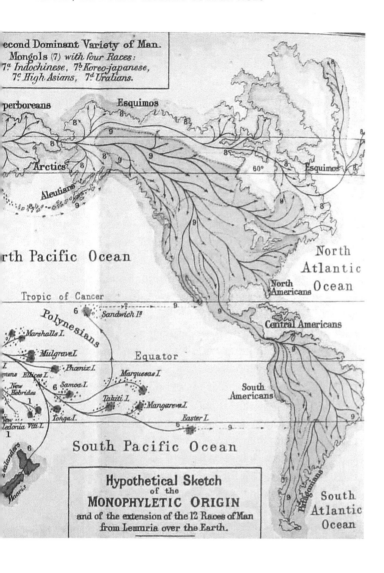

From the term 'ancestral home' it was a short way to characterizations of Lemuria as 'Tamil homeland' and 'motherland'. Over the years, Tamil nationalists gave the submerged continent different names: 'Kumarinatu', 'Tamilakam' and ultimately, in the 1930s, 'Kumari Kandam' – the word 'kumari' means 'virgin' or 'maiden' and so it symbolizes the purity of the Tamil language and culture before the coming of the Aryans. They connected Lemuria to legends created during an early Tamil Pandyan dynasty (being one of the three famous Tamil lineages, the other two being the Chola and the Chera), and as mentioned also in ancient and medieval Tamil and Sanskrit texts, about lands in the peninsula being lost to the ocean. The principal term used is *katalkol* or 'seizure by ocean' (by tsunami?), which attained a similar status among Tamils as the Judeo-Christian tradition's Deluge.

Tamil nationalists further argued that the first two (of three) Tamil literary academies (*sangams*) were held in Lemuria (the third *sangam* was held around present day Madurai). As many would do after him, V. G. Suryanarayana Sastri, Professor of Tamil and the first to campaign for the recognition of Tamil as a classical language, claimed in his *Tamil Mozhiyin Varalaru* or 'History of the Tamil Language' (1903) that all humans had descended from the ancient Tamils of Lemuria, which he labelled 'Kumarinatu'. Logically, this argument was accompanied by the idea that Tamil was the world's most ancient language, the primeval tongue of all of mankind. Although the continental drift theory rendered the idea of Lemuria obsolete, it remains popular among Tamil nationalists up to today. Since 1908, 'Kumari Kandam' is mentioned in the curriculum of south Indian Tamil schools and colleges. In 1981, the Tamil Nadu government sponsored a documentary film on 'Kumari Kandam', which depicted ancient Tamil cities with great palaces, mansions and gardens, full of arts, music and dance – and numerous similar images are still to be found on the internet today.

All in all, the Aryan invasion theory led to the notions of Aryan and Tamil Golden Ages among Hindus in north and south India respectively. That said, it may be argued that the nostalgic longing of Tamil Romantic nationalists for their past was deeper than that of north Indian Hindus for their Aryan past because, besides to British colonialism, they responded to Brahminical-Sanskritic domination at the same time. Anyhow, Hindu intellectuals in north and south India would increasingly discuss the historical and cultural differences between them. Interesting to mention in this context is the case of Abinas Chandra Das's *Rig-Vedic India* (1921). When there was a growing insistence during the early twentieth century that the Aryans were indigenous to India, he accepted Bal Gangadhar Tilak's theory that Aryans came from the Arctic. Most peculiarly, however, he did so by simply shifting the location of the North Pole to Punjab and the adjoining borderlands or Sapta-Sindhu, as it used to be called in Vedic times!

According to Das, Sapta-Sindhu was separated from Lemuria by the Rajputana Sea and there were absolutely no ties between the 'civilized' Aryas and the 'savage' Dravidians:

Whether this continent was the original cradle of mankind or not, there can be no doubt that man existed here from very early times, and that his creation in this continent was made possible only after the creation of anthropoid apes which were his nearest approach [*sic*]. We have already got evidence of the existence of Pliocene man in the valley gravels of the Narmada and of Miocene man in Upper Burma. It can, therefore, be safely surmised that man had existed in this continent long before the time when the greater portion of it was submerged in consequence of a violent cataclysm. Though Sapta-Sindhu was not directly connected with it, conditions similar to those of the lost continent must have prevailed there, which favored the creation of a family of human beings entirely different from that of the Southern Continent; and these were the progenitors of the Aryan race who, having been endowed with higher mental faculties, developed a civilization which was destined to dominate the whole world, and uplift the entire human race.[39]

After the submergence of Lemuria and the drying up of the Rajputana Sea, Das continued, a 'higher' Aryan civilization disseminated into the peninsula. Moreover, as a true Victorian colonial ethnologist, he stated that the 'primitive races' of south India had not really progressed beyond their ancestors who had once inhabited Lemuria. To the contrary, he underlined, they had 'little removed from the condition of anthropoid apes or brutes'.[40] Thus, the Aryan invasion theory did not only result into Romantic nationalist searches for ancient texts and Golden Ages, but also created a rift between Aryans and Dravidians that heavily influenced the making of modern India. Yet what about those other 'invaders', the Muslims? Did they too refer to a Golden Age now that the British had replaced them as rulers?

Islam's Lost Glory

Presently Aziz chaffed him, also the servants, and then began quoting poetry: Persian, Urdu, a little Arabic. His memory was good, and for so young a man he had read largely; the themes he preferred were the decay of Islam and the brevity of love. They listened delighted, for they took the public view of poetry, not the private which obtains in England. It never bored them to hear words,

---

39   A. C. Das, *Rig-Vedic India*, volume one, Calcutta: University of Calcutta, 1921: 97–98.
40   Ibid.: 102–103.

words; they breathed them with the cool night air, never stopping to analyse; the name of the poet, Hafiz, Hali, Iqbal was sufficient guarantee. India – a hundred Indias – whispered outside beneath the indifferent moon, but for the time, India seemed one and their own, and they regained their departed greatness by hearing its departure lamented, they felt young again because reminded that youth must fly.

E. M. FORSTER, *A Passage to India* (1924)[41]

The Revolt of 1857 was a defining moment for Indian Muslims. The two north Indian capitals of Indo-Islamic culture, Delhi and Lucknow, were heavily damaged and both the last Mughal Emperor, Bahadur Shah Zafar, and the last Nawab of Lucknow, Wajid Ali Shah, were exiled, to Burma and Calcutta respectively. As high court culture largely came to a halt, a Muslim intelligentsia familiar with modern print culture and often English-educated gradually took over the leadership of the community. At the same time, unsurprisingly, Muslim thinkers remained greatly attached to the Indo-Islamic culture they had grown up in. They generally believed in Hindu-Muslim amity and saw India as their motherland.[42] In the words of Zaka Ullah, the liberal teacher at Delhi College and one of the most distinguished scholars of his day:

> India is our mother country, the country which gave us birth. We have made our homes here, married her, begotten children here; and here on this soil of India we have buried our sacred dead. India, therefore, must needs be dearer to us than any other country upon earth. We should love this very soil, which is mingled with the dust of our ancestors. For a thousand years, our own religion of Islam has been intimately bound up with India; and in India, Islam has won some of the greatest triumphs for its own peculiar form of civilization. We should love, therefore, the history and government of India, which have been shaped by such great monarchs as Akbar the Great and his successors. I cannot bear to hear Indian Musalmans speaking without reverence and affection for India.[43]

---

41   Forster, *A Passage to India*: 9–10.
42   Mushirul Hasan, *A Moral Reckoning: Muslim Intellectuals in Nineteenth-Century Delhi*, New Delhi: Oxford University Press, 2003.
43   C. F. Andrews, *Zaka Ullah of Delhi*, with introductions by Mushirul Hasan and Margrit Pernau, New Delhi: Oxford University Press, 2003 (first published in 1929): 87.

Muslims, Zaka Ullah continued, should reject pan-Islamic ideas and remain loyal to the British instead:

> Let us love our Musalman brethren in other countries, and feel their joy and sorrows; but let us love with all our hearts our own country and have nothing to do with encouragement of those who tell us, that we, Musalmans, must always be looking outside India for our religious hopes and fulfilment.[44]

Nonetheless, in comparison to Hindus, and Bengalis in particular, Muslims had great difficulties adjusting to English education and finding jobs in the colonial administration. Furthermore, they were confronted by British writings, in which Muslims were described as outsiders to the subcontinent and informed about the contemporary fallen state of their own community through the census and other colonial reports. Undeniably, all this had an impact on the minds of Indian Muslims and, indeed, Hindus as well. By the 1880s, then, when Muslims were becoming increasingly aware of their minority status within India, the leaders of the community stood torn between two loyalties, namely, to its own complex future in a country dominated by Hindu majority politics and to pan-Islamic solidarity.

When Hindus, like Babu Shiva Prasad of Benares in the late 1860s, began to ask for the replacement of Urdu in *Nastaliq* by Hindi in *Devanagari*, both as administrative and national language, Sayyid Ahmad Khan (figure 19), the most influential Muslim leader of the second half of the nineteenth century and a close friend of Zaka Ullah, realized that the paths of the Muslims and the Hindus had to diverge. In this he understood the importance of modern education in English and, in 1875, after a visit to England, he established the Muhammadan Anglo-Oriental College in Aligarh. By this time Khan was still pro-Turkish, but this mainly because he thought that the Ottoman Sultan ruling over mixed Christian-Muslim populations could be a good ally of the British Queen ruling over an even more diverse population in India. In any case, at his 'Muslim Cambridge', he introduced the use of the Ottoman fez. In fact, this red felt hat with a tassel was adopted by (Indian) Muslim leaders as a symbol of the 'Muslim world',[45] but it originally was a traditional garb of orthodox Christian Greeks. Likewise, the crescent in the Ottoman flag

---

44   Ibid.: 88.
45   Cemil Aydin, *The Idea of the Muslim World: A Global Intellectual History*, Cambridge, Mass.: Harvard University Press, 2017.

FIGURE 19   Sayyid Ahmad Khan in Punjab, photographer unknown, c. 1890
                 SOURCE: WIKICOMMONS

became a symbol of Muslim identity. Following the Russo-Ottoman War of
1877–1878, when the British did not support the Turks, however, Khan became
fully committed to the strengthening of Muslim identity within British India.
In particular, he opposed Muslim participation in the INC because he believed
that Indian Muslims needed the protection of the British. In 1886, Khan for
the first time organized the All-India Muhammadan Educational Conference,
which subsequently met annually at different places to provide the Indian
Muslim community with a national platform and to promote modern education. Until the founding of the Muslim League in 1906, it was the principal
national organization of Indian Muslims.

   In addition, Sayyid Ahmad Khan advocated a modernized Urdu in the
Nastaliq script as the national language of Indian Muslims. Two of his great

admirers and associates, Muhammad Husain Azad and Altaf Husain Hali, were fundamental to the modernization of Urdu and its linking up to the Muslim nation. Both set out to replace the Indo-Persian concept of (*ghazal*) poetry of the traditional (Mughal) aristocracy, who greatly depended on ornate and exaggerated forms of expression, 'with what they understood to be the contemporary English one: a Wordsworth-like vision of "natural" poetry'.[46] Azad's *Ab-e Hayat* or 'Water of Life' (1880) was one of the most often reprinted and widely read Urdu books of the nineteenth century. It was the first attempt to establish an overview of the history of Urdu poetry in periods and schools, and it also had numerous collected anecdotes about Muslim writers and poets. In this way, Azad sought to keep alive the memory of the 'lost heaven' of the old Delhi culture that was destroyed during the Indian Revolt.[47] In the first book of literary criticism in Urdu, *Muqaddama-e-Shair-o-Shairi* or 'Introduction to Poetry and Poetics' (1893), Altaf Husain Hali 'mercilessly criticized the traditional poets because he felt that neither high-soaring mystical dreams nor complicated rhetorical devices could help Muslims face their basic duties and lead them towards a more glorious future'.[48] Both works are unique for their time as attempts to historicize Urdu poetry and aesthetics in its social and cultural contexts. To different extents, Azad and Hali refer to a Golden Age in which Urdu poetry still was 'honest' and 'natural', before it descended into a realm of musty mannerisms, hyperbole and convention. In their opinion, contemporary Urdu poets had to return to this former spirit if they aimed at improvement of the Muslim nation.

Hali became best known for his epic poem *Musaddas* (1879), subtitled 'The Flow and Ebb of Islam', in which he lamented the present condition of Indian Muslims in contrast to their past glories.[49] He originally dedicated the poem to the emerging Muslim nation, and it became a sort of anthem, of which parts were frequently recited to inaugurate sessions of Muslim voluntary organizations. Among elitist Indian Muslims, Hali's *Musaddas* generated a Romantic interest in historical Islam that was fed by a growing stream of publications – histories, biographies (of Prophet Muhammad) and historical

46   Frances W. Pritchett, *Nets of Awareness: Urdu Poetry and Its Critics*, Berkeley, CA: University of California Press, 1994: xvi.

47   Muhammad Husain Azad, *Ab-e Hayat: Shaping the Canon of Urdu Poetry*, translated and edited by Frances Pritchett in association with Shamsur Rahmani Farugi, New Delhi: Oxford University Press, 2001.

48   Annemarie Schimmel, *Islam in the Indian Subcontinent*, Leiden: Brill, 1980: 200.

49   Christopher Shackle and Javed Majeed, eds., *Hali's Musaddas: The Flow and Ebb of Islam*, New Delhi: Oxford University Press, 1997.

novels – and which mainly focused at two periods of Islam's victorious contact with Europe, namely, in the Iberian Peninsula and during the Ottoman
expansion. Abdul Halim Sharar became famous for his nostalgic sketches of
Lucknow life written between 1914 and 1916, *Guzishta Lucknow*, which was
subsequently published in English as *Lucknow: The Last Phase of an Oriental Culture*.[50] Lesser known remains the fact that he wrote several historical
novels about the great early Islamic past, of which *Malik-i Aziz aur Varjana*
(1888) is a rejoinder to Walter Scott's picture of Islam in his Waverley novel
The Talisman (1825).[51] Also Sayyid Amir Ali's *The Spirit of Islam* (1891) and *A
Short History of the Saracens* (1899) were extensively read. In 1877, Ali had
founded the Central National Muhammedan Association in Calcutta and it
later had 34 branches throughout the subcontinent from Madras to Karachi.
The organization played an important role in the modernization and political
consciousness of Indian Muslims but, in comparison to Sayyid Ahmad Khan's
work, it was rather restricted in its influence and achievements.

Particularly intriguing is the case of Muhammad Iqbal, the philosopher
and probably most renowned Urdu poet of the subcontinent. In 1904, before
he left for his three-years of study in Britain and Germany, he wrote 'Sare
Jahan se Accha', formally known as 'Taranah-i-Hind' (Anthem of the People
of Hindustan), a patriotic song for children in the *ghazal* style of Urdu poetry
that quickly became an anthem of opposition to British colonial rule, equally
among Muslims, Hindus and Sikhs:

> Better than the entire world, is our Hind,
> We are its nightingales, and it (is) our garden abode
>
> If we are in an alien place, the heart remains in the homeland,
> Know us to be only there where our heart is.
>
> That tallest mountain, that shade-sharer of the sky,
> It (is) our sentry, it (is) our watchman
>
> In its lap where frolic thousands of rivers,
> Whose vitality makes our garden the envy of Paradise.

---

50   Abdul Halim Sharar, *Lucknow: The Last Phase of an Oriental Culture*, translated and edited
      by E. S. Harcourt and Fakhir Hussain, London: Paul Elek, 1975.
51   Peter Hardy, *The Muslims of British India*, Cambridge: Cambridge University Press, 1972:
      176.

O the flowing waters of the Ganges, do you remember that day
When our caravan first disembarked on your waterfront?

Religion does not teach us to bear animosity among ourselves
We are of Hind, our homeland is Hindustan.

In a world in which ancient Greece, Egypt, and Rome have all vanished
Our own attributes (name and sign) live on today.

There is something about our existence for it doesn't get wiped
Even though, for centuries, the time-cycle of the world has been our
enemy.

Iqbal! We have no confidant in this world
What does any one know of our hidden pain?[52]

At the time of writing the poem, Iqbal still saw a future for Muslims within India. After his return from Europe, however, he had become an Islamic philosopher. In *Shikwa* or 'The Complaint' (1909), he not only nostalgically considered the past glories of Islam and attempted to wake up Indian Muslims – as Altaf Husain Hali had done in his *Musaddas* –, but he also went further by writing the poem in the form of a complaint to Allah for having let his followers down. Despite their weakness, Iqbal argued, Muslims had always been faithful to Him. The community's contemporary deplorable political state was therefore not a justified divine punishment, but an incomprehensible divine disillusionment. While the text equates God with the figure of the whimsical and unresponsive lover, however, the passionate accusations of infidelity against Him remain far removed from a lapse into atheism. To the contrary, precisely by complaining so bitterly, Muslims unequivocally affirm their unconditional love for God and His Messenger. In fact, the deeply moving and strangely satisfying experience of unreturned love is turned into a central pillar of Islamic identity itself – a move that undoubtedly represents the enchantment in strong emotions and Romantic self-pity prevalent at the time. Following a Nietzschean agenda, Iqbal ultimately holds up emotionalism and will-power as a shield against the tribulations of his time. Overall, he advocates the creation and cultivation of an uncompromising heroic self for the eventual recovery and salvation of the Muslim individual and com-

---

52   https://en.wikipedia.org/wiki/Sare_Jahan_se_Accha.

munity.[53] At the same time, significantly, 'while lauding the achievements of Muslim warriors and the civilizing role of Islam, the poet also reveals a not-too-veiled contempt for non-Muslims, particularly Hindus' and according to Khushwant Singh therefore this controversial poem may be regarded 'as the first manifesto of the two-nation theory'.[54]

In 1910, Iqbal wrote another song for children, 'Tarana-e-Milli' (Anthem of the Religious Community). It was composed in the same metre and rhyme scheme as 'Sare Jahan Se Achcha', but clearly renounced the sentiment of the latter, as exemplified by its first stanza for instance:

> Central Asia and Arabia are ours, Hindustan is ours
> We are Muslims, the whole world is our homeland.[55]

Iqbal's world view had changed; it had become both global and Islamic, as he confirmed in a lecture delivered by him at Aligarh in 1911:

> [...] the essential difference between the Muslim community and other communities of the world consists in our peculiar conception of nationality. It is not the unity of language or country that constitutes the basic principle of our nationality. It is because we all believe in a certain view of the universe and participate in the same historical tradition that we are members of the society founded by the Prophet of Islam.[56]

Elsewhere, he wrote that belonging to the Muslim nation meant 'like-mindedness not by domicile' and that 'the ideal territory for such a nation would be the whole earth'.[57] As a matter of fact, Iqbal first recited his *Jawab-i-Shikwa* or 'The Answer to the Complaint' (1913) in Lahore during a meeting that was organized to collect funds to help the Ottomans fighting against the Bulgarians. No doubt, Indian Muslim ideas of nationality were seriously tested with the outbreak of the First World War, with Britain and the Ottoman Empire in opposite camps. In the wake of the Morley-Minto reforms of 1909, which

---

53   See further: Ayesha Jalal, *Self and Sovereignty: Individual and Community in South Asian Islam Since 1850*, New Delhi: Oxford University Press, 2001 and Javed Majeed, *Muhammad Iqbal: Islam, Aesthetics and Postcolonialism*, London: Routledge, 2009.

54   Muhammad Iqbal, *Shikwa and Javab-i-Shikwa: Iqbal's Dialogue with Allah*, translated and introduced by Khushwant Singh, New Delhi: Oxford University Press, 2008 (first published in 1909 and 1913): 25.

55   https://en.wikipedia.org/wiki/Sare_Jahan_se_Accha.

56   As cited in Hardy, *The Muslims of British India*: 179.

57   Ibid.

granted separate electorates for Muslims, it furthered not only the making of a pan-Indian Muslim political constituency, but also led to the Khilafat Movement as a last attempt to reconcile Islamic identity with Indian nationality.

From the 1870s onward, Indian Muslim leaders referred increasingly to the Ottoman Caliph (*khalifa*), the protector of the holy cities of Mecca and Medina, as an authoritative reference point of the 'Muslim world'. In hindsight, the Romantic adherence to the outdated theory of the Caliphate (*khilafa*) remains rather surprising because Sultan Abdul Hamid II was defeated during the Russo-Ottoman War at the beginning of his reign in 1878. Even so, besides the fact that modern systems of transport and communication made Muslims, of which almost half were under British rule, increasingly aware of the 'Muslim world', the role of Jamal al-Din al-Afghani, the chief exponent of pan-Islamism, was important to this 'apparently naïve championship of a pan-Islamic cause already dried up at its source'.[58] Al-Afghani travelled widely in India for several years during two visits (1857–1865 and 1879–1882) and numerous influential Indian Muslim thinkers and rulers were inspired by his personality and writings. According to al-Afghani, the reassertion of Muslim identity and solidarity were prerequisites for the restoration of Indian cultural and political independence. He considered Sayyid Ahmad Khan as his main adversary because he opposed pan-Islamism and so isolated the Indian Muslims from the rest of the *Dar al-Islam* ('House of Islam').

Shibli Nomani was one of the many Indian Muslim intellectuals who came under al-Afghani's spell. He had worked together with Sayyid Ahmad Khan at Aligarh and wrote much about Islam's glorious past – including the series 'Heroes of Islam', for which he derived inspiration from Thomas Carlyle's *On Heroes, Hero-Worship, and the Heroic in History* (1841).[59] As a staunch supporter of pan-Islamism, Nomani wrote poems and articles decrying the British and other Western powers when the Ottomans were defeated in the Balkan Wars and urged Muslims to unite globally. In 1893, he visited Istanbul and received a medal from Sultan Abdul Hamid II. All in all, the Romantic historical writings of, amongst others, Nomani, Altaf Husain Hali and Abdul Halim Sharar coupled the idea of an Islamic Golden Age with the assumption that the 'Muslim world' existed before. As Cemil Aydin wrote:

> Thus the earliest Islamic text and history were yoked to an idea, the Muslim world, that would not have made sense in their own time. This new,

---

58 Gail Minault, *The Khilafat Movement: Religious Symbolism and Political Mobilization in India*, New York: Columbia University Press, 1982: 1.

59 Hasan, *A Moral Reckoning*: 222.

global narrative, a product of nineteenth-century geopolitics and fresh
scientific and political theories, was projected centuries into the past.[60]

Likewise inspired by al-Afghani were European-educated Indian Muslims
like Shaukat Ali, Muhammad Ali and Abul Kalam Azad. Their Khilafat Movement (1919–1924) took up the cause of the Ottoman Sultan as the Caliph of all
Muslims and was a Romantic quest to transcend the imperial world in which
Muslims increasingly felt left behind. Moreover, it became the first revolutionary mass movement in British India when the INC under Mahatma Gandhi and
the leaders of the Khilafat Movement promised to work together for the causes
of the Caliphate and *swaraj*. The anti-climax of course came with the abolishment of the Ottoman Caliphate in 1924. Yet, at the same time, the Khilafat
Movement had strengthened the pan-Indian Muslim audience whom Iqbal
aimed to reach in his presidential address to the Muslim League annual conference in Allahabad in 1930, when he supported a separate nation-state in the
Muslim majority areas of the subcontinent, an idea that inspired the creation
of Pakistan. The poet, indeed, had never believed in the Caliphate and, in 1922,
he was one of the few among Indian Muslims who praised the Turkish Grand
National Assembly's decision to end the Caliphate and appoint a new Caliph
stripped of any mundane authority. He later declared that among the Muslim
nations of the world Turkey alone had shaken off 'its dogmatic slumber, and
attained [...] self-consciousness' through the exercise of 'her right to intellectual freedom', while Muslims in India and elsewhere were solely 'repeating old
values, whereas the Turk [...] (was) on the way to creating new values'.[61]

After the downfall of the Khilafat Movement, the fate of Muslims in India
would become increasingly darker due to the rise of Hindu nationalist majority politics. Although they had repeatedly established their own cultural and
political organizations in response to what Hindus did, including of course
the Muslim League in 1906, as a minority community, Indian Muslims obviously could not afford to propagate something like Vivekananda's 'aggressive
Hinduism'. By and large, then, Muslim elites continued to look back to the glorious pasts of Islamic history, architecture, literature and music. As discussed
in Chapter Two, this nostalgic longing for the past, as well as the emphasis on
the importance of Urdu as a literary language, played a role in Indian cinema
at least until the 1970s.

---

60   Aydin, *The Idea of the Muslim World*: 73.
61   As cited in Jalal, *Self and Sovereignty*: 244–245.

CHAPTER 4

National Music, Art and Architecture

Music, Classicization and the Nation

To this day, Indian art music remains the non-Western world's main last stand in the face of the global hegemony of European music in its basic form, i.e. the use of equal temperament tuning and (functional) harmony, as well as different instruments and ensemble playing.[1] Hence, expectedly, since the late nineteenth century Indians – and a great number of Westerners – generally saw it as the critical essence of the nation's spiritual culture, whereby they romantically assumed that the tradition had largely survived colonialism unscathed. To the contrary, however, the patronage, performance practice and reception of Indian art music changed remarkably during the imperial encounter. Decisive to this transformation were the modern national music reforms by mostly upper caste Hindus. Yet, while the European Enlightenment search for the origins of language and music were closely intertwined in India, the roots of Indian national music reforms lay in the British colonial imagination. As Gerry Farrell wrote in his classic *Indian Music and the West* (1997):

> When India was discovered as a cultural entity by Orientalists in the late eighteenth century, the study of music, like language, had to suit their project of discovering and reconstructing a pristine Hindu past, free from Muslim influences. Hence the 'dead' music of Sanskrit texts was more revered than the living Indo-Muslim tradition.[2]

In particular, the work of William Jones was crucial to the Indian reception of the idea of 'Hindu music' and its degradation under Muslim rule. In *On the Musical Modes of the Hindus* (1792), he not only peddled the myth of Indian music being on the verge of extinction, but also, like other European Orientalists glorifying Sanskrit sources, directly combined it with the loss of the 'Hindu music' of a supposedly Golden Age.[3] Since the last decades of the nine-

---

1   Bob van der Linden, "Non-Western National Music and Empire in Global History: Interactions, Uniformities, and Comparisons", *Journal of Global History*, 10, 3, 2015: 431–456.

2   Gerry Farrell, *Indian Music and the West*, Oxford: Oxford University Press, 1997: 1–2.

3   William Jones, "On the Musical Modes of the Hindus" (first published in 1792) in Sourindro Mohun Tagore, ed., *Hindu Music from Various Authors*, Calcutta: I. C. Bose & Co, 1882: 125–160.

teenth century, then, Indian national music reformers disseminated Romantic nationalist beliefs of superiority (and partially so by referring to the authority of Sanskrit music theory treatises such as the *Natya Shastra*) about the antiquity, complexity and spirituality of Indian art music, whereby they repeatedly found support in the work of European Orientalist scholars and Theosophists on the way.

In India, a distinction is made between north Indian 'Hindustani' art music and south Indian 'Karnatak' art music. Although there is a great overlap between the two traditions, especially in music theory, Hindustani music mainly developed in a different manner because of the far more dominant interaction between Indic and Persian-Central Asian music in the north. During the colonial period, nonetheless, both music traditions underwent similar processes of musical standardization and institutionalization.[4] On the whole, Indian music reformers 'classicized' Hindustani and Karnatak music on a par with European classical music to make it modern, scientific and, indeed, national. Among other things, they did so by institutionalizing music schools, music conferences, canonical repertoire, concert arrangements and music theory (mostly based on Sanskrit treatises). Earlier, in fact, Indian elites generally associated musicians with low caste groups and looked down upon them. British officials and missionaries, as well as Indian (music) reformers, specifically stigmatized the south Indian female temple musicians and dancers (*devadasis*) and north Indian courtesans (*tawaifs* and *bajjis*) as 'dancing (*nautch*) girls' and, indeed, prostitutes (figure 20). Thus, music reformers not only turned Indian music into a symbol of national pride, but they equally made it 'respectable' for the emergent, often English-educated, Hindu (female) middle class, while a commercial market for music education and performance was created at the same time.

But the weightiest result of Indian national music reforms – and a truly unique event in global music history – was the transfer from Muslim 'minority' community to Hindu 'majority' community in terms of musicians, patronage and audiences that took place within the Hindustani music tradition in the context of the emergence of Hindu nationalism. On the whole, this 'Hinduization' of north Indian art music led to the marginalization of Muslim hereditary musicians (*ustads*) and their knowledge. Before the colonial era, indeed, Hindustani music had largely developed under Muslim patronage, above all the

4   Bob van der Linden, "Rhythms of the Raj: Music in Colonial South Asia" in Harald Fischer-Tiné and Maria Framke, eds., *Routledge Handbook of the History of Colonialism in South Asia*, London: Routledge, 2021: 373–385.

FIGURE 20   'Nautch', photographer unknown, 1863–1868
                 COURTESY OF THE J. P. GETTY MUSEUM, LOS ANGELES

Mughal court. For that reason, the north Indian music scene from the seventeenth until the early twentieth century was professionally dominated by
the *ustads*. Yet, to different extents, Hindu national music reformers such as
Sourindro Mohun Tagore, Vishnu Narayan Bhatkhande (figure 21) and Vishnu
Digambar Paluskar argued that the state of Hindustani music had declined
because it had fallen into the hands of the 'illiterate' *ustads*, whose knowledge and teaching of music was 'unscientific'.[5] Quite the reverse, however,
the whole nineteenth century was an important and creative period of tran-
sition for north Indian art music, with for example new instruments like the
sitar, *sarod* (a fretless, plucked lute) and *tabla* (a pair of tuneable hand played
drums), and relatively new genres, such as *khayal* and a modernized *thumri*,
replacing the instruments and styles associated with the Mughal court. Even

5   The notion of the deterioration of north Indian art music and the 'illiteracy' of its performers
    can also be found in pre-colonial Persian sources; yet it was the British colonial writers and
    Hindu national music reformers who specifically gave the narrative an anti-Muslim signifi-
    cance.

FIGURE 21   Vishnu Narayan Bhatkhande, photographer unknown
SOURCE: *The Report of the 4th All-India Music Conference Lucknow*, VOLUME
ONE, LUCKNOW: TALUQDAR PRESS, 1925: N.P.

so, in clash with the music practice and knowledge production of the Muslim traditional lineages, Tagore, Bhatkhande, Paluskar and other reformers aimed to revive 'Hindu music' as national music.

Vishnu Narayan Bhatkhande remains particularly important to the idea of Romantic nationalism in terms of knowledge production. For, in contrast to other Hindu music reformers, he was much more interested in the Hindustani music practice of his time and largely followed a 'salvage paradigm'. He directly questioned the common claim among Hindu music reformers and musicians – which is still often heard today – that North Indian art music had a continuity that went directly back to the Vedas, *Natya Shastra* and other Sanskrit (music theory) treatises. He based his argument on extensive fieldwork, during which he collected orally transmitted musical repertoire from contemporary, mostly Muslim performers from different lineages. This material resulted in the *Kramik Pustak Malika* (six volumes, 1919–1937), a collection of compositions in Bhatkhande's own version of the Indian *sargam* notation system,

FIGURE 22   'Maihar Band', photographer unknown
SOURCE: *The Report of the 4th All-India Music Conference Lucknow*, VOLUME
ONE, LUCKNOW: TALUQDAR PRESS, 1925: N.P.

which over time generally replaced all other existing systems. Also important
were the five All India Music Conferences convened by Bhatkhande between
1916 and 1926, at which scholars (mostly Hindu) and musicians (mostly Muslim) came together from all over India with the goal of regulating the standards
and boundaries of a national music. Above all, a national system of notation
and a uniform description of *ragas* (tonal frameworks for composition and
improvisation) were thought necessary. Somewhat contradictorily to this, but
again typical to the modern era, was the performance of the Maihar Band,
which combined Indian and European instruments, at the 1925 conference
in Lucknow (figure 22).[6] Ultimately, Bhatkhande had a definite influence on
modern Hindustani music teaching and practice through his writings, system
of *raga* classification, notation system and as the inspirator for the establishment of several north Indian music schools, including his own Marris College
in Lucknow in 1926.[7]

British Orientalist scholars approached south Indian art music differently.
In *The Music and Musical Instruments of Southern India and the Deccan* (1891),

6   The Mahair Band was established in 1918 by the illustrious musician Allauddin Khan, the
    guru of Ravi Shankar.
7   Presently it is known as the Bhatkhande Music Institute University.

Charles Day underlined that, in contrast to the north, south India had been ostensibly less affected by the Islamic interlude and that Karnatak music therefore was more authentic.[8] To the contrary, of course, south Indian music to some extent had also emerged as a result of the complex interaction between Indic and Islamic cultures, as attested for example by the shared cultural taste of Vijayanagar and Bijapur in the sixteenth and seventeenth centuries, as well as the influence of 'sufi musical lineages fostering a mystical devotion which transcended sectarian boundaries'.[9] Nonetheless, following Charles Day, south Indian music reformers assertively argued that Karnatak music embodied the more original 'Hindu music'. They too became preoccupied with music theory and music notation.

In *Oriental Music in European Notation* (1893), A. M. Chinnaswami Mudaliar, who was trained in European music and generally wanted to make Karnatak music known to the rest of the world (and his activities therefore may be compared with those of Sourindro Mohun Tagore in the north), notated a collection of south and north Indian melodies in staff notation and provided hints for harmonization. Together with the composer Subbarama Dikshitar, he compiled the encyclopaedia of Karnatak music, *Sangita Samprayada Pradarsini* (1904). Besides discussions of *ragas*, performance routines and biographies of musicians and authors of musicological treatises, this encyclopaedia includes numerous songs in staff notation with additional symbols to represent Karnatak music's typical trills, shakes and slurs, and glissandi. Vishnu Narayan Bhatkhande met Subbarama Dikshitar in 1904 and, afterwards, he not only took *Sangita Samprayada Pradarsini* as an example for his own work, but also based his renowned system of *raga* classification upon the ingenious symmetrical south Indian *melakarta* scheme of 72 *ragas*, which was first proposed by the theorist Venkatamakhi around 1620 at the Tanjore court.

All in all, a canon for Karnatak music was created on the basis of the heavily texted devotional compositions (*kritis*) – written almost exclusively in Sanskrit and Telugu, rather than in Tamil – of the Brahmin composers Tyagaraja, Syama Sastri and Muttusvami Dikshitar. Ever since, the compositions of this so-called 'Trinity', and especially of Tyagaraja, occupied the centre of most concerts and provided the model for composers. Mainly through the Madras Music Academy (1928), the standards for the teaching and perfor-

---

8   C. R. Day, *The Music and Musical Instruments of Southern India and the Deccan*, London: Novello, 1891: 5, 13.

9   Lakshmi Subramanian, *From the Tanjore Court to the Madras Music Academy*, New Delhi: Oxford University Press, 2006: 13.

mance of south Indian classical music were defined and disseminated, for example, through its journal and training college for teachers, as well as radio broadcasts. In comparison to what happened to modern Hindustani music, no doubt, national music reforms in south India led to stricter standardization of performance practice and repertoire. Simultaneously, although communal conflict between Hindus and Muslims was no issue in the south Indian music scene, the classicization of Karnatak music was accompanied by the marginalization of certain musical communities, often because of their lower caste status. I already mentioned the female temple musicians and dancers (*devadasis*), but the hereditary male temple musicians are another example. In addition, Tamil language nationalism became increasingly important to the canonization of Karnatak music. While the south Indian music scene during the previous four centuries had been dominated by music theory treatises in Telugu and Sanskrit, U. V. Swaminatha Iyer (figure 17) and others began to salvage and publish ancient Tamil music manuscripts. In response to the fact that the newly created Karnatak music canon excluded songs in Tamil, the mother tongue of the non-Brahmin majority, then, the *Tamil Isai Iyakkam* (Tamil Music Movement) successfully lobbied for the inclusion of Tamil repertoire. To a certain extent, this effort was strengthened by E. V. Ramaswamy's Self-Respect Movement.

The Theosophist reading of a Hindu Golden Age, and especially the superior place therein of the Brahmins, worked as a catalyst in the classicization of nationalist south Indian art music and dance. Most important was the role of the Theosophist, dancer and choreographer Rukmini Devi Arundale, wife of George Arundale, the third president of the Theosophical Society. After initial protests from the Brahmin orthodoxy against its performance on stage, Rukmini Devi appropriated the south Indian dance form *Bharatanatyam* from the *devadasis* to which it had been confined for many centuries. In line with the British civilizing mission, she removed its erotic elements and transformed it into a puritanical art form. Also, she introduced new combinations of musical instruments, set and lighting design elements, and customs and jewelry inspired by temple sculptures. In congruence with the Victorian idea of the 'sensitive' and 'intuitive' female spirit, Rukmini Devi generally emphasized the special relationship between women and the arts. In 1936, she established Kalakshetra (*kshetra*, womb or place, of *kala*, arts) at Adyar, as a cultural academy for the preservation of authentic and spiritual Indian music and dance.

Soon *Bharatanatyam* came to be seen as India's national classical dance. In chorus, Nataraja, the primarily south Indian appearance of the Hindu God Shiva as 'cosmic dancer', became not only the central icon for the revival

FIGURE 23   Sri Nataraj Puja, artist unknown, published by Ajanta Art Calendar, Calcutta,
                 n.d.
                 COURTESY OF PRIYA PAUL, NEW DELHI

of *Bharatanatyam* as a national dance but, partially due the publication of
Ananda Coomaraswamy's *The Dance of Siva* (1918), also for the 'grandeur of
ancient (specifically Hindu) Indian art, science, and religion' at large (figure 23).[10] Besides Nataraj, Hindu national music reforms generally resulted

---

10   Matthew Harp Allen, "Rewriting the Script for South Indian Dance", *The Drama Review*,
      41, 3, 1997: 83.

FIGURE 24   *Saraswati*, oil on canvas by Raja Ravi Varma, 1896
                SOURCE: WIKICOMMONS

in a growing visual dominance in Indian society of musical images of Hindu gods – including of Krishna playing the flute and of Saraswati with the *vina* (plucked string instrument) (figure 24) – and, in this way, Indian music was increasingly connotated with an Hindu aura.

Thus, while Indian nationalists proudly signified the ancientness, uniqueness and spirituality of the Hindustani and Karnatak traditions, these art music genres simultaneously became arenas for identity politics between the north and the south, Hindus and Muslims (mainly in the north), and Brahmins and non-Brahmins (mainly in the south). But what about non-art music? Inspired by the famous British folk song collector Cecil Sharp, Ananda Coomaraswamy argued that 'in spite of the neglect of Indian art-music in recent times, the folk-music of the people is still everywhere to be heard, and it is only in a living relation to this that a national school of music can be preserved'.[11] To a great extent, his viewpoint overlapped with that of Rabindranath Tagore, who partially on the basis of Bengali folk music composed an oeuvre of over 2,000 'modernist' songs, which generally came to be seen as representative for the Bengali nation and, as already remarked, include the future national anthems of India and Bangladesh.[12] While the efforts of Coomaraswamy and Tagore did not make folk music the basis for national music – as was the case in Europe –, it became increasingly important to the development of regional 'national' identities.

Several genres of devotional music (*kirtan*) to a certain degree were classicized as well. To give only two examples. During the early twentieth century, Professor Khagendranath Mitra of the University of Calcutta and his musical guru Nabadwip Brajabashi made the popular genre of Vaishanavite *kirtan* respectable for the Bengali elites. In their anthology of songs *Sri Padamrita-Madhuri* or 'The Sweet Elixer of Verse' (1910), they not only standardized and shortened songs, but also linked *kirtan* with Sanskrit aesthetic theory. Afterwards, the genre became perhaps even more important to Bengali national identity than the songs of Tagore.[13] The case of Sikh *kirtan* is particularly interesting because it concerns the devotional hymns of the Sikh holy scripture, the Guru Granth Sahib. This largest collection of sacred hymns in the world has compositions of several of the Sikh Gurus and, wholly in line with the *bhakti* tradition, of Hindu and Muslim saints (Sheikh Farid, Kabir, Ravidas and so on). In the wake of the Singh Sabha Reformation, the performance of these hymns became increasingly standardized – for instance with the harmonium replacing the use of different string instruments for accompaniment – and sanitized in line with the idea of spiritual music. Furthermore, as *kirtan* over time became an identity marker of the Sikh nation, Muslim musicians (*rababis*), who had performed *kirtan* since the time of the first Sikh Guru, Nanak, and his Muslim accompanist Mardana, were discarded.[14]

---

11   Ananda K. Coomaraswamy, *Essays in National Idealism*, New Delhi: Munshiram Manoharlal, 1981 (first published in 1909): 193–194.

12   Bob van der Linden, *Arnold Bake: A Life with South Asian Music*, London: Routledge, 2018: Chapter Three.

13   Ibid.: Chapter Two.

14   Bob van der Linden, *Music and Empire in Britain and India: Identity, Internationalism, and Cross-Cultural Communication*, New York: Palgrave Macmillan, 2013: Chapter 5.

Painting the Nation: from Raja Ravi Varma to *Swadeshi* Art and beyond

Although Indian music reformers and musicians overall remained indifferent to European music practice, to the contrary, Indian painters were overwhelmed by European 'naturalist' painting and the wide range of new materials (above all oil paint) and art examples, either in their original form or as reproduced in print.[15] Furthermore, unlike in the Indian music scene, the British directly interfered in the Indian art world by establishing four main art schools: Government School of Industrial Arts, Madras (1850), the Government College of Art and Craft, Calcutta (1854), Sir Jamsetjee Jeejeebhoy School of Art, Bombay (1857), and the Mayo School of Industrial Arts, Lahore (1875). In general, the colonial ruler looked down upon Indian arts and, hence, these schools were part of their civilizing mission. As the Governor of Bombay Presidency Sir Richard Temple, an amateur painter himself and advocate of modern arts schools in India, wrote in 1880:

> [Arts schools] will teach them one thing, which through all the preceding ages they have never learnt, namely drawing objects correctly, whether figures, landscape or architecture. Such drawing tends to rectify some of their mental faults, to intensify their powers of observation, and to make them understand analytically those glories of nature which they love so well.[16]

At the same time, however, it should be emphasized that the study and making of Indian arts and crafts was dominantly stimulated at the government art schools and to some extent led to a revival in this field. Students familiarized themselves with European art practices – including Romanticism, the sentimental and literary subject matter of academic painting – and Orientalist views on Indian art. Furthermore, after becoming teachers and/or artists, they proliferated their knowledge throughout the subcontinent. Conversely, colonial culture led to the rise of the Romantic individualist Indian artist creating new and meaningful forms of art that to a large extent represented (national) identity quests. This in contrast to pre-colonial times, when Indian artists had

15   Joachim K. Bautze, ed., *Interaction of Cultures: Indian and Western Painting 1780–1910*, Alexandria, Virginia: Arts Services International, 1998; Partha Mitter, *Art and Nationalism in Colonial India, 1850–1922: Occidental Orientations*, Cambridge: Cambridge University Press, 1994.
16   As cited in Mitter, *Art and Nationalism*: 32.

a humble (generally anonymous) position and the division between artists and artisans was largely ambiguous. The works produced by modern Indian artists reached wider national audiences through exhibitions and a growing number of art magazines with full colour illustrations. Specifically, Ramananda Chatterjee's *Prabasi* (since 1901 in Bengali) and *Modern Review* (since 1907 in English) were read widely by Indian elites and provided an intellectual forum for art criticism. In fact, the cover of the first issue of *Prabasi* shows Chatterjee's pan-Indian sentiment by proudly displaying 'a cultural prospectus of Indian architecture: Hindu, Buddhist, Muslim, Sikh and even Burmese (Burma being then under the Raj)'.[17]

At first, none embodied the Romantic image of the uncompromising artist more strikingly than Raja Ravi Varma, a minor south Indian prince from the state of Travancore (now Kerala).[18] This largely autodidact painter inventively merged Indian and European art practices. He started out as a fashionable portrait painter, who was appreciated by both the British rulers and the Indian aristocracy. Yet, he became truly famous for his historical paintings, in which he romantically brought to life the ancient Hindu epics and literary classics. This much to the acclaim of early Indian nationalists who saw in his paintings an inspiring new national imaginary. As Rabindranath Tagore wrote: 'The secret of their appeal is in reminding us how precious our own culture is to us, in restoring to us our inheritance. Our mind here acts as an ally of the artist. We can almost anticipate what he is about to say [...]'.[19] In 1894, as already remarked, Ravi Varma established his own Ravi Varma Fine Art Lithographic Press to mass-produce his historic paintings as oleographs. The company, for which he imported the machinery and experts from Germany, was led by the German master printer Fritz Schleicher, who in 1903 became its sole owner and led it to great financial success. Once again, in a largely illiterate country the role of visual imagery was even greater than printed texts in affirming common cultural values and aspirations that transcended region, religion, language and caste. Ramananda Chatterjee was crucial to Ravi Varma's emergence as national artist. He always wrote favourably about him and published large images of his paintings in full colour in *Prabasi* and *Modern Review*. Also, he composed an illustrated biography *Ravi Varma: The Indian Artist* (1903).

---

17   Mitter, *Art and Nationalism*: 121.
18   Ranjit Desai's Marathi biography of Raja Ravi Varma, of which an English translation appeared in 2013, served as the basis for the Hindi film *Rang Rasiya* ('Colours of Passion'), which was released in 2008 and the Malayalam film *Makaramanju* ('The Mist of Capricorn'), which was released in 2010 and subsequently dubbed in Tamil as *Apsaras* (2011).
19   Mitter, *Art and Nationalism*: 218.

Over the years, Ravi Varma befriended Indian nationalist leaders such as Dadabhai Naoroji, Gopal Krishna Gokhale and Annie Besant. In Calcutta, he was warmly received by Surendranath Banerjee, the Tagores and other members of the Bengali intelligentsia. Although he himself was never straightforwardly anti-colonial, some of his paintings provided nationalist hints or, in any case, were recognized as such by Indians. In 1870, Maharaja Visakham Tirunaal of Travancore commissioned Ravi Varma to paint *Sita Bhoopravesam* ('Sita's Ordeal'). The painting depicts a scene from the Ramayana, namely, 'an Ayodhya-returned Sita disappearing – in the arms of Bhoomi Devi – into the earth, unable to bear the questioning of her chastity after her abduction by Ravan'.[20] As Christopher Pinney argued, most Hindus familiar with the story would interpret the painting's message in view of their own times: '[...] the exile of Ram from Ayodhya as a deferment of just rule ("Ram Rajya"), Sita as the Motherland, and the rape of the Motherland by a foreign ruler'.[21] Similarly, Varma's *Kichak Sairandhri* or 'The Killing of Kichak' (1890),[22] depicting the stripping of Draupadi only to be saved by Hanuman, acquired a new meaning after a play about the same episode from the Mahabharata was banned by the British government in 1907. Although the play straightforwardly narrated the episode, everyone in the audience knew that Kichak was Lord Curzon, the man behind the partition of Bengal in 1905, Draupadi was India itself, and Yudhisthira and Bhima represented the 'moderate' and 'radical' wings of the Indian National Congress (INC) respectively.[23] In 1918, 'The Killing of Kichak' was one of the first Marathi films productions.

Also, Ravi Varma's Romantic depictions of women – the subject matter of the bulk of his paintings – were repeatedly dictated by his growing perception of Indian as one nation. To give two main examples. The ten paintings that he sent to the Columbian Exhibition in Chicago, where they won two awards, represented women from different Indian regions. As E. M. J. Venniyoor wrote:

> Ravi Varma chose women from all strata of Indian society, from all castes, creeds and regions, to highlight the rich variety of the country. He chose

---

20   Christopher Pinney, "Latrogenic Religion and Politics" in Raminder Kaur and William Mazzarella, eds., *Censorship in South Asia: Cultural Regulation from Sedition to Seduction*, Bloomington, IN: Indiana University Press, 2009: 34.

21   Ibid.

22   https://commons.wikimedia.org/wiki/File:Raja_Ravi_Varma,_Keechaka_and_Sairandhri ,_1890.jpg.

23   Christopher Pinney, *'Photos of the Gods': The Printed Image and Political Struggle in India*, London: Reaktion Books, 2004: 69.

women as his main theme for it is they, more than men, who carry with them the country's traditions in dress and customs and convey the even tenor of Indian life.[24]

Galaxy of Musicians (1889) is another attempt to allegorically portray India's unity in diversity.[25] The painting shows female musicians of diverse religious and geographical backgrounds, albeit in a largely imaginary manner as far as the combination of dresses and instruments is concerned. The work is of further interest because in making it Varma unintendedly perhaps brought to the fore the modern idea of the importance of music education for middle class Indian women as a sign of civilization. In chorus, Varma's choice of the *sari* to clothe the female characters of his historical paintings should be mentioned. For at the time, and even now, it was not a universal form of clothing for Indian women, yet into the twentieth century the *sari* increasingly came to be seen as India's national dress and undeniably Varma's paintings contributed to this.[26] In fact, his heroines generally created regional/national fashions for dressing styles and ornaments and thus had an enduring influence on Indian theatre and cinema.

Already before Ravi Varma's death in 1906, however, a powerful group of anti-colonial artists and intellectuals in Bengal propagated the creation of a 'true' nationalist Indian art. In particular, they denounced Varma's paintings as being Westernized and in opposition to the idea of Indian spirituality. The role of Ernest Binfield Havell, an English teacher of art and a follower of William Morris, was fundamental and indeed may be compared with that of Ernest Fenollosa, the teacher of Okakura Kakuzo, in Japan. Between 1896 and 1906, Havell was the director of Calcutta's Government College of Art and Craft and a trenchant critic of 'naturalist' painting. On the whole, he proclaimed that India's spirituality was reflected in its art. His *Indian Sculpture and Painting* (1908), which supported and defended Indian national unification from a cultural historical perspective, shocked English critics by describing its subject matter for the first time as 'fine art'. For the creation of a *swadeshi* style of art, he found an ally in Abanindranath Tagore.[27] The Mughal miniatures that

24   E. M. J. Venniyoor, *Raja Ravi Varma*, Trivandrum: Government of Kerala, 1981: 31.

25   https://commons.wikimedia.org/wiki/File:Raja_Ravi_Varma,_Galaxy_of_Musicians.jpg.

26   Venniyoor, *Raja Ravi Varma*: 27.

27   Abanindranath had been initiated into Indian art by Ravi Varma prints presented to him by his uncle Rabindranath and, even though he became the acclaimed, if somewhat reluctant leader of the nationalist Bengal School of Art, Abanindranath continued to admire Ravi Varma throughout his life.

Havell first introduced to him were a revelation to Tagore and had a powerful influence on his developing style. The collaboration between the two in recovering the principles of Hindu as well as Mughal art would become the principal axis of what came to be known as the Bengal School of Art, which contributed much to the cultivation of a modern Indian art. Like Havell, Tagore believed that Western art was materialistic in character and that India needed to return to its own traditions to recover spiritual values. Accordingly, he and his followers argued for a Romantic aesthetic that emphasized emotion (*bhave*) over form (*rupa*). Their art was to be created 'free of the trammels of education and training, free also of the demands of a profession and livelihood'.[28]

The members of the Bengal School not only rejected oil painting and naturalistic drawing as forged colonial impositions, but they also underlined links between pre-colonial and pan-Asian artistic practices. Their paintings were executed on paper, deployed 'Oriental' techniques – including the use of organic pigments, calligraphic brushwork and multiple washes of colour – and depicted historical or mythological themes from a glorious, pre-colonial Indian past.[29] Through his work with Okakura Kakuzo's students Yokoyama Taikan and Hishida Shunso, Abanindranath became familiar with the art of the Japanese Nihonga movement. Ultimately, this movement and the Bengal School adhered to a common Romantic nationalist aesthetic of both anti-realism and Asian spirituality. The first landmark in *swadeshi* art was Abanindranath's miniature painting *The Passing of Shah Jahan* (1902). It was awarded at the Delhi *durbar* exhibition of 1903 and shows the imprisoned Mughal Emperor gazing at the Taj Mahal, the celebrated mausoleum that he commissioned in memory of his wife (figure 25). The work depicts the idea of loss and its melancholy certainly had no precedent in Indian miniature painting. For Indian nationalists, both Hindus and Muslims, the painting's most relevant feature was its nostalgic evocation of history, which easily could be reinterpreted into the passing of Indian tradition under colonial rule. Decades later, because of its fame, a refurbished version of the painting was the obvious choice for the cover of the Shah Jahan-volume of the *Amar Chitta Katha* comic-series. During this period, in fact, Abanindranath made several paintings that were inspired by Mughal historic episodes. Conversely, his *Bharat Mata* (1905) (figure 7) – goddess-like, yet different from any known deity of the Hindu pan-

28   Tapati Guha-Thakurta, *Abanindranath, Known and Unknown: The Artist versus the Art of His Times*, Kolkata: Centre for Studies in Social Sciences, 2009: 7.

29   Natasha Eaton, "Swadeshi Color: Artistic Production and Indian Nationalism, ca. 1905–ca. 1947", *The Art Bulletin*, 95, 4, 2013: 623–641.

FIGURE 25   *The Passing of Shah Jahan*, oil on board by Abanindranath Tagore, 1902
                    SOURCE: WIKICOMMONS

theon – remains unique to the idea of the nation and Indian artistic creation
at large. With the goddess 'suspended in a yellowish-pink glow', it is also one
of the works for which he used the Japanese wash technique.[30]

In 1906, against heavy opposition, Havell appointed Abanindranath as
vice-principal of the Calcutta Art College. Accordingly, he trained numerous
students who would become famous artists themselves, including Nandalal
Bose, Surendranath Ganguly, Asit Haldar and Krishnappa Venkatappa. After
his resignation from the college in 1915, Abanindranath continued his activities within the Indian Society of Oriental Art, an '*avant garde* art salon' that
he had set up in 1907 as an alternative space to the college, albeit ironi-

---

30   Mitter, *Art and Nationalism*: 292.

cally under British patronage. The society published the art journal *Rupam*, which later became the *Journal of the Indian Society of Oriental Art*. Significantly, in 1902, as part of the historicist recovery of Indian heritage, Havell had singled out the narrative mural paintings at the Buddhist rock-cut *viharas* (monk's residences) and *chaityas* (prayer halls) built at Ajanta in central India (500 ACE) as the ideal example of Indian art. Ajanta's paintings had influenced Buddhist art throughout Asia, yet after the decline of Buddhism in India from the tenth century onwards, they had gradually faded from memory. An English officer rediscovered the frescoes during the early nineteenth century and in 1896–1897 they were documented by John Griffiths, the head of the Government Art School in Bombay. Students at the Calcutta Art College were encouraged to visit Ajanta. Over time, Nandalal Bose and others created Ajanta-inspired nationalist murals at Shantiniketan, the school and utopian community founded in 1901 by Rabindranath Tagore in rural Bengal, and elsewhere in a historicist style, with sources ranging from epics and mythology to historic figures such as Mirabai.

The works of the Bengal School reached Indian middle-class audiences through exhibitions in the country's main cities, where high-quality art prints were sold, and the proliferation of full-page colour plates of paintings in numerous art books and journals. In addition, *swadeshi* art was propagated by Havell, Ananda Coomaraswamy and Sister Nivedita in lectures and print – Nivedita's *The Function of Art in Shaping Nationality* (1906) and Coomaraswamy's *Art and Swadeshi* (1912) are two examples. Also, a good number of Romantic nationalist water colour illustrations that had been created by Abanindranath or under his supervision were reproduced in popular books such as Rabindranath Tagore's *The Crescent Moon* (1913) and *Gitanjali and Fruit-Gathering* (1918), *Hindus and Buddhists* (left unpublished at Nivedita's death and brought out by Coomaraswamy in 1913) and Coomaraswamy's *Buddha and the Gospel of Buddhism* (1916). Conversely, the Bengal School received support from London through Havell's India Society, which since 1910 promoted:

> the study and appreciation of Indian culture in its aesthetic aspects, believing that in Indian sculpture, architecture, and painting, as well as in Indian literature and music, there is a vast unexplored field, the investigation of which will bring about a better understanding of Indian ideals and aspirations, both in this country and in India.[31]

---

31   "The India Society", *The Times*, June 11, 1910: 18; as cited in Mary M. Lago, ed. *Imperfect Encounter: The Letters of Rabindranath Tagore and William Rothenstein*, Cambridge, MA: Harvard University Press, 1972: 7–8.

In 1911, the India Society had almost 200 members in Britain, India and the United States. Original members of the executive committee were Coomaraswamy and the painter William Rothenstein, who introduced Rabindranath Tagore and his work in Britain. It organized lectures and brought out publications such as its own journal *Indian Art and Letters*, Coomaraswamy's two volumes of *Indian Drawings* (1910 and 1912) and Rabindranath Tagore's *Gitanjali* (1912), the main work for which he received the Nobel Prize for Literature in 1913. Also, Havell was involved in Bengal School exhibitions in Britain and the Continent. Between 1909 and 1913, the India Society and Indian Society of Oriental Art kept in close contact, with Coomaraswamy travelling back and forth and Rothenstein visiting Calcutta.

By 1920, Abanindranath withdrew from the limelight as a nationalist artist and, according to art historian Tapati Guha-Thakurta, subsequently created his best works.[32] Yet, as a legacy of the Bengal School, his students secured teaching jobs at art institutions all over the subcontinent, including at Mayo School of Art, Lahore; Bharat Kala Bhavan, Benares; Shantiniketan Kala Bhavan; Jaipur School of Arts; Lucknow School of Art, Andhra Jatiya Kalashala, Masulipatam; Madras School of Arts and so on. For some time, late members of the Bengal School were inspired by European works in the *art nouveau* style, which they found ideologically attractive because 'their mood of disease and degeneration' offered 'ideal ingredients for a mythology of the defeated'.[33] Successively, however, Indian artists became more attracted to European modernism. The 1922 Bauhaus exhibition in Calcutta was obviously important here. Overall, they felt that the search for inspiration in primitive art and Eastern spirituality among the European avant-garde was much like their own struggle against colonial rule. This was also the time that Rabindranath Tagore began to paint his 'expressionist' works, which were successfully received in Germany in the 1930s, and Abanindranath's brother Gaganendranath created a new genre of poetic fantasy based upon Cubism.

More important to the discussion of Romantic nationalism, however, were the works of, amongst others, Nandalal Bose, Sunayani Devi and Jamini Roy (figure 26), who preferred eternal 'village India' over historicism and produced nationalist works in a 'primitivist' (folk) style as an authentic representation of the soul of the Indian nation. Over time, this primitivist urge among Indian artists would often led to a reassertion of regional identities in art.[34] The work

32   Guha-Thakurta, *Abanindranath*: 16–17.
33   Mitter, *Art and Nationalism*: 342.
34   Partha Mitter, *The Triumph of Modernism: India's Artists and the Avant-Garde, 1922–1947*, London: Reaktion Books, 2007.

FIGURE 26   *Manasa, The Snake Goddess* by Jamini Roy, c. 1920
             SOURCE: WIKICOMMONS

of Abdur Rahman Chughtai should be mentioned because of his contribution to Muslim Romantic nationalism in art. Trained by Samarendranath Gupta, a student of Abanindranath, at the Mayo School of Art in Lahore, this pan-Islamist 'was the first Muslim to use Muslim classics in a personal manner, conjuring up a fin-de-siècle voluptuous decadence to express Muslim feelings of degeneration under colonialism'.[35] He was a great admirer of the revivalist art of Abanindranath and the Bengal School, but expectedly thought that his own vision of the Islamic past was more authentic than the *swadeshi* works produced on similar themes. Finally, the historicist ideals of the Bengal School found an echo in the architecture of Rabindranath Tagore's Shantiniketan, of which the largely functional buildings have eclectic features, ranging from Buddhist gateways and columns to Mughal and Rajput style window openings. Revivalism indeed was central to Romantic nationalist architecture in India.

Revivalist Architecture of the Indian Nation(s)

As state power was in British hands, the conditions for the making of Romantic national architecture in India were evidently different from those in Europe. In

---

35   Mitter, *Art and Nationalism*: 332.

fact, besides the English language, the public buildings of British India belong to the most visible and lasting legacies of colonialism in the subcontinent – with 'Gothic' Bombay and Lutyens' New Delhi among its most famous examples.[36] To a large degree this can be explained by the fact that such public buildings as railway stations, government offices, (military) barracks, universities and museums were built primarily by the British (although often in a large part financed by Indian entrepreneurs) and are generally still in use today. On the other hand, it has much to do with the modernization of urban space in India. From the very beginning, the British refused to live in the overcrowded, unhealthy and intimidating cramped streets and alleys of Indian (walled) cities and towns. Instead, they inhabited their forts, 'white towns' (both in terms of European skin colour and the paint of the buildings) and well-planned cantonments and civil stations. Further, those who could afford it or were required to do so, like the members of the administration in Calcutta and later New Delhi, completed the yearly trek to the 'English-style' hill stations, to escape from the heat in the plains. Overall, British colonial architecture was pragmatically adjusted to the Indian climate, as best exemplified of course by the bungalow – that Anglo-Indian invention, which was subsequently adopted around the world, especially in the tropics –, and using local details and building materials. In turn, elitist Indians very soon took over much of the architecture and living habits of their colonial rulers.

Originally, colonial public buildings in India were erected in European 'Palladian-classical' and 'Gothic' styles. By the 1870s, however, the so-called 'Indo-Saracenic' style was added as one element of British self-identification with India's former rulers, especially the Mughals. Characteristic to this style, which defies definition as a pure single design and instead was a more complex phenomenon, are decorative features and details derived from the architectures of India's precolonial past as well as other exotic architectures of the Orientalist imagination, including 'Moorish' Andalusia. On the way, the British envisaged Indian architecture in religious terms and generally favoured the Islamic style over the Indic. Undoubtedly, this had much to do with the fact that they were attracted to architecture that, among other things, used arches, vaulting and domes, because these very building techniques were current in Europe as well. Instead, Indic architecture was largely alien to them because it was built on a post and lintel system, known as trabeated architecture. Regardless, the Indo-Saracenic style is often criticized for embodying a distinctively

36   Jon Lang, Madhav Desai and Miki Desai, *Architecture and Independence: The Search for Identity – India, 1880–1980*, New Delhi: Oxford University Press, 1997; Thomas R. Metcalf, *An Imperial Vision: Indian Architecture and Britain's Raj*, London: Faber and Faber, 1989.

European colonial imagination of India's architectural heritage. This is obviously true for most of the buildings in the style and especially so for the over-the-top palaces designed by and built under the supervision of British architects for Indian princes – Hindu and Sikh (maha)rajas as well as Muslim *nawabs* and *nizams* –, who enthusiastically adopted Indo-Saracenic architecture, partially to display themselves as rich and modern rulers.

Among the most interesting Indo-Saracenic palaces are those of Baroda and Kolhapur designed by Major Charles Mant of the Public Works Department. Both are from 1881 and include the presence of a soaring clock tower as a marker of the arrival of modern time discipline. Mant created the Kolhapur palace for the Maratha house descended from Shivaji (figure 27). Accordingly, he sought to incorporate local architectural elements and in doing so:

> He turned in part to the local temples of Kolhapur, but he derived inspiration as well from the *Jat* forts of Bharatpur and Mathura and the Jain temples of Ahmedabad, whose multiple clustered domes mount the Kolhapur skyline. Although Mughal forms are conspicuously absent, still the use of Gujarati and northern Indian elements in a building meant to symbolize Shivaji's Maharashtra testifies to the enduring eclecticism of British Indo-Saracenic design.[37]

Under the influence of the Arts and Crafts Movement, some British architects recognized and drew on continuous and living Indian legacies too. In particular, George S. T. Harris in Gwalior, Samuel Swinton Jacob in Rajasthan and John Lockwood Kipling in Lahore, and, later, to a lesser degree Vincent J. Esch in Hyderabad worked closely together with local master craftsmen and produced revivalist buildings that accentuated regional architectural styles.[38] Some Western educated Indian architects creatively continued to build in this tradition and, accordingly, had an influence on Indian Romantic nationalist architecture. Thus, on the one hand, the design context of the Indo-Saracenic style was more or less like the historicism that saturated nineteenth century Western architecture, namely, the looking back to the Renaissance, Gothic

---

37   Metcalf, *An Imperial Vision*: 112–113 ('*Jat*' refers to a north Indian caste).
38   Julius Bryant, "Colonial Architecture in Lahore: J. L. Kipling and the 'Indo-Saracenic' Styles", *South Asian Studies*, 36, 1, 2020: 61–71; Giles Tillotson, *The Tradition of Indian Architecture: Continuity, Controversy and Change since 1850*, New Haven: Yale University Press, 1989, "Vincent J. Esch and the Architecture of Hyderabad, 1914–36", *South Asian Studies*, 9, 1, 1993: 29–46 and "George S. T. Harris: An Architect in Gwalior", *South Asian Studies*, 20, 1, 2004: 9–24.

FIGURE 27   The New Palace at Kolhapur
SOURCE: C. C. DYSON, *From a Punjaub Pomegranate Grove*, LONDON: MILLS
& BOON, 1913: FRONTISPIECE

cathedrals and so on. Yet, on the other, in opposition to the situation in the West – and as nostalgically complained about by John Ruskin, William Morris and others –, individual craftsmanship was a continuing reality in India and sometimes, therefore, 'the Indo-Saracenic movement could go beyond revering the past, to engage with the living skills of the present'.[39]

What Indians decided to build themselves under colonial rule, however, is ultimately of greater significance for the discussion of Romantic nationalist architecture and cultivation of Indian culture at large. More than the Indian Princes, the main patrons of modern 'traditional' architecture were the Indian entrepreneurs whose fortunes were closely tied to the British. Under the Pax Britannica, they could display their affluence without fear and erected grand private houses in traditional styles, for which they to different degrees used new building materials and made modern adaptations. The painted houses of Shekhawati in Rajasthan and the grand mansions of the Chettiars in south India are two exceptional and divergent examples, but throughout the subcontinent private houses (called *havelis* in the north), with their characteristic

39   Tillotson, "George S. T. Harris": 23.

FIGURE 28   Holy Sikh Tank & Golden Temple at Amritsar, photographer
              unknown/probably Felice Beato, c. 1858–1861
              COURTESY OF THE METROPOLITAN MUSEUM OF ART, NEW YORK

inner courtyards rather than the outside verandas of the bungalow, continued
to be constructed in regional architectural styles up to the beginning of the
twentieth century.

More important in terms of historicist stylistic continuity remains the fact
that Indian merchants eagerly also institutionalized their wealth by spon-
soring the construction or maintenance of religious buildings, especially at
pilgrimage sites. For indeed, this centuries old practice grew remarkably under
colonial rule. Obviously, this was related to the societal stability provided by
the British regime and the expansion of the pilgrimage industry through the
introduction of the railways. But it also had much to do with the fact that religious communities during this period progressively distinguished themselves
from each other in different ways. Backed by colonial law, for instance, it now
became clear who was the owner of the grounds of the temple, mosque or gurdwara (Sikh place of worship) and this modern context undeniably boosted
further institutionalization, including standardization in architecture.

In this context, the earlier mentioned arrival of a modern Sikh identity
due to the Singh Sabha Reformation so far has remained undiscussed in
relation to Sikh (gurdwara) architecture. During the early twentieth century,
Singh Sabha reformers demanded control of Sikh shrines in opposition to

the British supported customary caretakers (the *mahants* and *pujaris* who in their eyes belonged to the Hindu fold). Accordingly, for instance, Hindu idols were removed of the grounds of the holiest Sikh shrine, the Golden Temple in Amritsar, and the buildings and the circumambulation path around the central tank were refurbished or destroyed and replaced by new ones. As Sikhs became more aware of their own history, then, gurdwaras at sites which marked important events in Sikh history were revamped in a common historicist style. Since the end of the nineteenth century, these gurdwaras were described in guidebooks as well and in this way the Punjab was steadily mapped as the historical territory of the Sikh nation. Moreover, when the 1925 Gurdwara Bill brought all the historical gurdwaras in India under the control of the Shiromani Gurdwara Parbandhak Committee, Sikh identity and the property of the land of the historical gurdwaras became one in view of colonial law.[40]

The process of standardization in Sikh architecture can specifically be traced through historical photographs of the Golden Temple. The oldest one known to me (figure 28) still shows that the buildings around the holy tank are anything but organized. Also, it includes Maharaja Ranjit Singh's palace that was demolished by the British and, in the 1860s, replaced by a Gothic clock tower that stood there for over 70 years. Successive photographs display the emergence of an increasingly homogenous complex. These developments at the Golden Temple architecture were adopted also as standard for (historical) gurdwaras in Punjab and beyond.

Without any doubt, Bhai Ram Singh, the celebrated Sikh architect and main student of John Lockwood Kipling, the father of Rudyard, at Lahore's Mayo School of Industrial Arts, played a role in the standardization of Sikh architecture. Lockwood was a strong propagator of the use of Indian arts and crafts and together with Ram Singh he worked on numerous revivalist buildings in Lahore.[41] Among Ram Singh's best-known work is Amritsar's Khalsa College (1892). While modern Hindu and Muslim reformers already had their own modern educational institutions, Singh Sabhaites argued that the Sikh community likewise needed one, especially for the teaching of Punjabi, the *Gurmukhi* script and Sikh history. With Khalsa College, Ram Singh aimed to

---

40   Anne Murphy, *The Materiality of the Past: History and Representation in Sikh Tradition*, New York: Oxford University Press, 2012.

41   The recording of Bhai Ram Singh's name on the foundation stone of Punjab University's Senate Hall in Lahore as its architect is the only instance where an Indian was credited with designing a colonial public building. In 1891, he created the Durbar Hall for Queen Victoria at Osborne House on the Isle of Wight. In 1910, he succeeded Kipling as the head of the Mayo School.

FIGURE 29   View of Benares with the mosque of Aurangzeb in the background,
               photographer unknown, published by Francis Frith & Co, c. 1850s–1890s
               COURTESY OF THE J. P. GETTY MUSEUM, LOS ANGELES

reflect Sikh identity in architecture and, as such, like the refurbished gurdwaras, it remains an example of regional historicist architecture that to a
certain extent transcends the Indo-Saracenic pastiche. Due to the Sikh concept of *seva* (selfless labour), however, little is known about Bhai Ram Singh's
involvement in the process of standardization of gurdwara architecture. Yet,
it can be safely assumed that with his standing and reputation as an architect, his services must often have been called upon. At least, it is known that
he designed the gurdwaras at Khalsa College, Lahore's Aitchison College and
two other ones built in memory of the Battle of Saragarhi in Amritsar and Fer-
ozepur.[42] Also, in 1906, Ram Singh created the marble railing around the tank
of the Golden Temple 'to prevent all danger to bathers from drowning'.[43]

Expectedly, the construction and renovation of temples became increasingly important to Hindu merchants and princes with the emergence of

---

42   Pervaiz Vandal and Sajida Vandal, *The Raj, Lahore and Bhai Ram Singh*, Lahore: National
        College of Arts, 2006: 229–230.
43   As cited in: Ibid.: 231.

Hindu nationalism. In contrast to modern Sikh gurdwara architecture, however, Hindu revivalist architecture materialized with great regional differences, especially between the north and the south. As in so many other instances, Hindus took an imagined Golden Age, before the advent of Islam, as the source of inspiration for their revivalist architecture. The case of Benares remains particularly intriguing. Although this city is usually depicted as ancient and timelessly Hindu, it has numerous Mughal buildings, including important mosques (figure 29), and temples and palaces in Mughal-style, mainly constructed by Marathas and Rajputs during the eighteenth and nineteenth century. Partially due to the impact of British historical and archaeological writings about the city, nonetheless, Benares was visually transformed into a Hindu pilgrimage centre, among other things through the (re)building of Hindu revivalist monuments, including at its famous Ganges waterfront.[44] The establishment of Benares Hindu University (BHU) in 1916 by the founder of the Hindu Mahasabha, Pandit Madan Mohan Malaviya, with great support from Annie Besant, should be mentioned in this context too. Supposedly, the plan of the university campus was based upon Vedic principles. Indeed, in architecture the slogan 'Back to the Shilpa Shastras' (traditional Hindu architectural guidelines) generally became the equivalent of the Hindu nationalist call 'Back to the Vedas'.

Among BHU's Hindu revivalist buildings, the most prominent landmark is the Shri Vishwanath temple (constructed between 1931 and 1966). It is an imagined replicate of the Kashi Viswanath temple, which originally stood in the heart of Benares but was destroyed several times by Muslim aggressors, including the Mughals under Emperor Aurangzeb. While it is empty inside, the temple has the entire Bhagavad Gita and extracts from other Sanskrit scriptures inscribed with illustrations on the inner marble walls of two floors. The famous entrepreneurial Birla family financed the construction of BHU's Shri Vishwanath temple, as they would do for a string of 'Birla temples' up to today, of which New Delhi's Lakshminarayan temple (1939) was the first and remains the best known. The latter was designed by Sris Chandra Chatterjee, the founder of the Modern Indian Architectural Movement.[45] His revivalist style mainly is an imitation of traditional symbology and elements stuck on functional structures – BHU's Shri Vishwanath temple fits this style as well – and it therefore may be seen as a variation of British Indo-Saracenic designs.

---

44   Madhuri Desai, *Banaras Reconstructed: Architecture and Sacred Space in a Hindu Holy City*, Seattle: University of Washington Press, 2017.

45   Samita Gupta, "Sris Chandra Chatterjee: The Quest for a National Architecture", *Indian Economic and Social History Review*, 28, 2, 1991: 187–201.

Even so, his work became very popular, especially among lay, mainly Hindu, Indians, 'who recognize its Indianness and take pride in it'.[46]

Another important Romantic nationalist shrine in Benares is the Bharat Mata temple, the very first temple dedicated to Mother India founded by Shiva Prasad Gupta, a staunch nationalist and Arya Samaji, and inaugurated by Mahatma Gandhi in 1936. Instead of an icon, as later Bharat Mata temples elsewhere in India would (in fact, besides of Hindu gods, the one in Haridwar has images of Annie Besant and Sister Nivedita), the temple solely houses a marble relief map of India, made to scale, with its topographic features shown in detail. Both at its entrance and on the inside walls it has the words Vande Mataram inscribed. Officially, the temple was established as a secular venue, where rituals were not allowed and open to people from all (religious) backgrounds. In reality, of course, the temple from the very beginning had a Hindu aura. As Sumathi Ramaswamy wrote:

> [...] the foundation stone for the temple was laid in April 1927 with the recitation of hymns from the Sanskrit scriptures and to the accompaniment of Hindu rituals of consecration; the inauguration ceremony took place on Vijaya Dashmi, one of the holiest days of the Hindu calendar; contemporaries frequently referred to the map enshrined in the building as the *murti* [icon]; and the building that houses the map, although not resembling a conventional temple, is after all referred to as *mandir* – the generic Hindi term for a Hindu house of worship.[47]

Predictably, the Bharat Mata temple was soon included in the Benares pilgrimage circuit, as was BHU's Shri Vishwanath temple later.

Most intriguing remains the building of revivalist Jain temples in the so-called north-western Indian Chaulukya style by traditional Hindu Brahmin Sompura architects.[48] Jains regard the reign of the Chaulukya dynasty during the eleventh to the thirteenth centuries, when it ruled parts of what are now Gujarat and Rajasthan, as a Golden Age in which their temple structures flourished. Since the nineteenth century, then, an ever increasing number of Jain temples have been most prominently renovated and/or rebuild, albeit to different extents, in the Chaulukya style, partially 'to counterbalance the often

---

46   Lang, Desai and Desai, *Architecture and Independence*: 134.

47   Sumathi Ramaswamy, *The Goddess and the Nation: Mapping Mother India*, Durham, NC: Duke University Press, 2010: 161, translation added.

48   For this and the next two paragraphs, I am indebted to John Cort for sharing his ideas and suggestions for literature.

strongly Islamicate style employed in Jain constructions during the sixteenth to eighteenth centuries'.[49] This was done largely under the patronage of the Anandji Kalyanji Trust and executed by Sompura builders and craftsmen, who originate from western India and claim to work in accordance with the Shilpa Shastras, whose descriptions and drawings however they do not slavishly follow. To the contrary, rather than to produce an authentic replica of a temple, they intend to capture its original spirit. While mainly working for religious trusts instead of the Archaeological Survey of India, Sompura architects further standardized the building of Jain temples by using marble and sandstone imported from Rajasthan.

Kasturbhai Lalbhai, industrialist, philanthropist and the chairman of the Anandji Kalyanji Trust between 1925 and 1975, was greatly guided by the English architect Claude Batley, the principal of Bombay's Jamsetjee Jeejeebhoy School of Art (1923–1943). In the footsteps of Lockwood Kipling, Batley strongly believed that Indian architects 'should use indigenous solutions in response to local conditions, rather than imitating imported architectural fashions' and he overall played an influential role in the development of modern architecture in India.[50] In this, he acknowledged Narmadashankar Muljibhai Sompura, one of the best known Sompura architects and the author of a standard textbook for temple construction and renovation, *Silpa Ratnakara* (1939), as his guru. Conversely, Kasturbhai Lalbhai was much advised in his activities by the architect and art historian M. A. Dhaky, who worked together with Sompura architects early in his career and as editor-in-chief canonized his ideas in the *Encyclopaedia of Indian Temple Architecture* (four volumes, 1983–1991).

Most significantly, in the wake of Jain architectural revivalism, Sompura architects and the Chaulukya style became fundamental to a broader Hindu nationalist temple architectural program. The best-known example is the newly constructed Somnath temple, a most important shrine for both Shiva and Krishna that was repeatedly destructed by Muslims. It became a Hindu nationalist symbol and its first phase, headed by Prabhashankar Oghadji Sompura, was completed under the patronage of the nationalist K. M. Munshi and India's first deputy prime minister Vallabhbhai Patel in 1951.[51] In fact,

49   Julia A. B. Hegewald, "The International Jaina Style? Maru-Gurjara Temples Under the Solankis, throughout India and in the Diaspora", *Ars Orientalis*, 45, 2015: 134.

50   John E. Cort, "Communities, Temples, Identities: Art Histories and Social Histories in Western India" in Michael W. Meister, ed., *Ethnography & Personhood: Notes from the Field*, New Delhi: Rawat Publications, 2000: 116.

51   For images of the nineteenth century ruins of the Somnath temple and the newly build one, see: https://en.wikipedia.org/wiki/Somnath_temple.

the Somnath temple is the model for the controversial Rama temple that was recently inaugurated by India's prime minister Narendra Modi in Ayodhya, and for which the design was made by Chandrakantbhai Sompura. The Sompura architect of one of the largest Hindu temples in the world, the Swaminarayana movement's Akshardam (2005) in New Delhi, was Virendrabhai Trivedi, whose company generally is involved in the restoration and building of numerous Hindu and Jain temples in India and around the world.

For, indeed, since the late twentieth century, the empire strikes back archi-tecturally in the West through the construction of an ever-growing number of Hindu and Jain temples, as well as Sikh gurdwaras. With the Hindu diaspora in mind, the Swaminarayan movement for instance constructed the largest Hindu temple in Europe, the Neasden temple (1995) in London. This temple too was designed by Chandrakantbhai Sompura, as were others in the West and Asia. To be clear, Sompura architects work most efficiently by assembly-line. Temples are still imagined and designed in a traditional manner, but the processes of sculpting stones and producing the temple parts is completely computerized. Afterwards, the manually finished prefabricated parts are trans-ported wherever they need to go in India and around the world, where the entire temple is put together on site by masons trained to do so.

But what about revivalist architecture among Indian Muslims? Again, there are regional differences. To begin with, the Indo-Saracenic buildings con-structed by the Muslim *nawabs* and *nizams* show many similarities with those of the Hindu (maha)rajas. During the nineteenth century, for instance, the *nawabs* of Junagadh State in Gujarat and of Bahawalpur State in Punjab (now Pakistan) correspondingly constructed buildings in a Gothic style (most likely as a response to the Gothic development of Bombay) and in an Italianate style. To the contrary, some of the architecture designed by Vincent J. Esch for the *nizam* of Hyderabad (India's largest Muslim Princely State) referred to the local architecture of the sultanates of the Deccan.[52] Most historicist were the female rulers (*begums*) of Bhopal State in central India.[53] Their gender notwithstand-ing, the Bhopal *begums* were granted to use the title *nawab* by the British, to whom they proved their loyalty before and after the 1857 Revolt, as well as during the Khilafat Movement.

Since Sikandar Begum (r. 1844–1868), the Bhopal *nawabs* aimed at a kind of Mughal Renaissance in their state, both in terms of religious reform and archi-

---

52   Tillotson, "Vincent J. Esch".
53   After Hyderabad, Bhopal was the second most important Muslim State, albeit with a predominantly Hindu population, in British India.

FIGURE 30   Shah Jahan, Begum of Bhopal, photographer unknown, 1872
                 COURTESY OF THE J. P. GETTY MUSEUM, LOS ANGELES

tecture. Overall, they projected themselves as the political and cultural inheritors of the Mughals, although Bhopal, unlike Hyderabad for example, never had been a Mughal province. In line with this, Sikandar Begum and her daughter and successor Shah Jahan Begum (r. 1868–1901) (figure 30) made several 'royal' tours through northern India, separately and together but always with a large following. In her *Taj al-Iqbal Tarikh-i Riyasat-i-Bhopal* (1873; English edition 1876: *The History of Bhopal*), Shah Jahan used the history of Bhopal state as well as her travels to link her rule and that of her predecessors to the earlier Mughal state. Besides other Mughal style buildings and gardens in Bhopal city, the two *begums* successively ordered the construction by architects from Delhi of two mosques that took the grand Jama Masjid (Friday Mosque) of Delhi as their example. Shah Jahan Begum even had a new city built at the edge of Bhopal, 'Shahjahanabad', named after the Mughal Emperor Shah Jahan under whose rule Delhi was known as the same. Her own vast palace complex was of course named after the famous mausoleum that Shah Jahan had constructed for his favourite wife: the Taj Mahal.[54]

Obviously, Muslim revivalist architecture was constructed beyond the Princely States as well. The buildings of Sayyid Ahmad Khan's Aligarh University and the Deoband School or Darul Uloom (1867), the leading Muslim *madrassah* of the subcontinent, refer to a great Indian Islamic past in different ways. Nakhoda Mosque (1926), the principal mosque of Calcutta, was built as an imitation of the mausoleum of Mughal Emperor Akbar at Sikandra near Agra, while its entrance is a pseudo-reproduction of the Buland Darwaza, the famous gateway to the Friday Mosque at Akbar's Fatehpur Sikri. The mosque's funder, Abdur Rahim Osman, was a shipping prince and, accordingly, 'Nakhoda' means 'Mariner'. He belonged to the Memon community of Hindus who since the fifteenth century converted to Islam under the influence of sufi *pirs* or spiritual guides and spread out over India from the Kutch area in Gujarat.

In sum, the British generally influenced the making of revivalist architecture in India by propagating the Indo-Saracenic style, establishing art schools as well as through their art historical and archaeological research. Yet, the revivalist constructions erected by both the British and Indians did not lead to the emergence of a definite Indian national architecture. To the contrary, modern Indian buildings in traditional style to a great extent remained characteristic to certain regions and/or communities. That said, and even though Indian elites subsequently favoured modernist architecture (from *art deco* to Le Corbusier's Chandigarh and beyond), revivalist buildings continue to be constructed up to the present, above all by Sompura architects in Chaulukya style.

---

54   Hanna L. Archambault, "Becoming Mughal in the Nineteenth Century: The Case of the Bhopal Princely State", *South Asia: Journal of South Asian Studies*, 36, 4, 2013: 479–495.

CHAPTER 5

Romantic Revolutions

The Return of the King

Following the death of Maharaja Ranjit Singh in 1839, his youngest son Duleep Singh became the last ruler of the Sikh Kingdom of the Punjab after surviving the bloody fights among his family members and the two Anglo-Sikh Wars. With the 1849 Treaty of Lahore, the nine-year-old Maharaja Duleep Singh was coerced by the British into signing away his Kingdom and giving the Koh-i-Noor, the world's most celebrated diamond, to Queen Victoria. He was separated from his mother, put under guardianship and sent into exile to Fatehgarh, halfway between Agra and Lucknow. After he voluntarily converted to Christianity, the maharaja was allowed to live in England, as he himself very much desired, and there he soon became a favourite of Queen Victoria. In the next decades, he divided his time between living the life of a London dandy, who was equally at home in boisterous theatre halls and conservative clubs, and that of a country squire, who organized grandiose shooting parties for the Prince of Wales and the great peers.

In 1859, however, Duleep Singh returned to India to meet his elderly mother Jindan Kaur. In Calcutta, to his own amazement, he was besieged by ex-members of his court and, more dangerous the British thought, by thousands of Sikh soldiers, who had just returned from the Second Opium War in China and had heard that their deposed maharaja was in town. Because he was afraid that all this would degrade his positive relationship with the British government, Duleep Singh immediately decided to return to London together with his mother. In 1863, he made another brief and less controversial trip to India (although again not to the Punjab) to depose his mother's ashes, as she wished, in accordance with Sikh rites. On his return, he married the German-Ethiopian Bamba Müller in Cairo and settled down with her at Elveden Hall in Suffolk, which was selected and purchased for him by the India Office. The maharaja transformed the run-down estate into an efficient game preserve and the house into a lavish pseudo-Oriental palace.

While Duleep Singh had found India a 'beastly place',[1] he could never forget that he was born a King. This even more so after he increasingly experienced

---

1   'From Maharaja Duleep Singh to Sir John Login, Spence's Hotel, Calcutta, February 1861 (letter 127)' in Ganda Singh, ed., *Maharaja Duleep Singh Correspondence*, Patiala: Patiala University, 1977: 84.

© BOB VAN DER LINDEN, 2024 | DOI:10.1163/9789004694804_007

harassment by importunate creditors and humiliating insults from the India Office. His pension proved insufficient for his princely lifestyle and the authorities accused him of keeping mistresses as well as being spendthrift and a gambler. Ultimately, Queen Victoria was also forced to distance herself from her beloved friend. Doubtlessly, the few years spent together with his mother had made Duleep Singh very conscious of his past. In 1861, he asked his guardian for a conversation about his private property in the Punjab as well as the Koh-i-Noor diamond, and he also requested him for the Punjab Blue Book.[2]

In the following decade, the maharaja repeatedly claimed more money from the India Office in replacement for what had been taken from him. He published letters in *The Times* about his pecuniary embarrassments and painful disappointments at the hands of the British government. In addition, he began to correspond with his cousin Sardar Thakur Singh Sandhanwalia, who informed him about his former private landed properties.[3] Thakur Singh was a central figure within the Sikh community. In 1873, he was one of the founders and the first president of the Amritsar Singh Sabha, the most important Sikh reformist organization. Ten years later, Duleep Singh invited Thakur Singh to come over to England, a visit that was two years postponed because the British did not allow it at first. Thakur Singh was accompanied, amongst others, by his two sons and a scripture reader (*granthi*), who daily read out to Duleep Singh from the Guru Granth Sahib and further instructed him in the tenets of the tradition.

After his confrontation with the India Office, the maharaja increasingly grieved the loss of his Kingdom and became determined to reconvert to the faith of his forefathers. Following the return of Thakur Singh's party to India, then, Duleep Singh decided to go and reside there with his family himself, partially because financially that would be more affordable than staying on in Britain. Also, his mother and Thakur Singh had reminded him of the rumours that circulated among Sikhs that related him to a prophecy by Guru Gobind Singh. It asserted that the latter would reincarnate as Deep Singh, live abroad for many years, but ultimately come back 'to correct the errors in which the Sikhs had fallen in their worship of God and the neglect of the Gooroo's [sic] tenets' and rule 'the land lying between Calcutta and the Indus'.[4] Accordingly, the maharaja sent a message to the newspapers in which he presented himself as the prophesied leader of the Sikhs and announced that he was on his way to

2   Lady Login, *Sir John Login and Duleep Singh*, London: W. H. Allen & Co, 1890: 463.
3   For the extensive list, see: 'From Sadhar Thakur Singh Sindhanwalia to His Majesty Maharaja Duleep Singh, 9 November 1883 (letter 162)' in Singh, ed., *Maharaja Duleep Singh Correspondence*: 117–124.
4   As cited in Michael Alexander and Sushila Anand, *Queen Victoria's Maharajah: Duleep Singh 1838–93*, London: Weidenfeld and Nicolson, 1980: 188.

FIGURE 31   Maharaja Duleep Singh by Antoine Claudet, Albumen carte-de-visite, c. 1864
             COURTESY OF THE NATIONAL PORTRAIT GALLERY, LONDON

India. Out of fear for a revolt, the British stopped Duleep Singh in Aden, where during his detention he nonetheless underwent the initiation rite (*khande ki pahul*) that made him a member the orthodox Sikh *Khalsa* fold.

By now, the maharaja's name was mentioned more than ever before in the Punjab. Copies of *The Annexation of the Punjaub and the Maharaja Duleep Singh* (1882) by a critic of British rule in India, Major Thomas Evans Bell, were distributed in the region, including in a *Gurmukhi* transcription arranged by Thakur Singh Sandhanwalia. Bengali nationalists wrote pamphlets and newspapers like *The Tribune* from Lahore carried articles in favour of the return of the Sikh King. A village in Lahore district refused to pay its land revenue, 'saying that tribute was due only to their King who was shortly to arrive in India'.[5]

---

5   D. Petrie, *Developments in Sikh Politics 1900–1911: A Report*, Amritsar: Chief Khalsa Diwan, n.d.: 19.

Duleep Singh's return was mentioned in speeches held in the bazaars and at the gurdwaras. He was among the twelve Sikh heroes depicted upon wood-cuts, and printed images of him were plentifully available.[6] Many traditional Sikh leaders such as Baba Khem Singh Bedi, a descendent of the first Sikh Guru Nanak, and Raja Bikram Singh of Faridkot actively broadcasted Duleep Singh's case or tried to cultivate ties with him. The fact that some Singh Sabha reformers advocated the return of their maharaja led to tensions within the movement. This especially came to the fore when on 31 October 1887, one of their satellite organizations, the Nanak Panth Prakash Sabha in Lahore, during its seventh anniversary 'displayed a garlanded portrait of the maharaja by the side of the Guru Granth Sahib'.[7] Yet, Sardar Thakur Singh Sandhanwalia was indubitably the most committed activist. He secretly visited Indian princes and numerous Sikh shrines to win support and funding, and he generally cre-ated an underground movement. Since the British were after him, however, he fled to French Pondicherry in 1886. There, he received a continuous stream of visitors, including envoys from Duleep Singh from Europe and Sikh soldiers from the Indian Army, and was appointed prime minister of the exiled Sikh State (*Khalsa Raj*).

From Aden, Duleep Singh decided not to return to Britain but to go to Paris instead. Also, he resigned the pension paid to him under the terms of the Treaty of Lahore. While plotting a rebellion that would throw the British out of India, the maharaja entered a shadowy Parisian world, which included Irish Fenians, Pan-Slavists and French Revanchists, who made a common cause of weakening the Russian-German alliance, which was underwritten by Britain. To all of them, Duleep Singh was attractive as a potential thorn in the side of the British. Subsequently, he became embroiled in the Byzantine conspiracies that linked the salons of Paris to the Great Game being played out between Britain and Russia at the Indian north-west frontier, as well as to the bazaars of Cairo.[8] Crucial was his contact with Fenian Patrick Casey, 'the apostle of dynamite' and a cousin of James Stephens, one of the founders of the Fenian Movement and the Irish Republican Brotherhood. Casey not only printed Duleep Singh's anti-British manifestos, but he also brought him into contact

---

6   W. H. McLeod, *Popular Sikh Art*, New Delhi: Oxford University Press, 1991: 19 and figures 2, 4 and 5.
7   Harbans Singh, ed., *The Encyclopaedia of Sikhism*, Patiala: Punjabi University, 1997, volume one: 294.
8   About this intellectual network: Christy Campbell, *The Maharajah's Box: An Imperial Story of Conspiracy, Love, and a Guru's Prophecy*, London: Harper Collins Publishers, 2000 and Faith Hillis, "The 'Franco-Russian Marseillaise': International Exchange and the Making of Antiliberal Politics in Fin de Siècle France", *Journal of Modern History*, 89, 1, 2017: 39–78.

with Russian agents who hoped to deploy the maharaja in a Franco-Russian alliance against Britain involving Russian military intervention in India. Simultaneously, Duleep Singh frequented the 'premier political salon in Paris' of Juliette Lamber (Madam Adam). A close friend and collaborator of the latter was the Russian Jewish-born Élie de Cyon, the chief agent in Paris of the Pan-Slavist and editor of the *Moscow Gazette* Mikhail Katkov, who advocated war with Germany and, if necessary, Britain. Katkov had a huge influence on Czar Alexander III. He sponsored Duleep's 1887 journey to Russia and remained his much-needed protector there. In fact, since the maharaja had no passport, he travelled to Moscow on Patrick Casey's.

Thus, Duleep Singh was at the centre of a highly diverse web of agents that created a master plan in which a combined Russo-Afghan force would invade India, precipitating revolts by the Sikh regiments and mutinies amongst the Irish soldiers. The armies of some Indian (Sikh) princes, it was further argued, would join them, while Bengalis would sabotage the railway system and Egyptian nationalists would obstruct the Suez Canal. Soon after his arrival in Russia, the maharaja wrote to the Czar about his plan 'to deliver some 250,000,000 of my countrymen from the cruel yoke of the British rule' with the help of a Russian military expedition, claiming that he was 'authorized' to offer three million pounds per annum from the Indian princes in tribute to him.[9] Apparently, the Czar showed interest in the scheme and, accordingly, Duleep Singh sent his loyal servant Arur Singh to the subcontinent to contact the 'brother Princes of Hindustan'. Soon, however, the British authorities came to know about the scheme and arrested the messenger.

Following this and, moreover, the death of both Michail Katkov and Thakur Singh Sandhanwalia in 1887,[10] Duleep Singh returned to Paris after having been less than a year in Russia. Almost bankrupt and bereft of political influence, he wrote to Queen Victoria, demanding the return of the Koh-i-Noor diamond with the intention of financing an Indian rebellion. For this same purpose, he launched 'The League of Indian Patriots' (an echo of the Boulangist 'Ligue des Patriotes') with Patrick Casey and James Stephens among its leaders. Yet, as happened before since early 1887, this initiative was stillborn because the maharaja's chief of staff in Paris, an Irish American double agent, shared his correspondence with the British prime minister.[11] In the following years, Duleep Singh suffered a massive stroke and, after a last emotional meeting with Queen Victoria, during which he asked her forgiveness, he died in 1893 as

---

9   'Duleep Singh to the Emperor of Russia, 10 May 1887 (letter 428)', in Singh, ed., *Maharaja Duleep Singh Correspondence*: 374–377.

10   Thakur Singh's sons continued to work for Duleep Singh's cause from Pondicherry.

11   The identity of this spy is the main discovery of Campbell, *The Maharajah's Box*.

a Christian, as he wished, and was buried at the churchyard on the fringe of Elveden Hall.

Duleep Singh's tragic tale of a duped, deprived and, finally, defeated King certainly fits the world of the 'tournament of shadows' played by the British and Russians at the Indian north-west frontier and which Rudyard Kipling so wonderfully described in *Kim* (1901). Of course, the maharaja was only a pawn in the Great Game, yet the essential truth about Anglo-Russian rivalry in Central Asia is that, despite the imperial fantasies entertained by its protagonists, there was never that much at stake. Likewise, in the 1870s and 1880s, few would have thought that the Dual Alliance between France and Russia would happen one day, but it did in 1894. Yet, what drove Duleep Singh to chase his fantastical destiny? It cannot have been a greed for money and/or power alone. Although he was more British than Indian, he still wanted to return to India, that 'beastly place'. No doubt, he had a Romantic longing for something that never had been or would be there. Most likely, his re-conversion to Sikhism was a sham, but he truly seemed to believe, like many Sikhs did, in Guru Gobind Singh's prophecy predicting his return as a King.

That said, Duleep Singh was probably the first Indian nationalist who attempted to reconcile the different interests of the Indian princes with that of the Sikh, Muslim and Bengali Hindu communities. Likewise, his attempt to build up an anti-colonial alliance shows an awareness of the need to organize internationally, although he probably came to this point only after realizing that all other avenues were closed to him. Simultaneously, Sikh hopes about the return of their King and, with it, the Golden Age of the Sikh Empire were real and might have inspired Duleep Singh in turn. Despite the failure of his mission, the maharaja has found an ever-growing place in Sikh memory ever since.[12] In 1999, in fact, the Prince of Wales unveiled a bronze equestrian statue of Duleep Singh, commissioned by the Maharaja Duleep Singh Centenary Trust, nearby Elveden Hall in Thetford, which by now has become a Sikh pilgrimage site. The inscription on the statue ends with: 'Even today, the Sikh nation aspires to regain its sovereignty', and it incorrectly states the maharaja's ultimate religious identity: 'He died in Paris having re-embraced the Sikh faith while still engaged in a struggle to reclaim his throne'. In 2017, a film about Duleep Singh, 'The Black Prince',[13] directed by Kavi Raz and starring the popular Punjabi singer Satinder Sartaaj, was released.

---

12 Tony Ballantyne, *Between Colonialism and Diaspora: Sikh Cultural Formations in an Imperial World*, New Delhi: Permanent Black, 2007: Chapter Three.

13 In 1858, Duleep Singh rented the house of Auchlyne from the Earl of Breadalbane. Among locals, he became known for his lavish lifestyle, shooting parties and love of dressing up in Highland costume, and he soon received the nickname 'the Black Prince of Perthshire'.

By and large, Maharaja Duleep Singh was an early participant in a geographically expanding, ideological diversifying and politically radicalizing network of anti-colonial activists and counter-cultural internationalists that emerged in the competitive world of empire. Soon this global network would produce Indian revolutionaries who propagated an end to colonial rule in India by any means and therefore were called 'seditionists', 'anarchists' or 'terrorists' by the British. Undeniably, their thinking was much influenced by the Japanese defeat of Russia and the partition of Bengal, as well as their interactions with anti-colonial revolutionaries (Irish Fenians in particular). Their hopes for Indian freedom increased with the outbreak of the First World War as well as the Russian Revolution, because it provided the possibility of forming deals with anti-British allies (Germans, Ottomans and Bolshevik Russians). In comparison to the world of Duleep Singh, Indian revolutionary nationalists were of course better organized, while meeting each other in 'India Houses' in London, New York and Tokyo, as well as on the Continent, especially in Paris and Berlin.[14] Even so, the mingling of their revolutionary thinking about freeing India from colonial rule with pan-Islamic, pan-Asian and other ideologies to a great extent was as imaginary as what Duleep Singh romantically dreamt about. Moreover, it had similar results, often because of the information delivered to the British by their Indian spies. As an example, the next section tells the remarkable life story of Muhammad Barkatullah, the main early twentieth century Indian intellectual who compounded pan-Islamist, pan-Asianist and Indian revolutionary thought, and was central also to establishing Indian nationalist activities in Japan.

Muhammad Barkatullah's Global Revolt

Although less known than for instance Shyamji Krishnavarma and Har Dayal,[15] Muhammad Barkatullah was undeniably as important in the world of Indian

---

14   Harald Fischer-Tiné, "Indian Nationalism and the 'World Forces': Transnational and Diasporic Dimensions of the Indian Freedom Movement on the Eve of the First World War",
      Journal of Global History, 2, 3, 2007: 325–344; Tim Harper, *Underground Asia: Global Revolutionaries and the Assault on Empire*, London: Allen Lane, 2020; Maia Ramnath, *Haj to
      Utopia: How the Ghadar Movement Charted Global Radicalism and Attempted to Overthrow
      the British Empire*, Berkeley, CA: University of California Press, 2011; Tilak Raj Sareen,
      Indian Revolutionary Movement Abroad (1905–1921), New Delhi: Sterling, 1979.

15   On Krishnavarma: Harald Fischer-Tiné, *Shyamji Krishnavarma: Sanskrit, Sociology and
      anti-Imperialism*, New Delhi: Routledge, 2014; on Har Dayal: Ramnath, *Haj to Utopia* and
      Benjamin Zachariah, "A Long, Strange Trip: The Lives in Exile of Har Dayal" in Virinder
      S. Kalra and Shalina Sharma, eds., *State of Subversion: Radical Politics in Punjab in the 20th
      Century*, London: Routledge, 2016: 188–217.

revolutionaries and one of the most widely travelled among them. His anti-imperialist internationalism is demonstrated by the wide range of his writings (in Urdu and English mainly) and his close collaboration over the decades with pan-Islamists, Irish American Fenians, Japanese pan-Asianists and, during the First World War, Ottomans and Germans, and then the Bolsheviks. Barkatullah was born and educated as an *alim* (Muslim scholar) in Bhopal. He continued his studies and learned English in Bombay. He was much attracted to the pan-Islamic ideas of Jamal al-Din Afghani, whom he apparently met and who particularly taught him that Islam was compatible with reason and freedom of thought.[16] From around 1887 until 1903, Barkatullah lived and worked in England, where he got involved in Muslim (pan-Islamic) activist networks, partially through his association with the British convert to Islam, Abdullah William Quilliam.[17] He became the first *imam* of Quilliam's Liverpool Muslim Institute and wrote extensively for his publications *The Crescent* and *The Islamic World*. Like Quilliam, Barkatullah argued that the British, as the ruler of most Muslims in the world, had to create a solid relationship with the Ottomans. By this time, he still saw a place for India within the British Empire, despite that he was critical of contemporary narrow-minded depictions of Islam and Muslims, as well as British policies in India.

In addition, Barkatullah befriended Shyamji Krishnavarma and other Indian nationalists and revolutionaries, and was impressed by the Irish nationalist call for Home Rule. He addressed a wide range of (radical) audiences, including that of the English Ethical Movement at the South Place in Finsbury, London. In general, he became acquainted with British leftists and alternativists, including Theosophists. Since he wrote critically about, among other things, British imperial policy against Turkey, nonetheless, he was put under surveillance by the authorities. Partly because of this (and the fact that he was invited to do so by Alexander Russell Webb, another eccentric Western convert

---

16   Humayun Ansari, "Maulana Barkatullah Bhopali's Transnationalism: Pan-Islamism, Colonialism, and Radical Politics" in Götz Nordbruch and Umar Ryad, eds., *Transnational Islam in Interwar Europe: Muslim Activists and Thinkers*, New York: Palgrave Macmillan, 2014: 183.

17   In 1894, Sultan Abdul Hamid II appointed Abdullah William Quilliam the first (and last) *Sheikh al-Islam* for the British Isles, a title that was acknowledged by Queen Victoria. Likewise, the Qajar Shah of Persia made the Englishman his consul. All in all, Quilliam stood at the centre of a pan-Islamic network and developed a reputation as a speaker about Islam. See further: Ron Geaves, *Islam in Victorian Britain: The Life and Times of Abdullah Quilliam*, London: Kube Publishing, 2010.

to Islam),[18] Barkatullah decided to set sail for New York, where he thought he would have more possibilities to mobilize Indians for nationalist action and pan-Islamism.

During his New York period (1903–1909), Barkatullah lectured widely and wrote numerous anti-imperial articles for the *North American Review* and other journals – for instance, about British hypocrisy and deceit in their political dealings worldwide and the fact that European powers hated the Ottoman Empire because it was Islamic. Also, he 'adopted the idea of the "white peril" popular in Japanese pan-Asianist literature and the Fenian trope of the "untrustworthy Anglo-Saxon"'.[19] Besides with Indian nationalist revolutionaries like Taraknath Das, he interacted with American counter-cultural figures, including African American anti-racists and again Theosophists. Among his closest collaborators were the Fenians John Devoy and George Freeman (born George Fitzgerald). Under Devoy, the Clan na Gael ('Family of the Gaels') organization, which was founded in New York in 1867 as a successor to the Fenian Brotherhood, became 'the most powerful republican organization on either side of the Atlantic'.[20] Further, he was the owner-editor of the newspaper and Clan na Gael-mouthpiece, *Gaelic American*, where George Freeman was co-editor. Devoy and Freeman cooperated with the India Houses in New York and London, and for instance reprinted articles from Krishnavarma's *The Indian Sociologist*. In 1906, Barkatullah and the Marathi Christian Samuel Lucas Joshi, with the help of Devoy and Freeman, established the Pan Aryan Association to propagate, among other things, Hindu-Muslim solidarity and Indo-Irish cooperation in the overthrow of British rule. The Association arranged lectures (by Madame Cama and others) and helped Indian students to find their way in America. Assumingly, Barkatullah's close association with Devoy and Freeman must have partially convinced him also of the necessity of the use of violence to achieve national sovereignty.

---

18   Following his conversion to Islam, Webb travelled widely in India, as well as in Egypt and Turkey. Also, he had a lifelong interest in Theosophy. Sultan Abdul Hamid II appointed him Honorary Turkish Consul in New York and, in 1893, he was the only representative of Islam at the World's Parliament of Religions in Chicago. Barkatullah wrote numerous articles about Islam and India for Webb's *The Muslim World*. See further: Umar Faruq Abd-Allah, *A Muslim in Victorian America: The Life of Alexander Russell Webb*, Oxford: Oxford University Press, 2006.

19   Samee Siddiqui, "Coupled Internationalisms: Charting Muhammad Barkatullah's Anti-Colonialism and Pan-Islamism", *ReOrient*, 5, 1, 2019: 36.

20   As cited in: Michael Silvestri, *Ireland and India: Nationalism, Empire and Memory*, Basingstoke: Palgrave Macmillan, 2009: 19.

In 1909, Barkatullah moved to Tokyo, which since the Russo-Japanese War had become a hub for students, (anti-colonial) intellectuals, revolutionaries and religious reformers from around Asia. He was urged to do so by George Freeman and especially Madame Cama and Krishnavarma from Paris. The latter two arranged his appointment as a teacher of Urdu at the School of Foreign Languages at Tokyo University through R. D. Tata of the prominent industrialist Tata family and one of the chief supporters of the Indo-Japanese Association. In Tokyo, Barkatullah threw himself into anti-imperialist lecturing and writing, mainly as the editor of the journal *Islamic Fraternity*. In general, he merged his pan-Islamism with pan-Asian thinking. He not only conversed with Japanese nationalists and pan-Asianist intellectuals like Okawa Shumei, but also with pan-Asian military strategists. At the India House in Tokyo, he invited members of the Japanese elite for lectures by Indian speakers and, as a pan-Asianist, he declared that 'India would regain her liberty one day through the combined assistance of China and Japan'.[21] Conversely, Barkatullah exchanged ideas about the 'world religion' status of Buddhism and Islam from a comparative perspective with the Zen Buddhist master Shaku Soen and the earlier mentioned global Buddhist missionary from Ceylon, Anagarika Dharmapala.[22] Both Buddhists had spoken at the World's Parliament of Religions in Chicago and Dharmapala's reformist Buddhism had largely come about through close cooperation with Theosophists. At the Chicago Parliament, 'despite the veiled fierceness of his growing Buddhist nationalism', however, Dharmapala was particularly admired as the 'Eastern Christ'.[23]

In 1911, Barkatullah travelled to St. Petersburg, Istanbul and Cairo, and reconnected himself with Krishnavarma and other revolutionary contacts. In the wake of the Balkan Wars of 1912–1913 and inspired by the Young Turks, he became completely convinced of the idea of overthrowing British rule in India with the help of the Ottomans and the Germans. Crucial here was his association with the Indian Ghadar ('Revolt') party,[24] a global Indian revolutionary network established in 1913 by predominantly Punjabi immigrants, and with Har Dayal among its leaders, on the West Coast of the United States and

---

21   Fischer-Tiné, "Indian Nationalism": 342.
22   Samee Siddiqui, "Parallel Lives or Interconnected Histories?: Anagarika Dharmapala and Muhammad Barkatullah's 'World Religioning' in Japan", *Modern Asian Studies*, 56, 4, 2022: 1329–1352.
23   Ruth Harris, *Guru to the World: The Life and Legacy of Vivekananda*, Cambridge, Mass.: The Belknap Press of Harvard University Press, 2022: 128.
24   With *Ghadar*, Ghadarites referred to the Indian Revolt of 1857, yet they extended the meaning of the term also to 'freedom'.

Canada. The masthead of its newspaper *Ghadar* (published in Punjabi, Urdu, Hindi and English) of which Barkatullah became the editor after Har Dayal was expelled from the United States, had the following motto: 'O People of India, Arise and Take up your Swords'. The movement's message soon spread to India and Indian diasporic communities around the world, and Barkatullah spoke on behalf of Ghadar in Japan.

When his contract at Tokyo University was not renewed due to pressure by the British government, Barkatullah returned to the United States in 1914. Following the famous Komagata Maru incident in Vancouver (see Chapter One, footnote 57) and the outbreak of the First World War, he emerged as one of the leaders of Ghadar. In his numerous speeches in the United States and Canada and in print, Barkatullah urged Indians to return to their homeland and launch an uprising against the British. Soon after Britain declared war against Germany, then, the following 'Declaration of War' appeared in *Ghadar* intended for Indians in the global diaspora:

> O Warriors! The opportunity you have been looking for has arrived. Arise, brave ones!
> Quickly [...] We want all brave and self-sacrificing warriors who can raise revolt [...]
>
> Salary: death
> Reward: martyrdom
> Pension: freedom
> Field of Battle: Hindustan.[25]

In 1915, Ghadarites boldly aimed to spark a violent rebellion across India, among other things, by robberies and attempts to persuade Indian troops to join their fold. Through their global network, and often with the help of German agents, with whom they had been in contact already before the War,[26] they exploited the neutrality of states such as the Dutch East Indies and Siam to smuggle arms and propaganda into British India. In the end, nonetheless,

---

25   As cited in: Ramnath, *Haj to Utopia*: 1.
26   In the United States, George Freeman served as a contact between Ghadarites and German agents, and generally Irish American revolutionaries played an important role to what led to the well-known 1917 'Hindu Conspiracy Case' against 35 persons, including 17 Indians and 9 German citizens, 'for violating American neutrality by using the United States as a base for German schemes to promote rebellion against the British Raj' (Silvestri, *Ireland and India*: 26).

FIGURE 32   Revolutionaries on mission: Muhammad Barkatullah, German medical officer
               Dr Karl Becker, Raja Mahendra Pratap and Turkish officer Kasim Bey on a
               Euphrates River boat, Mesopotamia, photographer unknown, 1915
               COURTESY OF THE STIFTUNG BIBLIOTHECA AFGHANICA, BUBENDORF

the Ghadar rebellion failed, mostly because plans were repeatedly foiled by
British spies.[27]

In that same year, Barkatullah arrived in Berlin on a German passport. As a
member of the Berlin Indian Independence Committee, he became involved
in the German-Ottoman scheme of a propagating a *jihad* against the British,
French and Russians by writing pamphlets in various languages and speaking to Indian Muslim prisoners of war to recruit them for this cause. He
joined the Oskar Niedermayer-Werner Otto Hentig mission (figure 32) together
with the maverick Indian revolutionary Raja Mahendra Pratap. This combined German-Turkish-Indian initiative aimed to persuade King Habibullah
of Afghanistan to declare war against the British. In Istanbul, the members of
the mission collected letters from the Sultan and, accompanied by Ottoman
agents and with large quantities of gold, arms and ammunition, they continued through Persia to Afghanistan. In Kabul, the Provisional Government
of India was established in December 1915, with Mahendra Pratap as president and Barkatullah as its prime minister. Besides publishing seditionist

27   By 1917, around 8,000 Ghadarites had returned to Punjab and by the end of the war
     more than 1,500 of them had been (temporarily) detained on suspicion of revolutionary
     activity.

newspapers, the Indian revolutionaries succeeded in recruiting Indians in Afghanistan and freeing Indian political prisoners in Kabul. Yet, Habibullah carefully safeguarded Afghanistan's neutrality and, despite the increasing bellicose opposition from within Afghan society, chose not to support the mission. Everything came to a complete standstill then with the signing of the Anglo-Afghan Treaty in 1919 by Habibullah's son and successor Amanullah Khan, which made Afghanistan into a buffer zone between British and Russian interests in the region.

In the meantime, Barkatullah and Mahendra Pratap had gone to Moscow to negotiate with the Bolsheviks. They were received by Lenin and, while being neither a communist nor a socialist, Barkatullah was impressed by the man and his ideology. Hence, in his subsequent writings and speeches in Tashkent and elsewhere (which were often held for the new propaganda bureau, Sovinterprop), he gave a pan-Islamic slant to the usual Bolshevik propaganda and overall tried to unite the Muslims of Central Asia for the anti-imperialist struggle. Yet, in 1922, Barkatullah had to depart for Germany for the treatment of an illness. Afterwards, he attended numerous European anti-imperial gatherings and met Indian nationalists like Jawaharlal Nehru. In particular, he became an ardent supporter of the revival of the Caliphate as a marker of the unity of the 'Muslim world'. For a long time, indeed, Barkatullah had been critical of Sultan Abdul Hamid's authoritarianism and, accordingly, in his last major work, *The Khilafat* (1924), he argued that the role of the Caliph had to be limited to that of being a spiritual leader alone. In 1925, he issued a declaration from Paris appealing to Muslims worldwide to send their representatives to Mecca and Medina and select their spiritual leader. Although one year later the General Islamic Congress for the Caliphate did indeed take place at the famous *Al-Azhar* Seminary in Cairo (without Barkatullah present), this initiative was unsuccessful. In the next year, Barkatullah told the Communist International (Comintern) leadership that the effort to lead revolution from outside India had failed: 'The whole thing falls into the hands of the English agents with the only result that the true Indian revolutionaries are being exposed and put to all sorts of trouble by the police'.[28] During his visit, together with Mahendra Pratap, to San Francisco for Ghadar's 1927 annual conference, then, Barkatullah died after long suffering from his chronic diabetes.

Surely, one should not be too idealistic about the global network of Indian revolutionaries in the context of anti-imperial internationalism, as some contemporary scholars undoubtedly are in their eagerness to revise the histori-

---

28   As cited in Harper, *Underground Asia*: 581.

ography of the Indian nationalist movement. For long periods, the uprooted lives of these cosmopolitan – but simultaneously no doubt often also narrow-minded – Indian revolutionaries were far from inspirational but, to the contrary, physically and emotionally challenging and, furthermore, without connectivity to the movement(s) of which they wished to form a part. Also, there were often quarrels within the network, as for example between Krishnavarma and both Har Dayal and Madame Cama in Paris.[29] In the very moment of unfolding events, things must have looked rather bleak and chaotic to them: a world full of mistranslations, misfortunes, deceitful alliances and schisms, wherein despite all the wheeling and dealing often little was achieved. Historical sources are problematic too. The British authorities generally tended to overinflate the impact of Indian revolutionaries in their numerous reports and no doubt subsequent Indian nationalist writings did the same. On the other hand, revolutionaries such as Raja Mahendra Pratap envisaged themselves as heroes in their own writings.[30] Be that as it may, the writings and speeches of Indian revolutionaries undoubtedly contributed to the fact that the Indian freedom call became an issue for debate around the world. Furthermore, they influenced Indian nationalists to be more radical, which in turn urged the British colonizers to allow more Indian participation in the colonial government.

Yet, how did Indian revolutionary ideas relate to Romantic nationalist thought? To begin with, they were all animated by a Romantic devotion to revolutionary resistance, while gaining inspiration from Italian, Irish and Russian revolutionaries, and in general followed unrealistic goals. Again, like Mazzini and other exiled European Romantic nationalists, they yearned for a triumphal return to their nation. Even though Mahatma Gandhi opposed their use of violence, he simultaneously recognized that Indian revolutionaries drew on the same principles as his non-violent *satyagraha* movement (about which more in the next section), namely, their love of their country, the principle of *swaraj* that guided them, and the willingness to suffer and sacrifice their lives. Expectedly, the slogan Vande Mataram was used by Indian revolutionaries worldwide. Since 1909, Madame Cama's Indian Society in Paris published the weekly paper *Vande Mataram* and earlier she had already co-designed the 'Flag of Indian Independence' with these very same words in *Devanagari*

---

29   Sareen, *Indian Revolutionary*: 43.

30   Raja Mahendra Pratap, *My Life Story of Fiftyfive Years: December 1886-December 1941*, Dehradun World Fedaration, 1947; Carolien Stolte, "'Enough of the Great Napoleons!' Raja Mahendra Pratap's Pan-Asian Projects (1929–1939), *Modern Asian Studies*, 46, 2, 2012: 403–423.

on it.[31] Significantly, the embryonic, but often intense, nationalism of Indian revolutionaries generally transcended divisions by religion, language, regional background, caste and class. Yet, at the same time, Vinayak Damodar Savarkar was one of the founders of the political ideology Hindutva and, over time, for instance, Har Dayal basically emerged as Hindu nationalist thinker too.

In contrast to Savarkar and Har Dayal (but not Krishnavarma), Muhammad Barkatullah preached Hindu-Muslim unity throughout his life. Moreover, partially because of his learned Muslim background, his Romantic nationalism was of a different kind. Barkatullah's Islamic universalist ideas are of particular interest. He generally argued that the Golden Age of Islam existed from the time of the Prophet Muhammad until that of the third Caliph Osman. By using reason, he continued, Muslims had to revive those earlier times by combining European technology and ideas with what was 'true' in Islam. Barkatullah particularly underlined that 'Muslim leaders had forgotten the egalitarian ethos inherent within Islam'.[32] Overall, he believed in the idea of 'spiritual Asia' but he simultaneously made it clear that Islamic universalism and Sufism in particular had as much to offer as Hinduism or Buddhism. Closely related was his notion of the importance of the Caliph as spiritual leader of the 'Muslim world'. Like other pan-Islamists, as well as Muhammad Iqbal (who, as already said, was certainly not a pan-Islamist), Barkatullah adhered to the novel conception of Islam as a universal religion comparable to the universalities of Christianity and the Enlightenment. The 'true' modern Muslim was, in his opinion, as enlightened and tolerant as the modern (Christian) Westerner. By propagating their modern visions of Islam, then, Barkatullah, Iqbal and others presented Islam as a 'world religion' along the lines of Protestant Christianity.[33]

---

31 Based on the so-called 'Calcutta Flag' of 1906, the green, yellow and red fields of the 'Flag of Indian Independence' (raised by Madame Cama at the Internationalist Socialist Conference in Stuttgart, Germany, in 1907) represent consecutively Islam, Hinduism and Buddhism. The crescent moon and the sun again symbolize Islam and Hinduism, respectively. The eight lotuses in the upper register represent the eight provinces of British India. In 1914, the design was adopted as the emblem of the Indian Independence Committee in Berlin and later it would serve as one of the templates for the current national flag of India.

32 Siddiqui, "Coupled Internationalisms": 30.

33 Tomoko Masuzawa, *The Invention of World Religions: Or, How European Universalism was Preserved in the Language of Pluralism*, Chicago: Chicago University Press, 2005.

Mobilization of the Masses: Gandhi and Ambedkar

Obviously, most Indians in the subcontinent were not aware of the existence of Indian revolutionaries in exile. Moreover, many of those who did often took their revolutionary programs with a grain of salt or, like Gandhi, contested their use of violence. Although revolutionary activities continued to be part of the freedom struggle during the coming decades (and, indeed, regularly so after clandestine contact with Indian National Congress (INC) members, including Gandhi),[34] the failure of the internationalist revolutionary movement was indisputably related to the fact that the anti-imperialism of Krishnavarma, Barakatullah and others was highly elitist. With its eclectic ideological make-up of pan-Asianist, pan-Islamist and other internationalist ideas, it stood far away from the (popular) cultural nationalism of the great majority of Indians, who simultaneously showed enormous loyalty to the British during the First World War. Most important, however, was the fact that Gandhi mobilized Indians on an unprecedented scale and made militant nationalism and socialist revolution the new main themes through his *satyagraha* ('truth force'), a philosophy as well as a method of mass agitation that prohibited the use of violence.

Gandhi condemned Madan Lal Dingra's assassination of Sir William Curzon Wyllie in London (as discussed in the Introduction) and, in response, he wrote one of his main publications, *Hind Swaraj* or 'Indian Home Rule' (1909), in the form of a dialogue between a 'reader' (an Indian revolutionary) and an 'editor' (Gandhi himself).[35] The pamphlet became the foundation of Gandhi's first *satyagraha* mass campaign against the Rowlatt Act of 1919 – the biggest anti-British upsurge in the subcontinent since 1857. The Act specifically targeted Indian revolutionaries by establishing wartime laws in peacetime India. Gandhi and Indian nationalist politicians claimed that this diverged from the liberal Montagu-Chelmsford constitutional reforms promised in exchange for India's cooperation and support during the First World War. Due to the 1919 *satyagraha*, the Rowlatt Act was never implemented at a national level and, during the following decades, Gandhi initiated three similar mass campaigns, namely, the Non-Cooperation Movement of 1920–1922, which overlapped,

34 Durba Ghosh, *Gentlemanly Terrorists: Political Violence and the Colonial State in India, 1919–1947*, New York: Cambridge University Press, 2017 and Kama Maclean, *A Revolutionary History of Interwar India: Violence, Image, Voice and Text*, New York: Oxford University Press, 2015.

35 M. K. Gandhi, *'Hind Swaraj' and Other Writings*, edited by Anthony J. Parel, Cambridge: Cambridge University Press, 1997.

albeit in thorny ways, with the Khilafat Movement; the Civil Disobedience Movement of 1930–1934; and the Quit India Movement of 1942. What is often forgotten, however, is that these *satyagrahas* were simultaneously accompanied by the use of violence by common Indians, revolutionaries and an increasingly repressive colonial state – although ultimately of course freedom was negotiated not seized.

The concept of *satyagraha* remains indeed a most intriguing example of the making of Romantic nationalist thought in the context of the global circulation of ideas. Finding common ground between the work of Tolstoy and *bhakti* poets like Tulsidas, Kabir and Mirabai, Gandhi developed it first in South Africa to counter the racial discrimination against Asian immigrants – for, to be clear, he himself continued to be racist towards black Africans.[36] While it is generally assumed that the Jain-Hindu concept of *ahimsa* (non-violence) was foundational to *satyagraha*, this was solely because Gandhi himself claimed it to be so. Only in the wake of the anti-Rowlatt Act campaign, he specifically reinterpreted the traditional meaning of *ahimsa* as 'non-injury' or 'non-killing' into 'non-violence'. In fact, he was the first person to consciously coin the English term 'non-violence' and to translate the Sanskrit word *ahimsa* into it and, hence, the term cannot be found in English dictionaries published before the Gandhian era.[37]

On the whole, Gandhi may be called a Romantic 'primitivist'. In *Hind Swaraj*, he argued that Indians should reject the 'disease' of European civilization, in particular its modern features such as railways, machinery and medicine.[38] Its adoption would lead to 'British rule without the British' even if India became independent. India's freedom, he argued, was not political independence from the British, but a revival of her moral roots and what he saw as the value of her own traditional civilization. To the contrary, he advocated self-sufficient Indian 'village republics' as the soul of the nation and as an

---

36   In 1897, for instance, Gandhi wrote to the Natal Legislative Assembly that Indians should not be 'dragged down to the position of a raw Kaffir' because both the English and Indians 'spring from a common stock, called the Indo-Aryan', and to authorize this statement he refers to Max Müller, Arthur Schopenhauer and William Jones. As cited by Arundhati Roy in B. R. Ambedkar, *Annihilation of Caste* (first published in 1936), edited and annotated by S. Anand and introduced with the essay 'The Doctor and the Saint' by Arundhati Roy, London: Verso, 2014: 67.

37   Eijiro Hazama, "Unravelling the Myth of Gandhian Non-Violence: Why Did Gandhi Connect His Principle of Satyagraha with the Hindu Notion of Ahimsa?", *Modern Intellectual History*, 20, 1, 2023: 116–140.

38   Simultaneously, however, he believed in the rule of modern law by which everyone is equally treated, bound to one another and to their government.

alternative to industrial capitalism. All this was imaginary, of course, because Gandhi had no knowledge of Indian village life when he wrote *Hind Swaraj* since he had only lived in towns in Kathiawar until his departure for London at the age of nineteen. Over time, he advocated ascetism and poverty as a means of moral resistance and self-sacrificing service to the nation in defiance of the decadent and materialist West, whose universal claims for the future of humanity had been simultaneously exposed by the First World War as being untruthful. It has been argued that this ideal of 'renunciation' had a background in the pietism of his traditional trading caste Vaishnavite upbringing.[39] Yet, at the same time, anti-materialism was a global phenomenon that was equally propagated by Western counter-cultural intellectuals, including some of Gandhi's heroes like Lev Tolstoy, Ralph Waldo Emerson and Henry David Thoreau, who themselves in turn were much inspired by Indian philosophy. More than these Westerners, nonetheless, Gandhi propagated poverty to become a cultural practice in India, a factor of national identity and an individual expression of self-realization.

Gandhi's idea of self-sufficient Indian village republics was to a great extent inspired by Henry James Sumner Maine's *Village Communities of the East and the West* (1871). Maine based his book on his experiences in India between 1862 and 1869 as (legal) advisor to the government, as well as on Orientalist accounts of the 'Indian village community', which he argued could shed light on the origins of the Teutonic *mark* and the Russian *mir* in terms of a common Aryan past. This debate about village communities had a parallel version in Russia, where it became the scholarly basis of the Narodnik movement, to which Tolstoy initially felt attracted. As already said, the Russian writer left a great impression on Gandhi's mind. Little known, however, remains the fact that Tolstoy himself came to a clear vision of the concepts of 'non-resistance' and the 'law of love' (he never used the term 'non-violence') after reading a German translation of Thiruvalluvar's *Tirukkural*.[40] It was through the Russian's 'A Letter to a Hindu' (1908) written to Taraknath Das, editor of the Indian newspaper *Free Hindustan*, in which the piece was published,[41] that Gandhi came to know about this earlier mentioned Tamil classic as well. Conversely, Tolstoy's planned community Yasnaya Polyana contributed to Gandhi's

---

39   Douglas Haynes, *Rhetoric and Ritual in Colonial India: The Shaping of the Public sphere in Surat City, 1852–1928*, New Delhi: Oxford University Press, 1992.

40   The first German translation of excerpts was made in 1803; Tolstoy probably read the first complete one by Karl Graul (1856).

41   Taraknath Das, a close associate of Muhammad Barkatullah, had his *Free Hindustan* published in New York by John Devoy's *Gaelic American* press.

Romantic vision of a 'village republic' at Sabarmati Ashram, which he established in Ahmedabad in 1917. Before that, Rabindranath Tagore had already
been influenced through his correspondence with the Russian in founding his
school at Shantiniketan.

To create self-sufficient Indian village republics, Gandhi began a rural
reconstruction program that envisaged participation in a moral, alternative
economy. Through the All-India Spinners' Association (1925) and the All-India
Village Industries Association (1934), he promoted *khadi* or homespun cotton – which to be clear was more expensive than imported cloth and its use
therefore required pecuniary sacrifice for the nation. Still today, India has its
government supported *khadi* retail stores, although these often function at a
loss. Within the subcontinent, the porous quality of coarse homespun, hard-
wearing fabrics was traditionally regarded as without power, boorish and even
impure. To the contrary, *swadeshi* songs lauded homespun cloth for their naturalness, purity and lack of sophistication, and generally associated it with the
authentic countryside of the (Bengali) Motherland. Likewise, Abanindranath
Tagore's *Bharat Mata* carries homespun cotton as an emblem of *swadeshi* aspiration (figure 7).

In general, the *khadi* movement 'sought to protect the values of indigenous
craft traditions against the impersonality of all mill production and the drab
uniformity of chemical dyes'.[42] In doing so, of course, it was to some degree
indebted to artistic revival communicated by the Arts and Crafts Movement.
Gandhi greatly admired John Ruskin, yet he went further than both the British
propagators of arts and crafts and the *swadeshi* nationalists by redefining the
production of cloth through spinning into a spiritual act – a moral duty that
was fundamental to the making of the nation, if not to a return to the Golden
Age of bucolic Indian village communities. Accordingly, numerous (popular)
images of him include a spinning wheel (*charkha*), although generally of the
modern portable box variant rather than the upright traditional one, as an
iconic symbol of the nation (figure 33). For a period, in fact, the traditional
charkha contended for a place in the national flag, but in the end Buddhist
Emperor Ashoka's *dharma* wheel (*chakra*) was chosen (figure 33).[43] While

42   C. A. Bayly, "The Origins of Swadeshi (Home Industry): Cloth and Indian Society,
      1700–1930" (first published in 1986), as reprinted in: C. A. Bayly, *Origins of Nationality in
      South Asia: Patriotism and Ethical Government in the Making of Modern India*, New Delhi:
      Oxford University Press, 1998, Chapter Six: 198.
43   Rebecca M. Brown, "Spinning without Touching the Wheel: Anticolonialism, Indian
      Nationalism, and the Deployment of Symbol", *Comparative Studies of South Asia, Africa
      and the Middle East*, 29, 2, 2009: 230–243.

FIGURE 33   Gandhi and Mother India by H. L. Khatri, published by Chimanlal Chhotalal &
Co, Ahmedabad, c. 1947

dress had always been a marker of caste, Gandhi aimed to introduce *khadi* also to create uniformity of appearance. White homespun became the uniform – as did the 'Gandhi cap' (see book cover), designed by the Mahatma himself – of the members of the INC. To the world, this undeniably presented a convincing visual image of the unity of the anti-imperialist Indian nation.

In the long-term, nonetheless, the anti-caste movements of, amongst others, Iyothee Thass, Jyotirao Phule, Periyar, Narayan Guru (who was active in Malabar and Travancore) and especially Bhimrao Ramji Ambedkar proved more important – both in terms of mass mobilization and revolutionary thought – to the development of modern India than Gandhi's *satyagrahas*.[44] Into the twentieth century, these anti-caste leaders became truly national heroes for lower castes and untouchables (called Dalits and officially 'Scheduled Castes' today). Obviously, they rebelled against traditional Indian society rather than against British rule, but they equally forged (and repeatedly so in a Romantic nationalist manner) what may be called lower caste and untouchable 'nations'. Due to their efforts, members of the last groups are nowadays occupying positions in the government. For instance, K. R. Narayan was India's vice-president (1992–1997) and president (1997–2002); K. G. Balakrishnan was India's Supreme Court's first chief justice (2007–2010); and between 1995 and 2012 the leader of the Bahujan Samaj Party, Mayawati, served four times as chief minister of Uttar Pradesh, the largest state of India. Unquestionably, the efforts of Ambedkar had the most profound long-term impact.[45] He was an untouchable himself but eventually studied in Britain and the United States. While Ambedkar is considered as the prime architect of the Constitution of India, his criticism of caste and Hinduism at large was definitely more important and, accordingly, statues of him are present in the village areas inhabited by untouchables throughout the subcontinent.

In his *Annihilation of Caste* (1936), Ambedkar was the first modern Indian thinker who asked for the eradication, rather than reform, of the caste system and, indeed, the Hindu tradition in general. Already for some years, he had been in serious debate about this with Gandhi and their discussion was included in the second edition of the book. Without any doubt, Ambedkar was Gandhi's most profound critic. While the Mahatma argued that caste could be the basis for collective harmony in society and found support for this in the Bhagavad Gita, to the contrary, Ambedkar saw it solely as an instrument

44   Christophe Jaffrelot, *India's Silent Revolution: The Rise of the Lower Castes in North India*, London: Hurst, 2003.

45   Christophe Jaffrelot, *Dr. Ambedkar and Untouchability: Analysing and Fighting Caste*, London: Hurst, 2005.

of oppression. Closely related, he was critical of Gandhi's Romantic idea of an India of village republics because it would only mean a return to squalor, poverty and ignorance for the vast mass of the people. Machinery and modern civilization, he argued, were 'indispensable for emancipating man from leading the life of a brute, and for providing him with leisure and for making a life of culture possible'.[46]

Like the Tamil anti-caste activist Iyothee Thass before him, Ambedkar became a Buddhist in 1956. Moreover, he led half a million of his untouchable followers doing the same in a public conversion ceremony. Still, he was critical of traditional Buddhist practices and precepts. Eventually, he went further than Thass and formulated his own form of neo-Buddhism, known as *navayana* ('new vehicle'), with a dominant focus on social equality and class struggle. In 1955, he founded the Bharatiya Buddha Mahasabha ('Buddhist Society of India'). His posthumously published *The Buddha and His Dhamma* (1957) became the central text of *navayana* Buddhism. Overall, Ambedkar reinterpreted the Buddhist past for the future in a utopian manner, whereby he romantically saw his *navayana* Buddhism as a movement working along the lines of the *bhakti* tradition. Also, he was responsible for the fact that the Ashokan wheel, rather than Gandhi's *charkha*, ended up on the flag of Independent India, partly because the symbol transcended Hindu-Muslim antagonism.

---

46   B. R. Ambedkar, *What Congress and Gandhi have done to the Untouchables*, Bombay: Thacker & Co, 1945: 283–284.

Epilogue

This book investigated the possibility of the use of Romantic nationalism as a comparative global concept by looking at the (British) Indian case. It argued that since the Enlightenment, European and Indian Romantic nationalist thought became closely intertwined and afterwards principally developed in similar ways, although due to the internal dynamics of Indian society things of course often worked out differently in the subcontinent at the same time. The theme of (Aryan) invasion became largely fundamental to both European and Indian Romantic nationalisms. On the one hand, it allowed original populations to claim the existence of a Golden Age before the coming of foreign intruders. On the other, invaders could declare that they were the harbingers of civilization. Thus, in Britain for instance, the Norman Conquest became a crucial point of reference for Romantic nationalists – as popularized in the stories about William the Conqueror, King Arthur, Ivanhoe, Richard Lionheart and Robin Hood – and the subsequent creation of British national identity was complemented by the simultaneous making of Irish, Welsh and Scottish national identities, as these Celtic peoples saw themselves as the original inhabitants of the isles. Likewise, in India, historical research led to a greater awareness and definition of the past of the nation, which at the same time was imagined in relation to other (internal) nations. Among other things, this resulted in the Aryan-Dravidian divide, the dominant notion of Muslims as 'invaders' and demarcations of different nations (Bengali, Maratha, Rajput, Sikh and so on).

Further, Joep Leerssen's earlier mentioned definition of European Romantic nationalism as 'the celebration of the nation (defined in its language, history and cultural character) as an inspiring ideal for artistic expression; and the instrumentalization of that expression in political consciousness-raising' has great resemblances in the Indian context. In relation to the first part of the definition, namely, 'the celebration of the nation (defined in its language, history and cultural character) as an inspiring ideal for artistic expression', this volume discussed a wide range of revivalist movements (in arts and crafts, music, architecture, folklore and so on) that romantically fed the cultivation of Indian national culture. Yet, a crucial point of divergence was that, while European Romantic nationalists often found the essence of the nation in folk traditions, in India this phenomenon largely remained the focus of regional nations alone – the main exception being the adherence of Rabindranath Tagore and others to the *bhakti* movement as the true soul of the Indian nation.[1] To the contrary, the north Indian Aryan and south Indian Tamil nations, as well as in a different way the Indian Muslim nation, predominantly discovered pride in past 'classical' Golden Ages. In this, both Aryan and Tamil Hindus were undeniably strengthened by the fact that Europeans had defined India as the original civilization of humanity. Rather than seeing themselves as backward peoples, Hindus found pride in being the heirs of a civilization that once had been a teacher to the world. For them, both their attention to the past and borrowing from modern knowledge was no more than reclaiming their patrimony. By rooting themselves in ancient and self-renewing moral communities, Hindus increasingly gained self-confidence in a fast-changing world and, accordingly, felt romantically inspired to dedicate themselves to the historical destiny of their nation(s).

In the context of the imperial encounter and the global circulation of ideas, the Indian Romantic celebration of national culture was more than 'an inspiring ideal for artistic expression'. While Indians directly experienced that their civilizational identity was under siege, cultivation of national culture became more important to them than for their European counterparts. Morally and spiritually, Indians armed themselves and their nation(s) by redefining their cultural traditions along modern lines. Moreover, in doing so, they found ways to take over state power on their own terms. Thus, in overlap with the second part of Leerssen's definition ('the instrumentalization of that expression in political consciousness-raising'), in India too, a (nostalgic) looking back to the past of the nation was followed by nationalist political agendas that invented the past and future at the same time. Here, as colonial subjects, Indian nationalists had obviously less space to move around in comparison to their European counterparts. Although Indian revolutionaries found alternative ways for their initiatives in a global underground network of anti-imperialist activists, they largely could not escape British surveillance.[2] That said, rather than suppressing the development of the Indian nation, imprisonment of Indian nationalists, who in British eyes behaved too radical, enhanced political conscious–raising among the wider population, as each imprisonment was breaking news and discussed widely.

----

1   Intriguingly, Johann Gottfried Herder, who is often seen as the founder of cultural nationalism, especially as propagator of the term 'folk' ('Volk'), remains unmentioned in the South Asian context.
2   Michael Silvestri, *Policing 'Bengali Terorism' in India and the World: Imperial Intelligence and Revolutionary Nationalism, 1905–1939*, New York: Palgrave Macmillan, 2019.

Simultaneously, Indian nationalists repeatedly were in conflict amongst each other. Mahatma Gandhi openly criticized revolutionary nationalists for their propagation of violent struggle. Shyamji Krishnavarma quarreled with both Har Dayal and Madame Cama in Paris. In fact, Rabindranath Tagore, who perhaps emerged as Asia's most famous early twentieth century global intellectual and, through his travels and writings, was a key figure in a network of counter-cultural intellectuals and artists worldwide, questioned nationalism at large because he believed Indians should not play the game of the West but, instead, had to stay true to themselves.[3] Over time and for different reasons, amongst others, Aurobindo Ghosh, Ananda Coomaraswamy and Abanindranath Tagore distanced themselves from the Indian nationalist movement.

Indian Romantic nationalism differed from its European equivalent because of the imperial encounter. In contrast to what happened in Europe, the Indian intelligentsia had to deal with colonial rule and modern European thought, science and technology in one go. In the process, they selectively refashioned European ideas and practices in the light of their own self-esteem, (regional) patriotisms and traditions, and it is this cultural continuity that makes Indian Romantic nationalism dissimilar. At the same time, the role of both European Orientalist knowledge production and the colonial state was crucial to the cultivation of modern Indian culture. The British fascination with Indian civilization, although repeatedly imaginary, was striking. Of course, the dominant position of Orientalist knowledge to the colonial state's activities (the census, land revenue reports, archaeological surveys and so on) had much to do with the control of the subcontinent and its inhabitants, yet every so often it was the work of individuals, such as William Jones and James Tod, who were genuinely and generally romantically interested in things Indian. All the same, following their preoccupation with Sanskrit texts, religion and caste in particular, the British defined Indian society in decisive ways. In their turn, Indian intellectuals became not only very familiar with European colonial/Orientalist knowledge, but they usually reinterpreted it from their own (moral) perspectives.

Thus, Indian Romantic nationalist thought was to a great extent the result of this complex interaction between colonial/Orientalist knowledge production and Indian intellectual appropriation. The Aryan-Dravidian divide, Golden

---

3 Bob van der Linden, *Music and Empire in Britain and India: Identity, Internationalism, and Cross-Cultural Communication*, New York: Palgrave Macmillan, 2013: 26–28; Rabindranath Tagore, *Nationalism*, with an introduction by Ramachandra Guha, New Delhi: Penguin, 2009 (first published in 1917).

Age thinking and a stricter political adherence to 'religion' and caste were some of its main consequences. In the end, however, Indian agency, rather than that of the British, was decisive in taking society into a future that both colonizer and colonized could not have foreseen. Indeed, due to the colonial context, the study of Romantic nationalism in India shows better than in the European case that the nation as a moral community is not build from scratch but, to the contrary, on the reinterpretation and cultivation of pre-modern tradition into national culture.

In addition, this book underlined that, at least from Ram Mohan Roy onwards, Indian Romantic nationalists actively participated in the global circulation of ideas. The positive reception and reinterpretation of Walter Scott's historical novels, Giuseppe Mazzini's ideas and the calls for both pan-Islamism and pan-Asianism in opposition to 'the West' were typical to the period. For all its emphasis on localism, the *swadeshi* movement was a rather global event that brought together Theosophists, Japanese and Indian pan-Asianists, as well as members of the Irish Literary Revival, the Arts and Crafts Movement and so on. To different degrees, all disparate individuals involved were critical about colonialism and industrial progress. While the Khilafat Movement ended with the abolishment of the Ottoman Caliphate, the Indian urge for pan-Asianism declined after Japan became increasingly militaristic. Well known is Rabindranath Tagore's criticism of Japanese nationalism spoken out during his tour of Japan in 1916 (figure 34).[4]

Even so, the linking up of Indian Romantic nationalism and pan-Asianism repeatedly came to the fore in the following decades. Tagore became fascinated with the idea of 'Greater India' or the fact that expanding land and maritime trade in Asia since around 500 BCE had resulted in the spread of Hindu and Buddhist traditions to Central and, especially through the south Indian Chola Empire, Southeast Asia. The term was popularized by Bengali scholars in the 1920s and by and large connected to the notion of Asian spirituality.[5] It resulted in Tagore's extensive 1927-tour through Southeast Asia. In chorus, Ananda Coomaraswamy in *History of Indian and Indonesian Art* (1926) located the pinnacle of India's 'greatest achievement in art' not in the subcontinent but on Java.[6] Later, India's first prime minister Jawaharlal Nehru

---

4 Tagore, *Nationalism*.

5 Susan Bayly, "Imagining 'Greater India': French and Indian Visions of Colonialism in the Indic Mode", *Modern Asian Studies*, 38, 3, 2004: 703–744; Carolien Stolte and Harald Fischer-Tiné, "Imagining Asia in India: Nationalism and Internationalism (ca. 1905–1940), *Comparative Studies in Society and History*, 54, 1, 2012: 65–92.

6 Ananda K. Coomaraswamy, *Swadeshi and Art*, Madras: Ganesh & Co, 1912: 3.

FIGURE 34   Rabindranath Tagore in Japan, photographer unknown, published by Bains
               News Service, 1916
               COURTESY OF THE LIBRARY OF CONGRESS, WASHINGTON

entered the international political stage as a pan-Asianist, for instance at the
1947 Asian Relations Conference in Delhi and the 1955 Afro-Asian Conference
in Bandung. His efforts ended of course with the Sino-Indian War of 1962.

Conversely, the propagation of Hindu universalism, especially since Swami
Vivekananda, and Islamic universalism (by Muhammad Iqbal, Muhammad
Barkatullah and others), as alternatives to Western moral claims to universalism bestowed upon the world by empire, was typical to Indian Romantic
nationalism and anti-colonial resistance at large. Indians thus aimed to change
the world through ideas that were partially informed by cultural traditions
and imaginaries. Yet, in doing so, they often reinterpreted their traditions,
literally and morally, in a Protestant manner into different 'world religions',
and this process continues up to today.[7] Hindutva propagators do not only
repeatedly put forward versions of Hindu universalism but, closely related and
expectedly, appropriate the notion of 'Greater India' in rather banal ways. The

---

7   Tomoko Masuzawa, *The Invention of World Religions: Or, How European Universalism was
    Preserved in the Language of Pluralism*, Chicago: Chicago University Press, 2005.

appearance of the idea of Indian spirituality is most significant in this context. Both Indians and Westerners referred to this essential feature of Indian
Romantic nationalist thought. The point, however, is that the idea originated
in Europe and its adoption by Indians was therefore a kind of 'reverse Orientalism'. Simultaneously, the concept remains something of an enigma because
Indians interpreted it in different ways. To begin with, Indian critiques of Western materialist progress echoed a mode of thinking that was widespread at the
time among Western (Romantic) philosophers and counter-cultural intellectuals (Theosophists and so on), who often felt alienated by the Christian Church
and, in its place, found spiritual solace in ideas from the ancient Sanskrit scriptures, such as reincarnation and the principle of *karma*.

Be that as it may, since Swami Vivekananda's smash hit speech at the
World's Parliament of Religions, an increasing number of Indian spiritual
gurus received great recognition in the West – something from which Gandhi,
Tagore and others undeniably profited. Although Vivekananda's 'aggressive
Hinduism' was the most extreme interpretation of Indian spirituality (even his
most devout followers Aurobindo Ghosh and Sister Nivedita eventually backed
off), it had the utmost long-term influence because it was largely adopted
by the advocates of Hindutva. Yet, numerous Hindu thinkers came up with
more ambiguous readings of Indian spirituality. To give but four examples.
Leading Indian nationalists reinterpreted the spiritual message of the Bhagavad Gita into a nationalist activist one that was surely less aggressive than
what Vivekananda propagated. Indian art music and *Bharatanatyam* dance
were redefined into national symbols of Hindu spirituality through modern
reforms, which not only brought music into the public sphere, but also to a
great extent disciplined the public behavior of performers and their practice.
Members of the Bengal School of *swadeshi* art explored new techniques to create spiritual national art works, while often preferring emotion over form. And
modern Hindu architects continue to adhere to the slogan 'Back to the Shilpa
Shastras' to provide an aura of spirituality to their newly build temples around
the world.

The case of Rabindranath Tagore deserves special mention. While he probably found most consolation in the spirituality of Bengali folk culture, he
simultaneously believed that the *bhakti* movement represented the soul of
the nation. In the end, however, he thought that the spiritual East was the necessary complement of the materialistic West and that nothing was exclusively
Western or Eastern anymore. In the view of the universal connectedness of
things, he believed that the West had to understand that 'the East has her con-

tribution to make to the history of civilization',[8] especially because the West had missed its own historicizing mission and had brought slavery rather than the envisioned freedom.[9] The future therefore, Tagore emphasized, was 'for those who are rich in moral ideals and not in mere things'.[10] Ultimately, he envisaged a scheme of things in which the best and the greatest thoughts and achievements of both the East and the West be offered to the welfare of humanity.

While Indian Romantic nationalist thought was elitist in its initial phase, in popular and recycled forms – as exemplified by several illustrations in this book – it soon mobilized wider audiences for the Indian nation(s) and this process continues until today. The enduring presence of legendary, albeit mainly Hindu, heroes in Indian cinema is one example and the idea of spiritual India – which particularly thrives in terms of yoga, as indeed both Swami Vivekananda and Aurobindo Ghosh would have liked it to happen – is another. Moreover, as to be expected in a country with a much greater linguistic diversity than Europe, the relationship between language and nation became increasingly important. Since the late nineteenth century, Indians had begun to identify themselves in modern ways with their regional nation based on language. Dissimilar from the European case, however, the desire for a distinct regional self and the development of an all-India national identity generally did not stand in opposition to each other. To the contrary, Indian unity was often strengthened by the numerous translations into local languages of for example: scriptures such as the Mahabharata and the Ramayana, novels (of Bankim Chandra Chatterjee, Rabindranath Tagore, Sarat Chandra Chatterjee and others) and the writings of nationalist leaders (Bal Gangadhar Tilak, Aurobindo Ghosh, Gandhi, Nehru and so on).

In chorus, the Indian National Congress (INC) was focused on national unity and, accordingly, downplayed any divisive demands on the way. Yet this situation changed when, during the Nehruvian era, the often newly created Indian states were confronted with an over-centralized national government, which represented a rigidifying alliance between the old colonial bureaucracy and Soviet-style planning. Ever since, regional nations have successfully lobbied for the creation of separate states based on language, including Orissa (Oriya), Tamil Nadu (Tamil), Punjab (Punjabi), Maharashtra (Marathi), Kerala (Malayalam), Andhra Pradesh (Telugu) and Karnataka (Kannada). In comparison to elsewhere in the world, Indian dedication to language has been rather

---

8   Tagore, *Nationalism*: 72.
9   Ibid.: 74.
10   Ibid.: 72.

extreme with Tamil and Telegu devotees committing suicide, respectively out of sheer Tamil language devotion and to demand a separate linguistic Telugu state.[11]

The Nation's Recoil

As in Europe, Aryanism surfaced as the grimmest legacy of Romantic nationalism in India. It transformed not only the Aryan-Dravidian linguistic difference into a racial one but, most significantly, also positioned Aryan Hindus in opposition to the Muslim 'invaders'. As discussed in Chapter Three, both the Aryan invasion theory and the search for the origins of the first Indians led to passionate discussions between north Indian Aryans and south Indian Dravidians. This debate only intensified after the archeological discovery of the Indus Civilization in 1924. The excavations at Harappa, Mohenjo-Daro and elsewhere in the northwestern parts of the subcontinent revealed an extensive urban culture with a population that used another language than Sanskrit, of which the script is still undeciphered. All this predated and hence directly questioned the theory of the arrival of a superior Aryan race bringing civilization to the subcontinent. But what was the continuity between the Indus Civilization and the later history of ancient India? Ever since, unsurprisingly, northern Hindus have argued that the Aryans had created the Indus Civilization, whereby they challenged the Aryan invasion theory at the same time. In their turn, as original habitants of the subcontinent, Tamils of course claimed the ancient urban culture in the Indus valley for themselves. In fact, they especially did so by emphasizing that Dravidian languages still exist in the Gangetic valley (Malto) and the Indus valley (Brahui), and that the *Rig Veda* contains traces of Dravidian languages (loanwords and retroflexion).[12]

Recently, the discussion has become even more heated because genetic research confirmed migrations of steppe pastoralists (with horses and spoke wheeled chariots, both of which were unknown to the Indus Civilization)

---

11   Lisa Mitchell, *Language, Emotion and Politics in South India: The Making of a Mother-Tongue*, Bloomington, IN: Indiana University Press, 2009: 1–2; Sumathi Ramaswamy, *Passions of the Tongue: Language Devotion in Tamil India, 1891–1970*, Berkeley, CA: University of California Press, 1997: 1. See also: Pritipuspa Mishra, *Language and the Making of Modern India: Nationalism and the Vernacular in Colonial Odisha, 1803–1956*, Cambridge: Cambridge University Press, 2020.

12   Nowadays philologists argue that the language of the Vedas is closely related to the language of the ancient Iranians, whose oldest text is the Avesta (c. 700 BCE).

into the subcontinent. Moreover, it underlined that the DNA of these invaders rapidly mixed with the local population during the long period of decline of the Indus Civilization, which was partially the result of environmental degradation and in any case not due to destruction by the invaders from the steppes. Accordingly, the geneticist David Reich wrote:

> The Hindutva ideology that there was no major contribution to Indian culture from migrants from outside South Asia is undermined by the fact that approximately half of the ancestry of Indians today is derived from multiple waves of mass migration from Iran and the Eurasian steppe within the last five thousand years.[13]

Earlier, however, Romila Thapar, the renowned Indian historian of ancient India, had already made the ultimate point about the relation between DNA analysis and the Aryan invasion theory (and indeed caste), namely, that Aryan is a cultural and linguistic category and not a racial and biological one.[14]

All the same, the Indian reality is that Hindutva chauvinists continue to use the ideology of Aryanism to distinguish Hindus from Muslims – as well as from lower castes and untouchables, and to a much lesser extent from Christians. As already mentioned, during the nineteenth century the term Arya conflated with that of (a) Hindu (Golden Age), and Hindu nationalists gained strength from this. Subsequently, in the wake of the establishment of the Muslim League (1906) and the Morley-Minto reforms (1909), several Hindu organizations were created to protect the rights of the Hindu community. The leaders of the Hindu Mahasabha and K. B. Hedgewar's Rashtriya Swayamsevak Sangh (RSS) criticized the INC as Muslim appeasers. To the contrary, they propagated the creation of a Hindu nation (*rashtra*), whereby they essentially saw Sikhs, Jains, Buddhists, lower castes and untouchables as Hindus, albeit in a hierarchical manner of course, with Brahmins at the top. Inspired by both European fascism and the idea of Maratha war bands led by Shivaji and his successors, the Maharashtrian Hedgewar also established squads of RSS storm troopers, of whom there are millions today. In *We, or the Nationhood Defined* (1939), Madhev Sadashiv Golwalker, the leader of the RSS from 1940 until his

---

13   David Reich, *Who We Are and How We Got Here: Ancient DNA and the New Science of the Human Past*, Oxford: Oxford University Press, 2018: 267. I am thankful to Erik van Ree for this reference and, moreover, for his comments on an earlier version of this book.

14   Romila Thapar, "Can Genetics Help Us Understand Indian Social History?", *Cold Spring Harbor Perspectives in Biology*, 6, 11, 2014: https://cshperspectives.cshlp.org/content/6/11/a008599.

death in 1973, straightforwardly rejected the Aryan invasion theory. This not only to strengthen the connection between the Hindu nation and territory, but specifically also to counter the appropriation of the theory by anti-caste movements. Among Hindutva chauvinists, this viewpoint of the indigenous-ness of the larger Aryan Hindu community (read: everyone except Muslims and Christians) became commonly accepted.

On the whole, the apostles of Hindutva 'took over the messianic, romantic, and insurrectionary aspects of Mazzini's thought and practice and made them their own'.[15] Indian revolutionary nationalists who were formerly seen as con-troversial by earlier generations of Indian nationalists, mainly of the INC, were redefined as Hindu national heroes, including Krishnavarma, Savarkar and Subhas Chandra Bose, who sought refuge in Hitler's Germany, imagined him-self as the *führer* of a free India and during the Second World War, with help of the Japanese, led the Indian National Army from Southeast Asia towards British India. As is well known, Mahatma Gandhi was killed by RSS member Nathuram Godse five months after the 1947 partition of British India into India and Pakistan – during which one million Indians lost their lives and almost twelve million lost their homes. According to Godse, Gandhi had favoured the political demands of Indian Muslims. When he later climbed the gallows, he carried a saffron flag,[16] a map of undivided India and, ironically, a copy of the Bhagavad Gita, Gandhi's 'spiritual dictionary'. Today, as a sign of the times, instead of Gandhi, numerous right-wing Hindus praise his murderer Godse. In fact, years before a volume about the Mahatma was published in the comic series *Amar Chitra Katha*, volumes about Savarkar and Subhas Chandra Bose already existed. Likewise, the series remediated revolutionary national-ists like Khudiram Bose, Bhagat Singh and Chandra Shekhar Azad.[17] Probably the greatest Hindutva hero, however, is the muscular and aggressive version of God Rama. An ever-increasing number of statues of him, and/or of his helper, the monkey God Hanuman, are to be found throughout the subcontinent and, naturally, the planned Rama statue in Ayodhya will be the tallest one in the world.

15   C. A. Bayly, "Liberalism at Large: Mazzini and Nineteenth-Century Indian Thought" in C. A. Bayly and E. F. Biagini, eds., *Giuseppe Mazzini and the Globalization of Democratic Nationalism, 1830–1920*, Oxford: Oxford University Press, 2008: 372.
16   Among Hindus (and Sikhs), the saffron flag is considered as a symbol of bravery. It served as the flag of the Marathas and subsequently was adopted by the RSS and the propagators of Hindutva in general.
17   Karline McLain, *India's Immortal Comic Books: Gods, Kings, and Other Heroes*, Blooming-ton, IN: Indian University Press, 2009.

While having been crucial to modern Indian history since the late nineteenth century, including in the INC, Hindu majority politics came straightforwardly out in the open with the growing dominance of the right-wing Bharatiya Janata Parishad (BJP), which is generally seen as the political arm of the RSS. From the 1990s onwards, it has been the major party in India besides the INC and, since 2019, it is the largest party in the Indian parliament. Many of its prominent leaders – such as current prime minister Narendra Modi, former prime minister Atal Bihari Vajpayee and senior leader L. K. Advani – are RSS members. In fact, since Modi was elected prime minister in 2014, Hindutva has mainstreamed into Indian politics. Furthermore, as a sort of 'counter revolution' of the Indian (upper caste) elites,[18] it has increasingly attracted Indians of lower caste and untouchable backgrounds (especially in the 2019 elections), who apparently felt their pride and sense of dignity restored, as Modi spoke about them as equal citizens of the 'Hindu nation' with a common enemy, namely, the Muslims. Earlier already, the BJP had courted alliances with castes categorized as 'Other Backward Class', groups that were asserting their rights in the reservations created by the implementation of the Mandal Commission in 1990. Once in power, it made evident attempts also to incorporate Ambedkar into the Hindutva pantheon.

Under BJP rule, reservations were extended to untouchables who had converted to Buddhism and Sikhism, but not to those who had done so to Christianity or Islam. As a matter of fact, despite that he committed himself to Hindutva, above all by being ruthlessly anti-Muslim, prime minister Narendra Modi is a Shudra and officially belongs to the 'Other Backward Class'. In view of his lower caste background, he increasingly projected himself as a charismatic populist 'father of the nation', a great unifier and a people's man. From 2014 onward, he relates emotionally to 'the poor', claiming that they are his priority, in the (at first monthly) radio program *Mann Ki Baat*. Thus, he appears to sacrifice his life for the people in actions devoid of all corruption. He has repeatedly called himself a fakir and, to confirm this image to the Indian public, he grew a white beard in 2020. By following this 'saintly politics', then, Modi adhered to the Indian Romantic nationalist idea of the selfless world renouncer, as did Mahatma Gandhi before him.[19]

The 2022 blockbuster *RRR* (*Raudram, Ranam, Rughiram*; Telugu for 'Rage, War, Blood'), directed by S. S. Rajamouli, reflects how Modi's Hindutva populism transcends regional and caste divisions. This originally Telugu film was

18   Christophe Jaffrelot, *Modi's India: Hindu Nationalism and the Rise of Ethnic Democracy*, Princeton, NJ: Princeton University Press, 2021: 457.
19   Ibid.: 463.

brought out simultaneously in Tamil, Kannada, Malayalam and Hindi. It fictionalizes the imagined interaction between two early twentieth century south Indian revolutionaries, Alluri Sitarama Raju (1897–1924) and Komaram Bheem (1901–1940),[20] who were of lower caste/tribal background and fought respectively against the Nizam of Hyderabad and the British. On the one hand, the film concerns the plight and resistance of the tribal (*adivasi*) communities of the peninsula. Yet, on the other, RRR borrows from the Ramayana and Mahabharata. The two protagonists are modelled after their namesakes from these epics. Alluri Sitarama Raju takes on the looks and guise of the Hindutva hero, God Rama, and Komaram Bheem is as muscular and immovable as Bhima from the Mahabharata. Also, the abduction of Sita, the central theme of the Ramayana is played out in reverse. Following a series of events, Raju is imprisoned but later saved by Bheem, who as a modern version of Hanuman carries a message from Raju's fiancée Sita. The final song and dance performance honours the national flag, albeit Madame Cama's 1907 'Flag of Indian Independence' adorned with the Vande Mataram slogan that is repeatedly chanted in the film. In chorus, it celebrates a selection of national heroes, including Subhas Chandra Bose, Vallabhbhai Patel and Bhagat Singh, as well as the legendary Rani of Jhansi and Shivaji. Expectedly, following the (inter)national success of RRR, Narendra Modi unveiled a 30-feet tall bronze statue of Alluri Sitarama Raju in Andhra Pradesh and stated that 'his indomitable courage inspires every Indian'.

By now, indeed, Hindutva propagandists have completely seized India's national song Vande Mataram. Since the 1920s, it was increasingly used already by Hindu chauvinists during anti-Muslim riots. Simultaneously, however, leading Muslims and secular Indians objected to the fact that some of its verses were idolatrous for addressing Mother India as a Hindu Goddess (Durga) and therefore anti-Muslim. Hence, at the time of Indian independence, solely the first two verses of Vande Mataram – which do not mention any Hindu deity and refer only abstractly to one's mother and motherland – were declared as India's national song, distinct from the national anthem, Tagore's Jana Gana Mana. From the very beginning of the controversy, nonetheless, Hindu nationalists, especially of the RSS, protested. Over the decades, they not only coined the slogan 'If you want to live in this country, you will have to sing "Vande Mataram"', but they also attempted to have the song sung in public schools

---

20   Earlier, two separate biographical (action) films in Telugu about Alluri Sitarama Raju, directed by V. Ramachandra Rao, and about Komaram Bheem, directed by Allani Sridhar, appeared respectively in 1974 and 1990.

as an expression of loyalty to the Indian nation. In the Hindutva era, new productions of Vande Mataram have become immensely popular. One 1998 clip sung by India's most famous Bollywood playback singer Late Mangeshkar (1929–2022) achieved cult status.[21] It is rather belligerent, full of marching, horseback riding and hosting of the flag in different Indian settings. Most interesting are its subtitles, which describe India's population as '700 million below the age of thirty!', followed by 'and home to 150 million peaceful Muslims'. In this way, then, Muslims were excluded from their rightful Indian citizenship and instead categorized as pacified others inhabiting the nation.[22]

Without any doubt, the anti-Muslim stand of Modi and Hindutva propagandists remains the most shocking feature of contemporary India. While reinforcing Orientalist stereotypes, for instance, Hindu chauvinists argue that the vulnerable daughters of Mother India should be kept away from the hands of 'hypersexual' and 'barbaric' Muslims, who falsely declare their love to Hindu women in order to convert them to Islam. Thus, by defending their women, they maintain that they are defending the purity of the nation. The introduction of the Citizenship Amendment Act of 2019 – which offers all undocumented migrants from Pakistan, Bangladesh and Afghanistan access to Indian citizenship as long as they are not Muslims – and, closely related, the detention camps for Muslim migrants in Assam only confirm the fact that Muslims are pariahs for the BJP government. By and large, the ever-increasing marginalization in this century of and, moreover, use of violence against Muslims (including random lynching) – besides the ever continuing brutality of high castes towards untouchables and tribals of course – brings to mind the comparison with the position of Jews in 1930s Nazi Germany. This book about Indian Romantic nationalism therefore also ends with a great sense of unease.

---

21 Late Mangeshkar's original version was featured in the film *Anandamath* (1952), after Bankim Chatterjee's novel, and was remixed for the clip.
22 Vande Mataram sung by Late Mangeshkar (music: Ranjit Barot/directors: Bala and Kanika), 1998: https://www.youtube.com/watch?v=c6PHJg9D_Sk.

Afterword

Joep Leerssen

The title of this book issues a bold challenge: *Romantic Nationalism in India*. Did Indian nation-building experience anything like 'Romanticism', and is this not an unwarranted projection of a European frame of analysis onto the South-Asian subcontinent? Bob van der Linden already hints at the way he wants us to understand that challenge by specifying 'Romantic nationalism' as a 'cultivation of culture' and by seeing its operative presence in India as part of a 'global circulation of ideas'. How and what that involves is explained in the book itself, which marks an exciting new step in the comparative, transnational and even trans-regional study of national movements.

Romantic nationalism is generally understood to be that assertion of the nation's claims to self-government which relies primarily, not on principles of social justice or political interest, but on a sense of an ideal essence characterizing the nation and setting it apart from all others. That sense of a separate, characteristic identity is typically based on cultural factors (history, collective memory, language, literature, traditions etc.); it is also predominantly expressed in cultural production.

More specifically, Romantic nationalism involves a 'cultivation of culture'. That recursive term implies that culture is not merely a behavioural ambience for social interactions and the ordering of life and its activities – something, in the words of Ernest Gellner, 'one can do without thinking about', such as speaking one's mother tongue or wearing one's clothes – but rather a culture consciously reflected upon, becoming self-aware as an acknowledged part of one's identity as opposed to that of others – such as rejecting the language of the imperial oppressor, or celebrating one's traditional costume. Culture as instrumentalized in the assertion of what is felt to be one's separate and characteristic identity becomes itself an object of consciousness-raising and cultivation. Hence the notion of a 'cultivation of culture', which lies at the heart of Romantic nationalism.

Much comparative work has in the last decades been done on the spread of Romantic nationalism across Europe in the century after Napoleon. It manifested itself across that entire continent, despite the massive socio-economic, political and cultural cleavages that divided its populations, from Reykjavík in Iceland to Tbilisi in Georgia and from Helsinki in Finland to Lisbon in Portugal. Whether the economy was agricultural and serf-based, or rapidly industrializing; whether there was an advanced public sphere carried by print capitalism

© BOB VAN DER LINDEN, 2024 | DOI:10.1163/9789004694804_009

and a dense media distribution, or bereft of printed matter with a high degree of illiteracy; whether the cultural centres gravitated to courts, monasteries or middle-class urban sociability; whether people identified as Protestants, Catholics, Orthodox, Jews or Muslims: across all those divides we see parallel developments, communicative transfers, entangled histories.

This runs counter to the sociopolitical study of nationalism, which tends to see national movements as a political response to a sociopolitical situation, locally circumscribed by societal and political parameters, and which sees the power of such movements in terms of their capacity to mobilize the masses and to challenge state power. But Romantic nationalism such as we encounter it in Europe was a repertoire as much as a movement, carried by the lettered and educated, culturally productive sections of the population (it would be a lazy simplification to call them by that slapdash word 'elite'), and it spread by communicative processes that were at most hindered, never altogether thwarted, by borders and boundaries between countries. Everyone read Walter Scott. The political mobilizing power of this cultivation of culture was limited; challenges to state power were often slightly quixotic, high-minded but unsuccessful. The power of Romantic nationalism was 'soft' rather than 'hard': not to mobilize or to challenge, but to inspire, to influence, to exercise leverage.

How European is this? The 'cultivation of culture' model has been operationalized on the basis of culture-historical data collected in Europe. Fields of culture that were 'cultivated' for the nation include history-writing, philology and folklore, the novel, theatre, classical and choral music, painting, architecture and applied/decorative arts. That is, to be sure, a very middle-class, and Europe-anchored lens. It cannot by default claim any general, 'global' applicability.

Many national movements worldwide succeeded without any need for Romantic idealism or a cultivation of culture. Resisting colonial expropriation and tyranny provided ample motivating and mobilizing power, even without the help of Walter Scott. But does that simply mean that 'Europe was different'? Here, then, lies a dilemma: to see Europe either as paradigmatic for the world at large, or as special and *sui generis*. That dilemmatic opposition needs to be deconstructed.

Operative factors that were at work in concentrated form across Europe include: the romantically heightened prestige of artists and intellectuals as an influential social group cutting across the divide between elite and masses, with the novel and music (to name but these) as important platforms; the status of national universities and archives as an ambience for nationally-focused forms of knowledge production; a historicist response to modernization emphasizing ethnic rootedness as a common social bond for 'the nation';

the rise of public display platforms for national culture such as the museum or exhibition fairs. It would be senseless to pretend that these were operative universally across the globe; but it would be equally senseless that they can only be encountered within Europe. Modernization and the rise of public spheres were transregional, truly global phenomena; but what about Romanticism?

The divide between 'Europe' and 'the rest of the world' is by default seen as part of a colonial order. But what does that mean? The relationships between Britain and India or Guyana; between Belgium and Congo; between Spain and Cuba; between Portugal and Angola; between France and Senegal or Algeria; between Denmark and Greenland; between Holland and Surinam or the Indonesian 'East Indies' … These were 'colonial' one and all, yet mutually they were very, very different indeed. For the colonial, enslaved subjects of Congo or Surinam, a 'cultivation of culture' was unachievable, but conditions were different in Calcutta, or Batavia/Jakarta. In some colonial societies, there were literate sections of the population with access to modern media maintaining a certain amount of control over the means of cultural self-representation. Their position was in some respects comparable to nationally-minded intellectuals in empires affected by 'Western' modernity, such as the post-Tanzimat Ottoman Empire or Meiji Japan. Conversely, there were, within the European landmass, imperial peripheries whose subaltern position was reminiscent of colonial domination: Finland, the Baltic Provinces, the Southern Caucasus and Tatar/Muslim communities in the Russian Empire; Ireland in the British Empire / United Kingdom; the Ottoman-dominated Balkan lands.

The black-and-white opposition is cross-hatched even further when we realize that it was in the metropolitan centres of such areas that the literate and culturally productive sections of society were active. The imperial capitals (Paris, Vienna, London) had their influx of artists and intellectuals, and students and activists, from the provinces and the colonies. And in the provincial and colonial capitals of the European empires, there is a sliding scale where Dublin and Calcutta, Reykjavík and Havana, Helsinki, Tbilisi, Batavia/Jakarta and Melbourne, are not all that dissimilar, despite the fact that some of these are located within, others outside Europe.

In the historical diffusion of Romantic nationalism the Europe/World divide is not all that absolute. And even that word 'diffusion' has misleading connotations: as if historical innovation emanates from one privileged place and thence radiates out to the passive trend-followers. To be sure, a time and a circumstance of origin can be identified for Romantic nationalism; but its spread was multidirectional, with multiple actors initiating, experiencing and sharing influences, and the division between sender and receiver was by no means clear-cut. Hegemon and colonized interactively created something that neither could have foreseen. It was, rather, a welter of circulating ideas, as Bob van der Linden terms it in this book's subtitle. The process took shape on the faultlines within and between empires: between the Romanov, Habsburg and Ottoman ones, between the French and German ones, and within and around Imperial Britain. The earliest trigger seems to have been the resistance against Napoleon. Repeated 'Loss of Empire' shocks or lost wars also provoked a turn towards national self-reflection. In the course of the century, various epicentres radiated the cultural habitus of Romantic nationalism into different, overlapping directions. The mode of dissemination was usually urban-based: spreading from city to city rather than from country to country. In this epidemiological spread, Dublin, Zagreb and Calcutta (as the case of Ram Mohan Roy shows) were affected early on, Barcelona and Helsinki slightly later, with a certain time-lag for cities like Tallinn and La Coruña, Tbilisi, Sofia and Istanbul.

In this circulation of ideas, the distinction between intra- and extra-European seems to make little sense. When studying the Africanism of Marcus Garvey, or the rise of Turkism among late-Ottoman intellectuals, or the novels of Bankim Chandra Chatterjee as manifestations of Romantic nationalism, two types of response would be equally unhelpful: either to see them as the passive trend-following epigons of a historical development 'Made in Europe', or else to assert their autonomous agency to the point of denying any involvement in the global circulation of ideas.

What I salute in this book is the brave and, in my opinion, hugely successful attempt to negotiate a middle course between those two extremes. It extends the idea of a 'cultivation of culture' to a complex of cultural communities in South Asia with their own, autonomously-descended and traditionally maintained cultural practices – ones not easily accommodated with the European taxonomy of cultural fields and genres. Bob van der Linden explores how a modernization process under the mortgage of colonialism affected different sets of religious and cultural traditions and *lieux de mémoire*, and different modes of cultural productivity, combining anti-colonial resistance with proudly-remembered ancient grandeur. The responses were nothing if not complex (or, for that matter, colourful), and range from the critically creative to the fanatically doctrinal, from the highly admirable to the deeply problematic – as, indeed, contemporary Hindutva nationalism plays its part in a troubling global wave of populist, intolerant nativism.

I am grateful to Bob van der Linden to have mapped the many, diverse and intriguing aspects of Indian culture in its relations to Indian nationalism. His application of the 'cultivation of culture' model enriches our understanding of Indian nationalism(s); and conversely, the Indian test-cases make us realize the breadth of cultural variations in which and through which the nation can be vindicated and nationalism can be propagated.

Bibliography

Abd-Allah, Umar Faruq, *A Muslim in Victorian America: The Life of Alexander Russell Webb*, Oxford: Oxford University Press, 2006.

Aboitiz, Nicole Cuunjieng, *Asian Place, Filippo Nation: A Global Intellectual History of the Philippine Revolution, 1887–1912*, New York: Columbia University Press, 2020.

Alexander, Michael, and Sushila Anand, *Queen Victoria's Maharajah: Duleep Singh 1838–93*, London: Weidenfeld and Nicolson, 1980.

Allen, Matthew Harp, "Rewriting the Script for South Indian Dance", *The Drama Review*, 41, 3, 1997: 63–100.

Ambedkar, B. R., *Annihilation of Caste* (first published in 1936), edited and annotated by S. Anand and introduced with the essay 'The Doctor and the Saint' by Arundhati Roy, London: Verso, 2014.

Ambedkar, B. R., *What Congress and Gandhi have done to the Untouchables*, Bombay: Thacker & Co, 1945.

Andrews, C. F., *Zaka Ullah of Delhi*, with introductions by Mushirul Hasan and Margrit Pernau, New Delhi: Oxford University Press, 2003 (first published in 1929).

Anonymous, "Ceylon Social Reform Society: Manifesto", *Ceylon National Review*, no. 1, January 1906: ii–iii.

Anonymous, *Bande Mataram Album*, Cawnpore: Prakash Pustakalaya, 1923.

Ansari, Humayun, "Maulana Barkatullah Bhopali's Transnationalism: Pan-Islamism, Colonialism, and Radical Politics" in Götz Nordbruch and Umar Ryad, eds., *Transnational Islam in Interwar Europe: Muslim Activists and Thinkers*, New York: Palgrave Macmillan, 2014: 181–209.

Archambault, Hanna L., "Becoming Mughal in the Nineteenth Century: The Case of the Bhopal Princely State", *South Asia: Journal of South Asian Studies*, 36, 4, 2013: 479–495.

Aydin, Cemil, *The Politics of Anti-Westernism in Asia: Visions of World Order in Pan-Islamic and Pan-Asian Thought*, New York: Columbia University Press, 2007.

Aydin, Cemil, *The Idea of the Muslim World: A Global Intellectual History*, Cambridge, Mass.: Harvard University Press, 2017.

Azad, Muhammad Husain, *Ab-e Hayat: Shaping the Canon of Urdu Poetry*, translated and edited by Frances Pritchett in association with Shamsur Rahmani Farugi, New Delhi: Oxford University Press, 2001.

Baier, Karl, "Swami Vivekananda: Reform Hinduism, Nationalism and Scientist Yoga", *Interdisciplinary Journal for Religion and Transformation in Contemporary Society*, 5, 2019: 230–257.

Ballantyne, Tony, *Orientalism and Race: Aryanism in the British Empire*, New York: Palgrave Macmillan, 2002.

Ballantyne, Tony, *Between Colonialism and Diaspora: Sikh Cultural Formations in an Imperial World*, New Delhi: Permanent Black, 2007.

Banerjea, Surendranath, *Speeches and Writings of the Hon. Surendranath Banerjea: Selected by Himself*, Madras: G. A. Natesan & Co, 1918.

Banerjea, Surendranath, *A Nation in the Making: Being the Reminiscences of Fifty Years of Public Life*, Bombay: Oxford University Press, 1963 (first published in 1925).

Banerjee, Himadri, "Bengali Perceptions of the Sikhs: The Nineteenth and Twentieth Centuries" in Joseph T. O'Connell, Milton Israel et al., eds., *Sikh History and Religion in the Twentieth Century*, Toronto: University of Toronto, Centre for South Asian Studies, 1988: 110–133.

Barucha, Rustom, *Another Asia: Rabindranath Tagore and Okakura Tenshin*, New Delhi: Oxford University Press, 2006.

Bautze, Joachim K., ed., *Interaction of Cultures: Indian and Western Painting 1780–1910*, Alexandria, Virginia: Arts Services International, 1998.

Bayly, C. A., *Origins of Nationality in South Asia: Patriotism and Ethical Government in the Making of Modern India*, New Delhi: Oxford University Press, 1998.

Bayly, C. A., "Ireland, India and the Empire: 1780–1914", *Transactions of the Royal Historical Society*, 10, 2000: 377–397.

Bayly, C. A., *The Birth of the Modern World, 1780–1914: Global Connections and Comparisons*, Oxford: Blackwell, 2004.

Bayly, C. A., "Liberalism at Large: Mazzini and Nineteenth-Century Indian Thought" in C. A. Bayly and E. F. Biagini, eds., *Guiseppe Mazzini and the Globalization of Democratic Nationalism, 1830–1920*, Oxford: Oxford University Press, 2008: 355–374.

Bayly, C. A., "India, the Bhagavad Gita and the World", *Modern Intellectual History*, 7, 2, 2010: 275–295.

Bayly, C. A., *Recovering Liberties: Indian Thought in the Age of Liberalism and Empire*, Cambridge: Cambridge University Press, 2012.

Bayly, Susan, "Imagining 'Greater India': French and Indian Visions of Colonialism in the Indic Mode", *Modern Asian Studies*, 38, 3, 2004: 703–744.

Besant, Annie, *The Bhagavad Gita or the Lord's Song*, London: Theosophical Publishing Society, 1895.

Bharati, Subramania, *Panchali's Pledge (Panchali Sabadham)*, translated by Usha Rajagopalan, Gurgaon: Hachette India, 2012 (first published in 1912).

Bhattacharya, Sabyasachi, *Vande Mataram: The Biography of a Song*, New Delhi: Penguin, 2003.

Bijlert, Victor A. van, "Tagore's Vision of the Indian Nation: 1900–1917" in Kathleen M. O'Connell and Joseph T. O'Connell, eds., *Rabindranath Tagore: Reclaiming a Cultural Icon*, Kolkata: Visva-Bharati, 2009: 46–62.

Blackburn, Stuart, *Print, Folklore, and Nationalism in Colonial South India*, New Delhi: Permanent Black, 2003.

Boehmer, Elleke, *Empire, the National, and the Postcolonial 1890–1920: Resistance in Interaction*, Oxford: Oxford University Press, 2002.

Bose, Sugata, "Nation as Mother: Representations and Contestations of 'India' in Bengali Literature and Culture" in Sugata Bose and Ayesha Jalal, eds., *Nationalism, Democracy, and Development: State and Politics in India*, New Delhi: Oxford University Press, 1997: 50–75.

Brown, Rebecca M., "Spinning without Touching the Wheel: Anticolonialism, Indian Nationalism, and the Deployment of Symbol", *Comparative Studies of South Asia, Africa and the Middle East*, 29, 2, 2009: 230–243.

Bryant, Julius, "Colonial Architecture in Lahore: J. L. Kipling and the 'Indo-Saracenic' Styles", *South Asian Studies*, 36, 1, 2020: 61–71.

Campbell, Christy, *The Maharajah's Box: An Imperial Story of Conspiracy, Love, and a Guru's Prophecy*, London: Harper Collins Publishers, 2000.

Casolari, Marzia, "Hindutva's Foreign Tie-Up in the 1930s: Archival Evidence", *Economic and Political Weekly*, 35, 4, 2000: 218–228.

Chadha, Kalyani, and Anandam P. Kavoori, "Exoticized, Marginalized, Demonized: The Muslim Other in Indian Cinema" in Anandam P. Kavoori and Ashwin Punathakbekar, eds., *Global Bollywood*, New York: New York University Press, 2008: 131–145.

Chakrabarty, Dipesh, "Romantic Archives: Literature and the Politics of Identity in Bengal", *Critical Inquiry*, 30, 3, 2004: 654–682.

Chandra, Sudhir, *The Oppressive Present: Literature and Social Consciousness in Colonial India*, New Delhi: Oxford University Press, 1992.

Chatterjee, Chanda, "Rabindranath Tagore's Use of Guru Gobind Singh as National Icon" in K. L. Tuteja and Kaustav Chakraborty, eds., *Tagore and Nationalism*, New Delhi: Springer, 2017: 257–266.

Chatterji, Bankimcandra, *Anandamath, or The Sacred Brotherhood*, translated and with an introduction and critical apparatus by Julius J. Lipner, New York: Oxford University Press, 2005.

Coomaraswamy, Ananda K., *Essays in National Idealism*, New Delhi: Munshiram Manoharlal, 1981 (first published in 1909).

Coomaraswamy, Ananda K., *The Indian Craftsman*, London: Probsthain & Co, 1909.

Coomaraswamy, Ananda K., *Swadeshi and Art*, Madras: Ganesh & Co, 1912.

Coomaraswamy, Ananda K., *The Dance of Siva*, New York: The Sunwise Turn, 1918.

Cort, John E., "Communities, Temples, Identities: Art Histories and Social Histories in Western India" in Michael W. Meister, ed., *Ethnography & Personhood: Notes from the Field*, New Delhi: Rawat Publications, 2000: 101–128.

Cousins, James H., *The Renaissance in India*, Madras: Ganesh & Co, 1918.

Cousins, James H., *The Cultural Unity of Asia*, Madras: Theosophical Publishing House, 1922.

Cousins, James H., and Margaret E. Cousins, *We Two Together*, Madras: Ganesh & Co, 1950.

Cousins, Margaret E., *The Music of Orient and Occident: Essays Towards Mutual Understanding*, Madras: B. G. Paul & Co, 1935.

Das, A. C., *Rig-Vedic India*, volume one, Calcutta: University of Calcutta, 1921.

Day, C. R., *The Music and Musical Instruments of Southern India and the Deccan*, London: Novello, 1891.

Derozio, H. L. V., *Poems of Henry Louis Vivian Derozio: A Forgotten Anglo-Indian Poet*, introduced by F. B. Bradley-Birt and with a new foreword by R. K. Dasgupta, Calcutta: Oxford University Press, 1980 (second edition; first published in 1923).

Desai, Madhuri, *Banaras Reconstructed: Architecture and Sacred Space in a Hindu Holy City*, Seattle: University of Washington Press, 2017.

Dutta, Nilanjana, "'Scott of Bengal': Examining the European Legacy in the Historical Novels of Bankimchandra Chatterjee", Unpublished PhD Dissertation: University of North Carolina, Chapel Hill, 2009.

Dwyer, Rachel, *Filming the Gods: Religion and Indian Cinema*, London: Routledge, 2006.

Eade, J. C., ed., *Romantic Nationalism in Europe*, Canberra: Australian National University, 1983.

Eaton, Natasha, "Swadeshi Color: Artistic Production and Indian Nationalism, ca. 1905–ca. 1947", *The Art Bulletin*, 95, 4, 2013: 623–641.

Ebeling, Sascha, *Colonizing the Realm of Words: The Transformation of Tamil Literature in Nineteenth-Century South India*, Albany: State University of New York Press, 2010.

Farrell, Gerry, *Indian Music and the West*, Oxford: Oxford University Press, 1997.

Fischer-Tiné, Harald, "Indian Nationalism and the 'World Forces': Transnational and Diasporic Dimensions of the Indian Freedom Movement on the Eve of the First World War", *Journal of Global History*, 2, 3, 2007: 325–344.

Fischer-Tiné, Harald, *Shyamji Krishnavarma: Sanskrit, Sociology and anti-Imperialism*, New Delhi: Routledge, 2014.

Fischer-Tiné, Harald, "Before Bollywood: Bombay Cinema and the Rise of the Film Industry in Late Colonial India" in Harald Fischer-Tiné and Maria Framke, eds., *Routledge Handbook of the History of Colonialism in South Asia*, London: Routledge, 2021: 359–372.

Forster, E. M., *A Passage to India*, London: Penguin, 1979 (first published in 1924).

Franklin, Michael J., *Orientalist Jones: Sir William Jones, Poet, Lawyer, and Linguist, 1746–1794*, New York: Oxford University Press, 2011.

Freitag, Jason, *Serving Empire, Serving Nation: James Tod and the Rajputs of Rajasthan*, Leiden: Brill, 2009.

Gandhi, M. K., *'Hind Swaraj' and Other Writings*, edited by Anthony J. Parel, Cambridge: Cambridge University Press, 1997.

Geaves, Ron, *Islam in Victorian Britain: The Life and Times of Abdullah Quilliam*, London: Kube Publishing, 2010.

Ghosh, Durba, *Gentlemanly Terrorists: Political Violence and the Colonial State in India, 1919–1947*, New York: Cambridge University Press, 2017.

Gooptu, Sharmistha, *Bengali Cinema: 'An Other Nation'*, London: Routledge, 2011.

Guha, Ranajit, *History at the Limit of World-History*, New York: Columbia University Press, 2002.

Guha, Sumit, *History and Collective Memory in South Asia, 1200–2000*, Seattle: University of Washington Press, 2019.

Guha-Thakurta, Tapati, *Abanindranath, Known and Unknown: The Artist versus the Art of His Times*, Kolkata: Centre for Studies in Social Sciences, 2009.

Gupta, Samita, "Sris Chandra Chatterjee: The Quest for a National Architecture", *Indian Economic and Social History Review*, 28, 2, 1991: 187–201.

Halbfass, Wilhelm, *India and Europe: An Essay in Understanding*, New Delhi: Motilal Banarsidass, 1990 (first published in 1988).

Hardy, Peter, *The Muslims of British India*, Cambridge: Cambridge University Press, 1972.

Harper, Tim, *Underground Asia: Global Revolutionaries and the Assault on Empire*, London: Allen Lane, 2020.

Harris, Ruth, *Guru to the World: The Life and Legacy of Vivekananda*, Cambridge, Mass.: The Belknap Press of Harvard University Press, 2022.

Hasan, Mushirul, *A Moral Reckoning: Muslim Intellectuals in Nineteenth-Century Delhi*, New Delhi: Oxford University Press, 2003.

Hawley, John Stratton, *A Storm of Songs: India and the Idea of the Bhakti Movement*, Cambridge, MA: Harvard University Press, 2015.

Hay, Stephen N., *Asian Ideas of East and West: Tagore and His Critics in Japan, China, and India*, Cambridge, MA: Harvard University Press, 1970.

Haynes, Douglas, *Rhetoric and Ritual in Colonial India: The Shaping of the Public Sphere in Surat City, 1852–1928*, New Delhi: Oxford University Press, 1992.

Hazama, Eijiro, "Unravelling the Myth of Gandhian Non-Violence: Why Did Gandhi Connect His Principle of Satyagraha with the Hindu Notion of Ahimsa?", *Modern Intellectual History*, 20, 1, 2023: 116–140.

Hegewald, Julia A. B., "The International Jaina Style? Maru-Gurjara Temples Under the Solankis, throughout India and in the Diaspora", *Ars Orientalis*, 45, 2015: 114–140.

Hillis, Faith, "The 'Franco-Russian Marseillaise': International Exchange and the Making of Antiliberal Politics in Fin de Siècle France", *Journal of Modern History*, 89, 1, 2017: 39–78.

Hroch, Miroslav, "National Romanticism" in Balázs Trencsényi and Michal Kopeček, eds., *Discourses of Collective Identity in Central and Southeast Europe 1770–1945, vol-*

ume two: National Romanticism: The Formation of National Movements, Budapest: Central European University Press, 2007: 4–18.

Hughes, Stephen Putnam, "Tamil Mythological Cinema and the Politics of Secular Modernism" in Birgit Meyer, ed., *Aesthetic Formations: Media, Religion, and the Senses*, New York: Palgrave Macmillan, 2009: 93–116.

Hutchinson, John, "Cultural Nationalism" in John Breuilly, ed., *The Oxford Handbook of the History of Nationalism*, Oxford: Oxford University Press, 2013: 75–94.

Inden, Ronald, *Imagining India*, Bloomington, IN: Indiana University Press, 2000 (second edition; first published in 1990).

Iqbal, Muhammad, *Shikwa and Jawab-i-Shikwa: Iqbal's Dialogue with Allah*, translated and introduced by Khushwant Singh, New Delhi: Oxford University Press, 2008 (first published in 1909 and 1913).

Irschick, Eugene F., *Politics and Social Conflict in South India: The Non-Brahman Movement and Tamil Separatism, 1916–1929*, Berkeley, CA: University of California Press, 1969.

Jaffrelot, Christophe, *India's Silent Revolution: The Rise of the Lower Castes in North India*, London: Hurst, 2003.

Jaffrelot, Christophe, *Dr. Ambedkar and Untouchability: Analysing and Fighting Caste*, London: Hurst 2005.

Jaffrelot, Christophe, *Modi's India: Hindu Nationalism and the Rise of Ethnic Democracy*, Princeton, NJ: Princeton University Press, 2021.

Jalal, Ayesha, *Self and Sovereignty: Individual and Community in South Asian Islam Since 1850*, New Delhi: Oxford University Press, 2001.

Jones, William, "On the Musical Modes of the Hindus" (first published in 1792) in Sourindro Mohun Tagore, ed., *Hindu Music from Various Authors*, Calcutta: I. C. Bose & Co, 1882: 125–160.

Joshi, Priya, *In Another Country: Colonialism, Culture, and the English Novel in India*, New York: Columbia University Press, 2002.

Karl, Rebecca E., *Staging the World: Chinese Nationalism at the Turn of the Twentieth Century*, Durham, NC: Duke University Press, 2002.

Kolff, D. H. A., *Naukar, Rajput, Sepoy: The Ethnohistory of the Military Labour Market in Hindustan, 1450–1850*, Cambridge: Cambridge University Press, 1990.

Kopf, David, *British Orientalism and the Bengal Renaissance*, Berkeley, CA: University of California Press, 1969.

Kopf, David, *The Brahmo Samaj and the Shaping of the Modern Indian Mind*, Princeton, NJ: Princeton University Press, 1979.

Lago, Mary M., ed. *Imperfect Encounter: The Letters of Rabindranath Tagore and William Rothenstein*, Cambridge, MA: Harvard University Press, 1972.

Lang, Jon, Madhav Desai and Miki Desai, *Architecture and Independence: The Search for Identity – India, 1880–1980*, New Delhi: Oxford University Press, 1997.

Laursen, Ole Birk, "'I have only One Country, it is the World': Madame Cama, Anti-colonialism, and Indian-Russian Revolutionary Networks in Paris, 1907–17", *History Workshop Journal*, 90, 2020: 96–114.

Leerssen, Joep, *National Thought in Europe: A Cultural History*, Amsterdam: Amsterdam University Press, 2018 (third revised and expanded edition; first published in 2006).

Leerssen, Joep, "Nationalism and the Cultivation of Culture", *Nations and Nationalism*, 12, 4, 2006: 559–578.

Leerssen, Joep, ed., *Encyclopedia of Romantic Nationalism in Europe*, two volumes, Amsterdam: Amsterdam University Press, 2018.

Linden, Bob van der, *Moral Languages from Colonial Punjab: The Singh Sabha, Arya Samaj and Ahmadiyahs*, New Delhi: Manohar, 2008.

Linden, Bob van der, *Music and Empire in Britain and India: Identity, Internationalism, and Cross-Cultural Communication*, New York: Palgrave Macmillan, 2013.

Linden, Bob van der, "Non-Western National Music and Empire in Global History: Interactions, Uniformities, and Comparisons", *Journal of Global History*, 10, 3, 2015: 431–456.

Linden, Bob van der, *Arnold Bake: A Life with South Asian Music*, London: Routledge, 2018.

Linden, Bob van der, "Rhythms of the Raj: Music in Colonial South Asia" in Harald Fischer-Tiné and Maria Framke, eds., *Routledge Handbook of the History of Colonialism in South Asia*, London: Routledge, 2021: 373–385.

Linden, Bob van der, *Cultivating Sikh Culture and Identity: Art, Music and Philology*, London: Routledge, forthcoming.

Login, Lady, *Sir John Login and Duleep Singh*, London: W. H. Allen & Co, 1890.

Maclean, Kama, *Pilgrimage and Power: The Kumbh Mela in Allahabad, 1765–1954*, New York: Oxford University Press, 2008.

Maclean, Kama, *A Revolutionary History of Interwar India: Violence, Image, Voice and Text*, New York: Oxford University Press, 2015.

Majeed, Javed, *Muhammad Iqbal: Islam, Aesthetics and Postcolonialism*, London: Routledge, 2009.

Masuzawa, Tomoko, *The Invention of World Religions: Or, How European Universalism was Preserved in the Language of Pluralism*, Chicago: Chicago University Press, 2005.

Max Müller, Friedrich, *Biographies of Words and the Home of the Aryas*, London: Longmans, Green, and Co., 1888.

Max Müller, Friedrich, *Auld Lang Syne, volume two: My Indian Friends*, New York: C. Scribner's Sons, 1899.

McLain, Karline, *India's Immortal Comic Books: Gods, Kings, and Other Heroes*, Bloomington, IN: Indiana University Press, 2009.

McLeod, W. H., *Popular Sikh Art*, New Delhi: Oxford University Press, 1991.

Metcalf, Thomas R., *An Imperial Vision: Indian Architecture and Britain's Raj*, London: Faber and Faber, 1989.

Minault, Gail, *The Khilafat Movement: Religious Symbolism and Political Mobilization in India*, New York: Columbia University Press, 1982.

Mishra, Pankaj, *From the Ruins of Empire: The Revolt Against the West and the Remaking of Asia*, London: Allen Lane, 2012.

Mishra, Pritipuspa, *Language and the Making of Modern India: Nationalism and the Vernacular in Colonial Odisha, 1803–1956*, Cambridge: Cambridge University Press, 2020.

Mitchell, Lisa, *Language, Emotion and Politics in South India: The Making of a Mother-Tongue*, Bloomington, IN: Indiana University Press, 2009.

Mitter, Partha, *Art and Nationalism in Colonial India, 1850–1922: Occidental Orientations*, Cambridge: Cambridge University Press, 1994.

Mitter, Partha, *The Triumph of Modernism: India's Artists and the Avant-Garde, 1922–1947*, London: Reaktion Books, 2007.

Murphy, Anne, *The Materiality of the Past: History and Representation in Sikh Tradition*, New York: Oxford University Press, 2012.

Neumayer, Erwin, and Christine Schelberger, eds., *Raja Ravi Varma: Portrait of an Artist (The Diary of C. Raja Raja Varma)*, New Delhi: Oxford University Press, 2005.

O'Hanlon, Rosalind, *Caste, Conflict and Ideology: Mahatma Jotirao Phule and Low-Caste Protest in Nineteenth-Century Western India*, Cambridge: Cambridge University Press, 1985.

Okakura Kakuzo, *The Ideals of the East with Special Reference to the Art of Japan*, London: John Murray, 1903.

Owen, Nicholas, "The Soft Heart of the British Empire: Indian Radicals in London", *Past and Present*, 220, 1, 2013: 143–184.

Pal, Bipin Chandra, *The Soul of India: A Constructive Study of Indian Thoughts and Ideals*, Calcutta: Choudhury and Choudhury, 1911.

Pal, Bipin Chandra, *Memories of My Life and Times*, Calcutta: Modern Book Agency, 1932.

Pandit, Mimasha, *Performing Nationhood: The Emotional Roots of Swadeshi Nationhood in Bengal, 1905–12*, New Delhi: Oxford University Press, 2019.

Patel, Dinyar, *Naoroji: Pioneer of Indian Nationalism*, Harvard: Harvard University Press, 2020.

Pernau, Margrit, *Emotions and Modernity in Colonial India: From Balance to Fervor*, New Delhi: Oxford University Press, 2019.

Petrie, D., *Developments in Sikh Politics 1900–1911: A Report*, Amritsar: Chief Khalsa Diwan, n.d.

Pinney, Christopher, *'Photos of the Gods': The Printed Image and Political Struggle in India*, London: Reaktion Books, 2004.

Pinney, Christopher, "Latrogenic Religion and Politics" in Raminder Kaur and William Mazzarella, eds., *Censorship in South Asia: Cultural Regulation from Sedition to Seduction*, Bloomington, IN: Indiana University Press, 2009: 29–62.

Pratap, Raja Mahendra, *My Life Story of Fiftyfive Years: December 1886-December 1941*, Dehradun World Fedaration, 1947.

Pritchett, Frances W., *Nets of Awareness: Urdu Poetry and Its Critics*, Berkeley, CA: University of California Press, 1994.

Rai, Lala Lajpat, "Shivaji (1896)", excerpts translated from Urdu, in B. R. Nanda, ed., *The Collected Works of Lala Lajpat Rai*, volume one, New Delhi: Manohar, 2004: 335–368.

Rai, Lala Lajpat, "Swami Dayanand (1898)", excerpts translated from Urdu, in B. R. Nanda, ed., *The Collected Works of Lala Lajpat Rai*, volume one, New Delhi: Manohar, 2004: 371–418.

Rai, Lala Lajpat, "The Message of the Bhagavad Gita (1908)", in B. R. Nanda, ed., *The Collected Works of Lala Lajpat Rai*, volume three, New Delhi: Manohar, 2004: 329–353.

Raj, Kapil, *Relocating Modern Science: Circulation and the Construction of Knowledge in South Asia and Europe, 1650–1900*, New York: Palgrave Macmillan, 2007.

Raj, Kapil, "The Historical Anatomy of a Contact Zone: Calcutta in the Eighteenth Century", *Indian Economic and Social History Review*, 48, 1, 2011: 55–82.

Ramaswamy, Sumathi, *Passions of the Tongue: Language Devotion in Tamil India, 1891–1970*, Berkeley, CA: University of California Press, 1997.

Ramaswamy, Sumathi, *The Lost Land of Lemuria: Fabulous Geographies, Catastrophic Histories*, Berkeley, CA: University of California Press, 2004.

Ramaswamy, Sumathi, *The Goddess and the Nation: Mapping Mother India*, Durham, NC: Duke University Press, 2010.

Ramnath, Maia, *Haj to Utopia: How the Ghadar Movement Charted Global Radicalism and Attempted to Overthrow the British Empire*, Berkeley, CA: University of California Press, 2011.

Ranade, M. G., *Rise of the Maratha Power*, Bombay: Punalekar, 1900.

Raychaudhuri, Tapan, *Europe Reconsidered: Perceptions of the West in Nineteenth-Century Bengal*, New Delhi: Oxford University Press, 2002 (second edition; first published in 1989).

Raychaudhuri, Tapan, *Perceptions, Emotions, Sensibilities: Essays on India's Colonial and Post-Colonial Experiences*, New Delhi: Oxford University Press, 1999.

Reich, David, *Who We Are and How We Got Here: Ancient DNA and the New Science of the Human Past*, Oxford: Oxford University Press, 2018.

Rigney, Ann, "Cultural Memory Studies: Mediation, Narrative, and the Aesthetic" in Anna Lisa Tota and Trever Hagen, eds., *Routledge International Handbook of Memory Studies*, London: Routledge, 2016: 65–76.

Rudolph, Lloyd I., and Susanne Hoeber Rudolph, *Romanticism's Child: An Intellectual History of James Tod's Influence on Indian History and Historiography*, New Delhi: Oxford University Press, 2017.

Sareen, Tilak Raj, *Indian Revolutionary Movement Abroad (1905–1921)*, New Delhi: Sterling, 1979.

Sarkar, Abhishek, "The Scottish 'Ploughman Poet' Among the Bengali Intelligentsia: Appreciating Robert Burns in Colonial Bengal", *Scottish Literary Review*, 11, 2, 2019: 101–124.

Schimmel, Annemarie, *Islam in the Indian Subcontinent*, Leiden: Brill, 1980.

Schwab, Raymond, *The Oriental Renaissance: Europe's Rediscovery of India and the East, 1680–1880*, with an introduction by Edward W. Said, New York: Columbia University Press, 1984 (first published in French in 1950).

Sekhon, Sant Singh, and Kartar Singh Duggal, *A History of Punjabi Literature*, New Delhi: Sahitya Akademi, 1992.

Shackle, Christopher, and Javed Majeed, eds., *Hali's Musaddas: The Flow and Ebb of Islam*, New Delhi: Oxford University Press, 1997.

Sharar, Abdul Halim, *Lucknow: The Last Phase of an Oriental Culture*, translated and edited by E. S. Harcourt and Fakhir Hussain, London: Paul Elek, 1975.

Siddiqui, Samee, "Coupled Internationalisms: Charting Muhammad Barkatullah's Anti-Colonialism and Pan-Islamism", *ReOrient*, 5, 1, 2019: 25–46.

Siddiqui, Samee, "Parallel Lives or Interconnected Histories?: Anagarika Dharmapala and Muhammad Barkatullah's 'World Religioning' in Japan", *Modern Asian Studies*, 56, 4, 2022: 1329–1352.

Silvestri, Michael, *Ireland and India: Nationalism, Empire and Memory*, Basingstoke: Palgrave Macmillan, 2009.

Silvestri, Michael, *Policing 'Bengali Terorism' in India and the World: Imperial Intelligence and Revolutionary Nationalism, 1905–1939*, New York: Palgrave Macmillan, 2019.

Singh, Ganda, ed., *Maharaja Duleep Singh Correspondence*, Patiala: Patiala University, 1977.

Singh, Harbans, ed., *The Encyclopaedia of Sikhism*, four volumes, Patiala: Punjabi University, 1997.

Singh, Harleen, *The Rani of Jhansi: Gender, History, and Fable in India*, Cambridge: Cambridge University Press, 2014.

Sreenivasan, Ramya, *The Many Lives of a Rajput Queen: Heroic Pasts in India, c. 1500–1900*, Seattle: University of Washington Press, 2007.

Srivastava, Gita, *Mazzini and His Impact on the Indian Nationalist Movement*, Allahabad: Chugh Publications, 1982.

Stolte, Carolien, "'Enough of the Great Napoleons!' Raja Mahendra Pratap's Pan-Asian Projects (1929–1939), *Modern Asian Studies*, 46, 2, 2012: 403–423.

Stolte, Carolien, and Harald Fischer-Tiné, "Imagining Asia in India: Nationalism and Internationalism (ca. 1905–1940), *Comparative Studies in Society and History*, 54, 1, 2012: 65–92.

Subramanian, Lakshmi, *From the Tanjore Court to the Madras Music Academy*, New Delhi: Oxford University Press, 2006.

Tagore, Rabindranath, Rabindranath Tagore, *Nationalism*, with an introduction by Ramachandra Guha, New Delhi: Penguin, 2009 (first published in 1917).

Tagore, Rabindranath, Rabindranath Tagore, *The Home and the World*, New Delhi: Penguin, 2005 (first published in 1919).

Talbot, Cynthia, *The Last Hindu Emperor: Prithviraj Chauhan and the Indian Past, 1200–2000*, Cambridge: Cambridge University Press, 2016.

Thapar, Romila, "The Theory of Aryan Race and India: History and Politics", *Social Scientist*, 24, 1–3, 1996: 3–29.

Thapar, Romila, "Can Genetics Help Us Understand Indian Social History?", *Cold Spring Harbor Perspectives in Biology*, 6, 11, 2014: https://cshperspectives.cshlp.org/content/6/11/a008599.

Tilak, B. G., *Orion or Researches into the Antiquity of the Vedas*, Bombay: Mrs. Radhabdi Atmaram Sagoon, 1893.

Tilak, B. G., *The Arctic Home in the Vedas*, Poona City: Messrs. Tilak Bros. Gaikwar Waida, 1925 (first published in 1903).

Tillotson, Giles, *The Tradition of Indian Architecture: Continuity, Controversy and Change since 1850*, New Haven: Yale University Press, 1989.

Tillotson, Giles, "Vincent J. Esch and the Architecture of Hyderabad, 1914–36", *South Asian Studies*, 9, 1, 1993: 29–46.

Tillotson, Giles, "George S. T. Harris: An Architect in Gwalior", *South Asian Studies*, 20, 1, 2004: 9–24.

Trautmann, Thomas R., *Aryans and British India*, Berkeley, CA: University of California Press, 1997.

Trautmann, Thomas R., *Languages and Nations: Conversations in Colonial South India*, Berkeley, CA: University of California Press, 2006.

Vandal, Pervaiz, and Sajida Vandal, *The Raj, Lahore and Bhai Ram Singh*, Lahore: National College of Arts, 2006.

Veer, Peter van der, *Imperial Encounters: Religion and Modernity in India and Britain*, Princeton, NJ: Princeton University Press, 2001.

Venniyoor, E. M. J., *Raja Ravi Varma*, Trivandrum: Government of Kerala, 1981.

Williams, Louise Blakeney, "Overcoming the 'Contagion of Mimicry': The Cosmopolitan Nationalism and Modernist History of Rabindranath Tagore and W. B. Yeats", *American Historical Review*, 112, 1, 2007: 69–100.

Woods, Jeannine, *Visions of Empire and Other Imaginings: Cinema, Ireland and India 1910–1962*, Bern: Peter Lang, 2011.

Zachariah, Benjamin, "A Long, Strange Trip: The Lives in Exile of Har Dayal" in Virinder S. Kalra and Shalina Sharma, eds., *State of Subversion: Radical Politics in Punjab in the 20th Century*, London: Routledge, 2016: 188–217.

Zastoupil, Lynn, *Rammohun Roy and the Making of Victorian Britain*, New York: Palgrave Macmillan, 2010.

Index